Stress and Quality of Working Life

The Positive and The Negative

edited by

Ana Maria Rossi
International Stress Management Association

James Campbell (Jim) Quick
The University of Texas at Arlington

Pamela L. Perrewé
Florida State University

INFORMATION AGE PUBLISHING, INC.
Charlotte, NC • www.infoagepub.com

Library of Congress Cataloging-in-Publication Data

Stress and quality of working life : the positive and the negative / edited
by Ana Maria Rossi, James Campbell (Jim) Quick, Pamela L. Perrewé.
    p. cm. – (Stress and quality of working life)
 Includes bibliographical references.
 ISBN 978-1-60752-058-0 (pbk.) – ISBN 978-1-60752-059-7 (hardcover)
1. Job stress. I. Rossi, Ana Maria. II. Quick, James C. III. Perrewe,
Pamela L.
 HF5548.85.S747 2009
 158.7'2–dc22

                                      2009002235

Printed in the United States of America

CONTENTS

SECTION 1

THE ORGANIZATIONAL AND INDIVIDUAL COSTS
OF OCCUPATIONAL STRESS

SECTION 2

MITIGATING THE NEGATIVE EFFECTS OF OCCUPATIONAL STRESS

SECTION 3

UNDERSTANDING AND EXAMINING WORK LIFE QUALITY

PREFACE

The consequences of occupational stress have been felt more strongly and markedly in spite of an increasing number of international studies and research on the subject. According to data published by The American Institute of Stress (AIS), the United States spend around US$ 300 billion/ year due to the consequences of stress and according to estimates, in Brazil these expenses account for 3.5% of the GDP/year.

This situation begs the following questions: Where is all knowledge about stress acquired over the past decades being placed? What is missing in the programs implemented by companies that want to manage stress? Why is it that in spite of all efforts the desired results cannot be achieved?

Excess strain became something so common in today's society that more than a threat to the quality of life, it has become a threat to life itself. Therefore, it is important to understand the level it can reach and develop strategies accordingly, trying to find new choices.

In order to provide alternatives to some of these issues, the Brazilian branch of the International Stress Management Association (ISMA-BR) was founded in the year 2000, a non-profit organization with the mission of doing research on stress and disseminating the most updated theories, practices and technology applications for its diagnosis and treatment.

However, facing the situation in which corporate stress is one of the big culprits of the loss of workers' quality of life, maybe it is high time we make another leap and decrease the costs of stress to corporations, making use of more efficient actions that deal with the core of the issue.

Although quality of life is everyone's responsibility, companies will certainly be able to benefit from the implementation of preventive programs, avoiding paying the high price caused by absenteeism, sick leaves, reduc-

Stress and Quality of Working Life, pages vii–viii
Copyright © 2009 by Information Age Publishing
All rights of reproduction in any form reserved.

tion in production and low quality work. Thus, this is a win–win situation, for companies and employees.

In this regard, it is important to have an additional tool to get information on stress and to help companies and workers act more accurately to improve quality of life and cut healthcare costs which is the main topic of this book. Here you will find the experience and opinion of some of the best professionals in this field in the world. ISMA-BR wishes you a lot of success in this challenge.

Ana Maria Rossi, Ph.D.
President of ISMA-BR

FOREWORD

Is job stress a global epidemic? Some say "yes" while others say "no." Regardless, the methods and practices of preventive stress management are now available worldwide and are needed. Macik-Frey, Quick, and Nelson (2007) reported job stress as a major occupational health concern in major economies, such as the United States, Europe, Japan, and Brazil. Pendey, Quick, Rossi, Nelson, and Martin (in press) have found that bullying has emerged as a major cause of stress for people at work. The National Institutes of Health in the United States is funding a major collaborative, multi-year study of work–family dynamics due to the significant spillover effects from work to home and home to work. Job stress effects are not isolated in the workplace. The 2008 Gallup-Healthways Well-Being Index, based on the World Health Organization's definition of health, inaugural test in the U.S. found that a majority of Americans are struggling with stress, health, and well-being. This Well-Being Index is designed for use in countries around the world for testing their health and well-being. A survey conducted by the Brazil Chapter of the International Stress Management Association (IS-MA-BR) showed that 70% of economically active Brazilians suffer from too much tension in their daily lives (Rossi, 2006). Pendey et al. (in press) find that job stress causes adverse physiological effects and suffering for individuals while generating a significant economic burden for companies due to worker disability, absenteeism, productivity problems, and turnover.

This volume offers twelve chapters organized into three major sections that address occupational stress and quality of working live. The authors are an internationally renowned team of scholar-research-practitioners who are grounded in applied science and clinical practice. Section 1 includes five chapters that address the organizational and individual costs of occupational stress. The costs are humanitarian and economic; both human suffer-

Stress and Quality of Working Life, pages ix–xi
Copyright © 2009 by Information Age Publishing

ing and financial burdens are important. Section 2 includes three chapters that focus on ways to mitigate the negative effects of occupational stress. We must help those who are suffering but we must do more by preventing distress where we can and building on positive, strength factors where possible. Section 3 includes four chapters that examine and expand our understanding of work life quality. Work life quality is so important because of the effects it has on workers and leaders, to include the spillover impact into families and communities.

Section 1 includes Chapters 1 through 5. Chapter 1 by world-renowned authorities Michael Leiter and Christina Maslach provides us with a longitudinal and in-depth look at burnout and workplace injuries. Burnout continues to be a major cost of job and occupational stress for so many professionals and workers around the world. Chapter 2 by Mina Westman and her colleagues brings our attention to the challenges of international business travel, with the effects it has on the travelers and their spouses. Safety and security are only part of the puzzle that travelers must solve to journey in a healthy, effective way. Chapter 3 by Sarah DeArmond and Peter Chen brings out attention to the understudied issue of workplace sleepiness and sleep deprivation. We see the range of adverse consequences caused by this important yet under-recognized problem. Chapter 4 by Sheena, Johnson, Cary Cooper, and their colleagues takes a cross-occupational look at work-related stress. Stress is not uniform; either in causes or consequences, across occupations and this comparative study provides an important perspective. Chapter 5 by Duílio deCamargo offers important insight into mental illness that is work-related. Drawing on psychiatry and occupational medicine, we are given an in-depth look from the Brazilian perspective. While Section 1 does not exhaust the list of occupational stress costs, it provides core coverage.

Section 2 includes Chapter 6 through 9. Chapter 6 by Marilyn Macik-Frey and her Goolsby Leadership Academy colleagues presents a healthy model of leadership from a positive health perspective. This chapter is based on in-depth interviews with senior executives in many industries. Chapter 7 by Kelly Zellars, Pamela Perrewé, and their colleagues brings attention to the powerful neutralizing effects that political skill can have to reduce negative affect and both psychological and physiological strain. Political skills can be learned without compromising ethical integrity. Chapter 8 by Roberto Cardoso and colleagues offers insight into the reverse side of the stress response, which is the relaxation response, as elicited through meditation. Life goes in cycles as do we, so for every stress there must be an accompanying recovery for us to stay healthy. Section 2 covers an essential, but not exhaustive, coverage of keys tools for combating job stress.

Section 3 includes Chapters 9 through 12. Chapter 9 by Bob Gatchel and Andy Baum is anchored in a biopsychosocial model and looks at biobehavioral mechanisms of stress and quality of life and work. These leading healthy psychologists are well anchored with their work in medical centers, thus bridge several domains of knowledge. Chapter 10 by Irvin Schonfeld and Farrell helps us better understand the many methods that researchers can use in getting a handle on occupational stress and quality of work life. There is no one measure or a single standard for workers or companies to use in "taking their temperature" with regard to stress on the job. Chapter 11 by Káthia Cunha points out that there is a tension between high levels of production and improvements in quality of work life. Chapter 12 by Ana Cristina Limongi-França proposes an integration of the concepts of health promotion and work life quality. Section 3 covers valuable information for enhancing our understanding of work life quality.

These thirteen chapters, organized into three sections, highlight both core knowledge and new developments within the rapidly growing field of research on stress and the quality of working life. We believe this information can help to raise awareness of the causes and costs of occupational stress and poor quality of working life. Further, this should provide a challenge, some incentive, and renewed insight for organizations in Brazil and elsewhere to begin thinking about and acting in ways that lead to a less stressful environment for their workforce.

REFERENCES

Gallup-Healthways Well-Being Index. (2008). National Well-Being Index finds majority struggling (news release), Washington, D.C., 29 April.

Macik-Frey, M., Quick, J.C., & Nelson, D.L. (2007). Advances in occupational health: From a stressful beginning to a more positive future. *Journal of Management, 33*, 809–840.

Pendey, A., Quick, J.C., Rossi, A.M., Nelson, D.L., & Martin, W. (in press). Stress in the Workplace: A Ten-Year Review of the Science, 1997–2007. In R. Contrada and A. Baum (Eds.), *Handbook of Stress Science*.

Rossi, A.M. (2006). *Autocontrole—nova maneira de gerenciar o estresse*. Rio de Janeiro: Best Seller.

SECTION 1

THE ORGANIZATIONAL AND INDIVIDUAL COSTS
OF OCCUPATIONAL STRESS

CHAPTER 1

BURNOUT AND WORKPLACE INJURIES

A Longitudinal Analysis[1]

Michael P. Leiter
Acadia University

Christina Maslach
University of California, Berkeley

ABSTRACT

Employees (N = 682) in 37 work units of the administrative services sector of a large USA organization completed two annual surveys of burnout, workload, and supervision. These surveys were linked to workplace injury rates for the work units as recorded by the organization's human resources office during the subsequent year, for each of the two years of the study. The longitudinal analysis found that workload and exhaustion predicted the incidence of injuries during the subsequent year. Multiple regression analyses established that exhaustion mediated the relationship of workload with injury rate and that Year 1 injuries mediated the relationship of Year 1 exhaustion on Year 2 injury rates. Implications of burnout for workplace safety are considered.

Stress and Quality of Working Life, pages 3–18
Copyright © 2009 by Information Age Publishing

3

In 2001, nearly 4 million employees in the USA experienced workplace injuries, with over $45 billion in direct and indirect costs. The major cause of injuries during this period was overexertion, accounting for 27.3% of that total (Liberty Mutual, 2003). In addition to their direct harm, workplace accidents undermine the quality of worklife. They define the workplace as unsafe and introduce doubts about the organization's concern for employees.

Many factors can increase the risk of workplace injuries. Of particular interest for the current study is the role of psychological factors, such as the experience of job stress. There is a well-documented link between stress and negative health outcomes, including cardiovascular disease, muscularskeletal problems, and infections. Job stress is also predictive of various behavioral responses, such as problems with family relationships and self-damaging behaviors. What is particularly noteworthy here is that job stress can also impair job performance, by reducing one's capacity for complex physical skills and by impairing cognitive functioning (see Kahn & Byosiere, 1992; Sauter & Murphy, 1995). This research literature suggests that the experience of job stress may place workers at greater risk for an accident on the job.

BURNOUT

One type of job stress that has been studied in recent years is burnout, which involves a prolonged response to chronic interpersonal stressors on the job (Maslach, 1982; Maslach & Leiter, 1997). The three key dimensions of burnout are exhaustion, cynicism, and a sense of professional ineffectiveness. These three dimensions have a structured interrelationship, in that exhaustion, occurring in response to environmental demands, leads to cynicism, which in turn diminishes professional efficacy. This structured relationship defines burnout as a syndrome rather than as a coincidental cluster of symptoms.

Burnout symptoms tend to manifest themselves in normal persons who do not suffer from prior psychopathology or an identifiable organic illness. As such, burnout seems to fit the diagnostic criteria for job-related neurasthenia (Schaufeli, Bakker, Hoogduin, Schaap, & Kladler, 2001). As one would expect from the research on stress and health, the exhaustion dimension of burnout has been correlated with various self-reported physical symptoms of stress: headaches, gastrointestinal disorders, muscle tension, hypertension, cold/flu episodes, and sleep disturbances (see Leiter & Maslach, 2000a, for a review). Although there has been less research on how job burnout affects one's home life, studies have found a fairly consistent negative "spillover" effect (Maslach, 2004).

Burnout has been associated with various forms of negative responses to the job, including job dissatisfaction, low organizational commitment, absenteeism, intention to leave the job, and turnover (see Schaufeli & Enzmann, 1998, for a review). People who are experiencing burnout can have a negative impact on their colleagues, both by causing greater personal conflict and by disrupting job tasks. Thus, burnout can be "contagious" and perpetuate itself through informal interactions on the job. When burnout reaches the high cynicism stage, it can result in higher absenteeism and increased turnover. Furthermore, burnout is linked to poorer quality of work, as people shift to doing the bare minimum, rather than performing at their best. They make more errors, become less thorough, and have less creativity for solving problems. For example, studies have found that nurses experiencing higher levels of burnout were judged by their patients to be providing a lower level of patient care (Leiter, Harvie, & Frizzell, 1998; Vahey, Aiken, Sloane, Clarke, & Vargas, 2004), while another study found that the risk of patient mortality was higher when nurses had a higher patient workload and were experiencing greater burnout (Aiken, Clarke, Sloane, Sochalski & Silber, 2002).

Research has also linked burnout with employees' perceptions of occupational safety. Aircraft maintenance personnel experiencing aspects of burnout reported feeling more at risk for workplace hazards (Leiter & Robichaud, 1997). Other research found health care workers' reports of abusive interactions to be related to the exhaustion and cynicism components of burnout (Leiter, Frizzell, Harvie, & Churchill, 2001). Although these self-reported results indicate that exhausted workers feel more at risk, they do not establish that such workers are actually more susceptible to harm. Other research has established that fatigue, resulting from prolonged effort or extended shifts, aggravates the risk of workplace accidents (Liao, Arvey, & Butler, 2001; Rosa, 1995). This research has not associated fatigue with measures of burnout. To date, there has not been any research that links experienced burnout to independent measures of health outcomes, such as the utilization of health care services, the filing of workers' compensation claims, or the incidence of workplace accidents.

The current study is an attempt to address that gap by assessing the relationship between self-reported burnout and objective records of workplace injuries. Of the three burnout dimensions, exhaustion appears to be most relevant for this particular outcome variable. Physical exhaustion can interfere with performance of intricate or effortful tasks, and mental fatigue can interfere with attention to complex tasks. The potential of exhaustion to inhibit performance—especially performance in demanding and risky situations—suggests that the exhaustion component of burnout may serve as an effective predictor of workplace accidents.

MEDIATION MODEL OF BURNOUT

A mediation model presents the experience of burnout as a subjective state, responsive to the work environment in a way that inhibits key work outcomes (Leiter & Maslach, 2004, Maslach & Leiter, 1997). This model identifies six areas of worklife (workload, control, reward, community, fairness, and values) in which incongruencies, or mismatches, between the work environment and employees' personal aspirations or expectations have the potential of aggravating burnout. The general hypothesis is that worklife incongruencies directly affect employees' thoughts and feelings about their job. In turn, the experience of exhaustion, cynicism, and inefficacy has an impact on performance, health, and well-being. In addition to burnout's role in mediating the impact of worklife incongruencies on outcomes, the model identifies specific mediating relationships among the six areas of worklife and among the three components of burnout (see Leiter & Maslach, 2004, for a complete description of these relationships and relevant empirical evidence).

Workload is the area of worklife most directly associated with exhaustion. Excessive work demands arising from the quantity of work, the intensity of deadlines, or the complexity of work exhaust personal energy. The Mediation Model proposes that excessive workload relates to injury rates through its relationship with exhaustion: exhausting workers' energy is the route through which excessive workload increases their susceptibility to workplace injuries.

CURRENT STUDY

The current study focused on whether the burnout dimension of exhaustion is associated with an increased vulnerability to workplace accidents. The first set of hypotheses concerned longitudinal relationships of exhaustion and workload with incidence of injuries. As noted above, exhaustion was expected to be associated with higher accident rates in the subsequent 12 months because of the deleterious impact of fatigue on performance.

> **Hypothesis 1:** *Exhaustion is positively related to the incidence of workplace injuries during the following year (1–12 months). This hypothesis was tested for both Year 1 and Year 2.*

> **Hypothesis 2:** *Exhaustion at Time 1 is positively related to the incidence of workplace injuries during the following second year (13–24 months).*

> **Hypothesis 3:** *Workload incongruencies are positively related to the incidence of workplace injuries during the following 12 months*

Hypothesis 4: *Exhaustion enhances the prediction of the future year's injuries by the previous year's injuries. The fourth hypothesis concerned the extent to which exhaustion contributed to the prediction of injuries in the long term, in contrast to predicting injuries in the immediate future. Confirming this hypothesis would indicate a long-term relationship of exhaustion that goes beyond the year-to-year consistency in injury rates across organizational units. Rejecting the hypothesis would limit the relationship of exhaustion and injuries to the immediate future.*

Hypothesis 5: *Exhaustion mediates the relationship of workload with injuries.*

The fifth hypothesis reflects a process in which excessive workload prompts exhaustion, which in turn leads to a greater susceptibility to injuries at work.

METHOD

The staff of a business and administrative services division of a large North American university participated in an annual assessment process, as part of its attempt to deal with a series of organizational issues. The assessment utilized a checkup survey process that is designed to produce a high level of employee participation within the organization, with a minimum goal of a 70% response rate (see Leiter & Maslach, 2000b for details of this organizational checkup process). The survey included measures of the six domains of worklife, the three dimensions of experienced job burnout, and several management variables. For each year of this annual assessment, records were maintained of workplace injuries within the organizational units, thus allowing an analysis of the relationship between employee experience and subsequent risk of injury.

Participants

The organizational units in this business and administrative services division comprised a wide range of personnel providing accounting and purchasing services, maintenance of physical plant and extensive grounds, a printing operation, and safety monitoring. Some units were as small as three individuals, with the largest comprising 77 individuals. Both the total number of employees and the participation rate declined slightly over the two surveys: there were 992 in Year 1 (87% response rate), and 812 in Year 2 (83% response rate).

Within this sample, the analysis focused on the 37 units for which there were complete data on all the variables in the study for each of the two years. Due to the organizational restructuring between Year 1 and Year 2, some units had inconsistent membership over this interval. They were dropped from the analysis.

The sample included 682 employees working in the 37 organizational units. The participants include 415 males (60.9%), and 259 females (38.0%), with 1.2% responses missing. Age ranges were 18–29 (120, 17.6%), 30–39 (124, 18.2%), 40–49 (217, 31.8%), 50–59 (179, 26.8%), and 60 or older (28, 4.1%), with 2.1% responses missing. In terms of cultural origin, participants reported African (126, 12.6%), Asian (136, 19.9%), European (208, 30.5%), Latino (102, 15.0%), Middle Eastern (5, 0.7%), Native American (42, 6.2%), Multiracial (32, 4.7%), Pacific Islander (11, 1.6%), with 8.8% responses missing. Job groupings were non-supervisory staff (552, 80.9%), first-line supervisor (68, 10.0%), middle to upper management (43, 6.3%) with 2.8% responses missing. At Year 1, time on the job ranged from less than 6 months (114, 16.7%),6 months–1 year (96, 14%), 1–2 years (77, 11.3%), 2–5 years (101, 14.8%), 5–10 years (73, 10.7%), 10–15 years (95, 13.9%), 15–20 years (48, 7.0%), 20–25 years (39, 5.7%), more than 25 years (30, 4.4%), with 1.3% responses missing. In terms of career status, participants were ongoing career employees (556, 81.5%) and casual employees (117, 17.2%) with 1.3% responses missing.

Procedure

The current study comprised two surveys at one-year intervals (October 2001 and October 2002). A census survey distributed to all employees in the organization assessed their perception of their work environment and their level of experienced burnout. Over the same period, records of reported injuries, as well as lost working days resulting from these injuries, were maintained by the personnel office of the organization.

Participation in the survey was voluntary, anonymous, and confidential. Each year, respondents completed questionnaires on machine-scanned response sheets during scheduled sessions over a two-week period. Translators were available in some sessions for participants who had difficulty reading English.

The survey was fully supported by top administration who, in their survey introduction, pledged that the aggregated responses would be made public and would be used to help design interventions that would improve working conditions. A strategic planning group, which was composed of staff from various units and levels of responsibility, was responsible for the oversight of the survey process. The annual results were shared with each unit in the division, who were charged with developing and implementing initiatives that would address the specific areas of worklife that had been identified as problematic for that unit.

Measures

Two measures assessed the survey elements of the study: worklife areas and burnout,. Organizational records provided data on workplace injuries.

Because the survey was anonymous, the researchers could not link the injury data to the survey data on an individual level. Prior research addressed this challenge by linking survey and performance data based on organizational units, rather than individuals (Leiter, Harvie, & Frizzell, 1998; Vahey, et al, 2004). The opportunity to make these unit links occurred because the two data sources were collected within the same time frame, using the same definition of organizational units, and included a large enough number of units that there was sufficient power to correlate the two sources of data. Thus, the data were summarized on the level of the work unit for each year of the survey. Survey assessments and injury data were each averaged within work units and linked by work unit and survey year. The analysis linked units' scores on exhaustion, cynicism, and workload for each of the two surveys with their scores on injury incidence for the subsequent 12 months.

Worklife Areas

The Areas of Worklife Scale (AWS; Leiter & Maslach, 2004) comprises 29 items that produce distinct scores for each of the six areas of worklife: workload (6), control (3), reward (4), community (5), fairness (6), and values (5). Only the items regarding workload were used in this analysis. The items are worded as statements of perceived congruence or incongruence between oneself and the job. Thus each subscale includes positively worded items of congruence, e.g., "I have enough time to do what's important in my job" (workload) and negatively worded items of incongruence, e.g., "I do not have time to do the work that must be done." Respondents indicate their degree of agreement with these statements on a 5-point Likert-type scale ranging from 1 (strongly disagree), through 3 (hard to decide), to 5 (strongly agree). The scoring for the negatively worded items is reversed. For each of the six subscales, larger scores indicate a higher degree of perceived alignment between the workplace and the respondent's preferences. Conversely, lower scores indicate more perceived misalignment or misfit between the worker and the workplace. The AWS items were developed from a series of staff surveys conducted by the Centre for Organizational Research & Development (Leiter & Harvie, 1998; Maslach & Leiter, 1997) as a means of assessing the constructs underlying our analysis of the six areas of worklife. The scale has yielded a consistent factor structure across samples (Leiter & Maslach, 2004). A factor analysis of the data in this study for the AWS items replicated the established AWS factor structure.

Burnout

The Maslach Burnout Inventory–General Scale (MBI–GS; Schaufeli, Leiter, Maslach, & Jackson, 1996) measures the three dimensions of the burnout syndrome: exhaustion, cynicism, and efficacy (reversed). The items are framed as statements of job-related feelings (e.g., "I feel burned out from my work", "I feel confident that I am effective at getting things done"), and are rated on a 6-point frequency scale (ranging from "never" to "daily"). Burnout is reflected in higher scores on exhaustion and cynicism, and lower scores on efficacy. Developed from the original MBI (Maslach & Jackson, 1981), which was designed for human service occupations, the MBI–GS is a 16-item measure that evaluates burnout among people in all occupations. Thus, the MBI-GS was appropriate for the wide range of employees within the participating organization. A factor analysis of the data in this study for the MBI-GS items replicated the established MBI-GS factor structure.

The strategy in this study averaged scores on the exhaustion and cynicism scales of the MBI–GS across individuals in a work unit. These scores provide indicators of an overall level of exhaustion and cynicism within that work unit. This construct is an appropriate level of analysis because the MBI–GS was developed primarily to assess social systems, rather than as an instrument for individual clinical diagnosis. As a unit average, exhaustion and cynicism scores reflect an overall tendency of a group regarding the energy and involvement they bring to their work.

Injuries

The organization recorded workplace injuries, including the date, type of injury, employee injured, work unit, and number of missed working days. The injury data were available for the 12 months following each survey. An injury was operationally defined as an incident that generated a report that was registered with the health and safety office of the human resource department in the organization, in response to a policy that required employees and their supervisors to report all physical harm to employees occurring at work. Some injuries required medical interventions and up to a year of sick leave; some required no intervention. In Year 1, employees reported 209 injuries; in Year 2 they reported 166 injuries. Adjusting the 682 participants by the annual response rates (87% and 83% respectively), the injury rate per employee was 27% in Year 1 and 20% in Year 2.

This injury rate is much higher than those reported in government reports (e.g., US Department of Labor, 2004) because the organization used a more comprehensive definition of an injury. The organization has an assertive approach to recording injuries that counts a relatively large number of minor incidents that would elsewhere go unreported. As an indication of this contrast, the US Department of Labor notes that 53% of injuries counted in their system result in at least one day of lost work (US Department of Labor, 2004). Only 33% of the injuries in this organization resulted in any lost work days, suggesting that the organization's injury rate is reported at 1.60 (.53/.33) times that of industry data by including a large number of relatively minor injuries requiring no time off work. Adjusting the injury rate regarding this overall indicator of severity produces a comparable injury rate in Year 1 of 16.5% and in Year 2 of 12.5%. This remains a relatively high injury rate, but one that is comparable to other industries.

The types of injuries reported for each year are displayed in Table 1.1. The variable used in this study was the annual injury incidence rate for each unit, i.e., the unit's average number of injuries per employee over the course of 12 months following the survey. The injury measure was structured as an incidence frequency. It was not weighted for severity. The primary hypothesis of the study was that the exhaustion dimension of burnout predicts the incidence of injury, not its severity. The organizational records did not include a gauge of severity, per se, only the type of injury. A given type of injury could have various levels of severity. Also, the type of injury is confounded with the type of work conducted by members of this occupationally diverse workforce. The number of lost days following an injury was not an appropriate measure. Its distribution, with units reporting lost days ranging from 0 to 300 resulted in a kurtosis of 3.39, indicating a distribution unsuitable for correlational analysis. Most importantly, the study tests the proposal that chronic exhaustion increases a workers' susceptibility to committing errors at work; there is no compelling argument that greater exhaustion leads to injuries of greater severity. The appropriate measure for this study is one with the greatest sensitivity to the occurrence of an injury, not a measure of injury severity.

RESULTS

Table 1.2 displays statistics for all variables for Time 1 and Time 2. Each table includes for each construct the means, standard deviations, kurtosis, and correlations based on scores for the 37 units. In parentheses, the table

TABLE 1.1 Types of Injury

Nature of Injury	Year 1	Year 2	Total
Abrasions	9	5	14
Allergy	1	1	2
Avulsion	3	1	4
Bite	7	3	10
Conjunctivitis		1	1
Contusion/Bruise	25	13	38
Dermatitis	3	8	11
Emotional Stress	2	5	7
Fainting	1	1	2
Foreign Object	1	1	2
Fracture	4	4	8
Hearing Loss/Tinnitus	1		1
Hernia	2		2
Infection	1		1
Internal Organ	2		2
Laceration(s)	13	16	29
Multiple Injuries		2	2
Nausea/Vomiting		1	1
Not Classified	4		4
Other	2	1	3
Overuse	16	13	29
Pain	9	7	16
Physical Contact	1		1
Poisoning		1	1
Puncture	3	6	9
Respiratory Disorder	4	3	7
Rupture	2		2
Strain or Sprain	81	72	153
Tendonitis	3		3
Thermal		1	1
Total	200	166	366

also displays the standard deviation based on the individual scores to indicate the difference in range between the individual (N = 622) and unit (N = 37) based scores. There is no alpha for the injury constructs as they are based on single item indicators. Alpha levels indicate acceptable levels of inter-item consistency.

Hypothesis 1 was confirmed for both time samples: exhaustion was correlated with injuries at Time 1 ($r = .35$, $p < .05$; see Table 1.2) and at Time 2

TABLE 1.2   Descriptive Statistics and Correlations

	Mean	S. D. (Full Sample)	Alpha	Kurtosis	Exhaustion T1	Workload T1	Injuries T2	Exhaustion T2	Workload T2
Injuries T1	0.33	0.31		0.45	.35*	−.43**	.41**	.48**	−.46**
Exhaustion T1	2.20	0.59 (1.57)	.89	1.41		−.76**	.30	.68**	−.44**
Workload T1	3.12	.37 (0.84)	.73	1.38			−.39*	−.72**	.74**
Injuries T2	0.30	0.29		−0.68				.43**	−.34*
Exhaustion T2	2.42	0.66 (1.57)	.90	0.38					−.68**
Workload T2	3.03	0.42 (0.84)	.75	1.51					

($r = .43$, $p < .01$; see Table 1.2 Hypothesis 2 was confirmed in that Time 1 exhaustion was correlated with Time 2 injuries ($r = .30$, $p < .05$). Hypothesis 3 was confirmed in that workload was correlated with injuries in Time 1 ($r = −.43$, $p < .01$; see Table 1.2) and at Time 2 ($r = −.33$, $p < .05$; see Table 1.2). The variables were generally consistent over time, with the lowest correlation between Time 1 and Time 2 injuries ($r = .41$, $p < .01$) and the highest for Time 1 and Time 2 workload ($r = .74$, $p < .01$).

A multiple regression tested Hypothesis 4 to determine the extent to which exhaustion enhanced the prediction of Time 2 injuries beyond the prediction provided by Time 1 injuries (adjusted $R^2 = .141$; $F_{(1,35)} = 6.88$, $p < .01$). After entering injuries as a predictor, neither exhaustion nor any other variable in the study enhanced the prediction of Time 2 injuries (see Table 1.3). Thus Hypothesis 4 was not supported.

TABLE 1.3   Time 1: Capacity to Enhance Time 1 Incident's Prediction of Time 2 Injuries

	Beta	t	Sig.		
Time 1 Injuries	.37	2.75	.01		
	Beta in	t	Sig.	Partial Correlation	Tolerance
Exhaustion	.18	1.11	.27	.19	.88

A multiple regression tested Hypothesis 4 to determine the extent to which Time 1 injuries mediated the relationship of exhaustion with Time 2 injuries following Baron and Kenny's (1986) procedure that defines mediation by (1) a significant zero-order correlation between the predictor and the dependent variable, (2) a significant regression coefficient between the mediator and the dependent variable, and (3) reduction of the relationship of the predictor with the dependent variable after entering the mediator in a regression. As noted above, the first condition is met with the correlation of exhaustion with Time 2 injuries; the second condition was met with (adjusted R^2 = .141; $F_{(1,35)}$ = 6.88, $p < .01$). After entering injuries as a predictor, neither exhaustion nor any other variable in the study enhanced the prediction of Time 2 injuries (see Table 1.3). Thus Hypothesis 4 was not supported.

A multiple regression for each of the two years tested Hypothesis 5 to determine the extent to which Time 1 exhaustion mediated the relationship of Time 1 workload with injuries following Baron and Kenny's (1986) procedure that defines mediation by (1) a significant zero-order correlation between the predictor and the dependent variable, (2) a significant regression coefficient between the mediator and the dependent variable, and (3) reduction of the relationship of the predictor with the dependent variable after entering the mediator in a regression. As noted above, the first condition is met with the correlation of exhaustion with Time 2 injuries; the second condition was met with exhaustion predicting Time 1 injuries (adjusted R^2 = .097; $F_{(1,35)}$ = 4.89, $p < .05$) and Time 2 injuries (adjusted R^2 = .159; $F_{(1,35)}$ = 7.81, $p < .01$). After entering exhaustion as a predictor, workload did not enhance the prediction of injuries (see Table 1.4 and Table 1.5). In both analyses, the partial correlations for workload were not significant after exhaustion was entered.

TABLE 1.4   Time 1: Capacity to Enhance Exhaustion's Prediction of Injuries

	Beta	t	Sig.		
Exhaustion	.35	2.21	.03		

	Beta in	t	Sig.	Partial Correlation	Tolerance
Workload	−.38	−1.60	.12	−.26	.43

TABLE 1.5   Time 2: Capacity to Enhance Exhaustion's Prediction of Injuries

	Beta	t	Sig.		
Exhaustion	.43	2.80	.01		

	Beta in	t	Sig.	Partial Correlation	Tolerance
Workload	−.08	−0.38	.70	−.07	.53

DISCUSSION

The results of this analysis confirm a direct relationship of the exhaustion component of burnout with the frequency of workplace injuries occurring in the subsequent year. These findings are remarkable in their capacity to provide a significant link between self-reported burnout and independent organizational records on workplace injuries maintained by the personnel office of the organization. Further, the study provided support for exhaustion's mediation role, consistent with the Mediation Model proposed by Leiter and Maslach (2004). These results provide a major contribution to research on burnout by establishing longitudinal predictive relationships between burnout and objective measures of injury incidence in the workplace.

The results of this study extend previous research linking burnout to self-reported indicators of ill health. The links of exhaustion with injury were established across two distinct sources of data. Employee surveys on two occasions provided self-report measures of exhaustion and workload. Organizational records of workplace injuries over the year following each survey provided information on units. These conditions assure that the relationships established with injuries are robust, as the injury incidence data are collected through a completely different methodology, compiled during the year following the survey.

The mediation analysis extends the Mediation Model of burnout (Leiter & Maslach, 2004). The analysis confirmed exhaustion's role in mediating the longitudinal relationship of workload with injuries. This finding is consistent with the model's prediction that burnout mediates the relationship of various worklife problems with key work outcomes. The mediating relationship is consistent with the proposal that a primary route through which problematic work settings have a detrimental impact on performance, health, and safety is through their impact on workers' state of energy.

Despite its clear advance over other research in this field, the current study has limitations to be addressed in future studies. If the study were to be replicated over multiple organizations, the results would have greater generalizability, although it should be noted that the study sample was composed of a diverse mix of work settings, including business offices, machine shops, outdoor maintenance, and management. A much larger number of organizational units would also permit the analysis to examine more complex longitudinal relationships, such as exhaustion's mediation of workload and the impact of injury rates on subsequent levels of exhaustion. The scope of the present study is not sufficiently large to permit examination of such complex relationships within the context of the longitudinal relationships of burnout with workplace injuries.

In conclusion, this study constitutes a major contribution to the research on burnout, demonstrating a longitudinal relationship of exhaustion with objective measures of workplace injuries. The longitudinal nature of the study strengthens the argument that the exhaustion component of burnout leads to diminished performance and greater susceptibility to harm. As such, exhaustion can serve as an indicator of risk: work units with high levels of exhaustion are more likely to experience workplace accidents and injuries over the subsequent year. As the average incident in this study was nearly one injury for every three employees, the study was focusing on a serious issue in a large organization. From the perspective of risk management and concern for employees, these results emphasize issues of consequence for employers.

ACKNOWLEDGMENT

This research was supported by a grant from the Social Sciences and Humanities Research Council of Canada.

REFERENCES

Aiken, L. H., Clarke, S. P., Sloane, D. M., Sochalski, J., & Silber, J. H. (2002). Hospital nurse staffing and patient mortality, nurse burnout, and job dissatisfaction. *Journal of the American Medical Association, 288*(16), 1987–93.

Baron, R. M. & Kenny, D. A. (1986). The Moderator-mediator variable distinction in social psychological research: Conceptual, strategic, and statistical considerations. *Journal of Personality and Social Psychology, 51,* 1173–1182.

Kahn, R. L., & Byosiere, P. (1992). Stress in organizations. In M. D. Dunnette & L. M. Hough (Eds.), *Handbook of Industrial and Organizational Psychology, Vol. 3* (pp. 571–650). Palo Alto, CA: Consulting Psychologists Press.

Leiter, M. P., Frizzell, C., Harvie, P., & Churchill, L. (2001). Abusive interactions and burnout: Examining occupation, gender, and the mediating role of community. *Psychology and Health, 16,* 547–563.

Leiter, M. P., & Harvie, P. (1998). Conditions for staff acceptance of organizational change: burnout as a mediating construct. *Anxiety, Stress, & Coping, 11,* 1–25

Leiter, M. P., Harvie, P. & Frizzell, C. (1998). The correspondence of patient satisfaction and nurse burnout. *Social Science & Medicine, 47,* 1611–1617.

Leiter, M. P. & Maslach, C. (2000a). Burnout and health. In A. Baum, T. Revenson, & J. Singer (Eds.) *Handbook of health psychology* (pp. 415–426). Hillsdale, NJ: Lawrence Earlbaum.

Leiter, M. P. & Maslach, C. (2000b). *Preventing burnout and building engagement: A complete program for organizational renewal.* San Francisco: Jossey Bass.

Leiter, M. P., & Maslach, C. (2004). Areas of worklife: A structured approach to organizational predictors of job burnout. In P. Perrewé & D. C. Ganster, (Eds.), *Research in occupational stress and well being: Vol. 3. Emotional and physiological processes and positive intervention strategies* (pp. 91–134). Oxford, UK: JAI Press/ Elsevier.

Leiter, M. P., & Robichaud, L. (1997). Relationships of occupational hazards with burnout: An assessment of measures and models. *Journal of Occupational Health Psychology, 2,* 1–11.

Liao, H., Arvey, R. D., & Butler R. J. (2001). Correlates of Work Injury Frequency and Duration Among Firefighters. *Journal of Occupational Health Psychology, 6*(3), 229–242.

Liberty Mutual Institute for Safety (2003). From research to reality: 2003 annual report of scientific activity. Retrieved October, 14, 2004, http://www.liberty-mutual.com/research-institute-report2003/html/index.html

Maslach, C. (1982). *Burnout: The cost of caring.* Englewood Cliffs, NJ: Prentice-Hall.

Maslach, C. (2004). Understanding burnout: Work and family issues. In D. F. Halpern & S. G. Murphy (Eds.), *Changing the metaphor: From work-family balance to work family interaction* (pp. 99–114). Mahwah, NJ: Lawrence Erlbaum.

Maslach, C., & Jackson, S. E. (1981). *The Maslach Burnout Inventory (research ed.).* Palo Alto, CA: Consulting Psychologists Press.

Maslach, C., & Leiter, M. P. (1997). *The truth about burnout.* San Francisco, CA: Jossey-Bass.

Maslach, D., Schaufeli, W. B., & Leiter, M.P. (2001). Job burnout. *Annual Review of Psychology, 52,* 397–422.

Rosa, R. R. (1995). Extended workshifts and excessive fatigue. *Journal of Sleep Research, 4*(S2), 51–56.

Sauter, S. L., & Murphy, L. R. (Eds.). (1995). *Organizational risk factors for job stress.* Washington, DC: American Psychological Association.

Schaufeli, W. B., Bakker, A. B., Hoogduin, K., Schaap, C., & Kladler, A. (2001). The clinical validity of the Maslach Burnout Inventory and the Burnout Measure. *Psychology and Health, 16,* 565–582.

Schaufeli WB, & Enzmann D. (1998). *The burnout companion to study & practice: A critical analysis.* Philadelphia, PA: Taylor & Francis.

Schaufeli, W. B., Leiter, M. P., Maslach, C., & Jackson, S. E. (1996). The Maslach Burnout Inventory—General Survey. In C. Maslach, S. E. Jackson, & M. P. Leiter (Eds.), *MBI Manual (3rd edition).* Palo Alto, CA: Consulting Psychologists Press.

United States Department of Labor (2004). *Workplace Injuries And Illnesses In 2003.* http://www.bls.gov/news.release/osh.nr0.htm (accessed 2 January 2005).

Vahey, D. C., Aiken, L. H., Sloane, D. M., Clarke, S. P., & Vargas, D. (2004). Nurse burnout and patient satisfaction. *Medical Care, 24*(2), 57–66.

CHAPTER 2

THE IMPACT OF INTERNATIONAL BUSINESS TRIPS ON THE TRAVELERS AND THEIR SPOUSES

Mina Westman, Dalia Etzion and Shoshi Chen
Tel Aviv University, Israel

ABSTRACT

The present chapter, which embeds business travel and crossover research, examines the effects of business trips, which are an ever increasing feature of globalization, on personal well-being and the family domain. In contrast to past research with its focus on the negative psychological and physical consequences of the stress of business traveling, the focus of this chapter is on the positive repercussions. Thus, the current study examined the antecedents of engagement[1] (vigor) and the crossover of engagement (vigor) from business travelers to their spouses and vice versa in a sample consisting of 275 business travelers and their working spouses. The business travelers (21% of them females) were required to travel abroad several times a year within the framework of their jobs.

---

1   In the current study we focus on one component of engagement—vigor

Stress and Quality of Working Life, pages 19–39
Copyright © 2009 by Information Age Publishing
All rights of reproduction in any form reserved.

19

We found that the number of trips of the travelers and their trip control as well as their business trips satisfaction and their work-family conflict were positively related to their engagement (vigor). For spouses, only their perception of travelers' trip control and their work-family conflict were positively related to the engagement. Furthermore, we found a uni-directional crossover of engagement from the spouses to the business travelers. We discuss the implications of these findings and suggest avenues for future research.

One of the consequences of globalization has been an increase in the number of international business trips for the organization. International business travelers are people whose work involves a large number of visits to foreign countries. Thus, business travel is an essential part of their work and for some, traveling is a kind of career in itself. However, there is scant research on the effect of the trips on the travelers and their families and the crossover effects of experiences between them.

Most researchers on business travel regard such trips as a source of stress to the travelers (e.g., DeFrank, Konopaske & Ivancevich, 2000) and their families (Dimberg, Striker, Nordanlycke-Yoo, Nagy, Mundt & Sulsky, 2002; Espino, Sundstorm, Frick, Jacobs & Peters, 2002). In the current chapter we review the literature on travel stress but highlight the positive impact of business trips on the individuals and their families.

Focusing on the positive aspects of business trips, the current chapter related to the antecedents of positive experience-vigor, and the crossover of vigor from business travelers to their spouses and vice versa. The main objectives of this chapter were; to examine the impact of demands and resources on the vigor of the travelers and their spouses; to examine the impact of resources on business travelers' trip satisfaction; to examine the impact of work-family conflict (WFC) on the vigor of the travelers and their spouses; and to test the crossover of vigor between business travelers and their spouses In the current study we drew on the research literature from both the crossover and the business trips domains.

INTERNATIONAL BUSINESS TRIPS

Business trips are characterized by high demands. According to the Job Demands-Resources (JD-R) model (Bakker & Demerouti 2007), job demands refer to physical, psychological, social, or organizational aspects of the job that require sustained physical and/or psychological effort or skills and are therefore associated with certain physiological and/or psychological costs. Job demands are not necessarily negative; however, they may turn into job stressors when meeting those demands requires high effort.

DeFrank, Konopaske and Ivancevich (2000, p. 59) define travel stress as the "perceptual, emotional, behavioral and physical responses made by an individual to the various problems faced during one or more of the phases of travel." They identify specific travel stressors for three phases of the trip: pre-trip stressors, trip stressors and post-trip stressors.

Pre-trip stressors include trip planning and work arrangements. According to DeFrank et al. (2000) some executives push themselves to tie as many loose ends as possible prior to departure, which may result in stress. Home and family issues: Most married business travelers find extended absences from home to be difficult. *Trip stressors* include characteristics of the travel, the air travel itself and travel logistics (e.g., communication infrastructure), job-related factors and cultural differences. According to DeFrank et al. (2000), unmet expectations and the need for rapid cultural adjustment can result in stress. *Post-trip issues* can be caused by job demands (e.g., problems faced both at work and at home during the traveler's absence). DeFrank et al. (2000) concluded that all these stressors, caused by business travel, disturb the efficient functioning of the traveler and, as a result, decrease the organizational success. Dimberg et al. (2002) found that the physical and psychological impact on the traveler is especially substantial when traveling is frequent, as this prevents easy adaptation and setting in to new routines.

Dimberg et al. (2002) found that the physical and psychological impact on the traveler is especially substantial when traveling is frequent, as this prevents easy adaptation and settling in to new routines.

THE WORK–FAMILY INTERFACE AND BUSINESS TRAVEL

Little empirical research has been conducted on the work-family interface of business travelers. Work-family conflict occurs when demands associated with one domain are incompatible with the demands associated with the other domain. Such conflict may arise because performance of one role absorbs time, creates strain, or is behaviorally incompatible with performance of another role (Etzion & Bailyn, 1994; Greenhaus & Beutell, 1985).

For people engaged in business travel as part of their job, these two domains are inseparable and potentially stressful. Work-family conflict is affected by the structural characteristics of the two roles. The literature on the impact of international business travel on the families is sparse. Furthermore, to the best of our knowledge, there is no research focusing on the impact of the family on the business travelers.

Several researchers have focused on the effects of international business trips on the family. Leider (1991) claimed that the temporary separation places a strain on family relationships. Therefore, the longer the trip, the more intense is the stress. He labeled the three stress points: *1: Letting go.* The period leading up to departure is a time of stress for the traveler and the family, as both parties anticipate the upcoming separation. *2: Separation.*

Chronic travel separation brings out feelings of loneliness. Being away, travelers cannot deal with issues relating to their children. *3: Reentry.* Reentry is the point at which the implications of having been absent become clear. For some, both work and home life continued smoothly in their absence, while others face disruptions on one or both fronts upon reentry. Leider (1991) concluded that for many frequent travelers, these three processes never seem to stop.

CONSEQUENCES OF SHORT BUSINESS TRIPS

A business trip seems to be a dual experience, consisting of hassles and uplifts, losses and gains, all impacting the well-being of the travelers. These contradicting effects suggest that research must focus on variables that contribute to the satisfaction or dissatisfaction with the trip and the crossover of negative and positive experiences and moods between spouses

Negative Impact. Several researchers found that business trips resulted in high levels of stress and psychological disorders (Dimberg et al., 2002) and physical and psychological health problems (Rogers, 1998). Striker et al. (1999) found that social, job, and emotional concerns such as the impact of travel on the family, workload upon return and sense of isolation contributed the most to the traveler's stress.

The findings of Espino et al. (2002) indicated that frequent trips increased the strain on the family and, as a by-product, contributed to the stress of the travelers. By rendering the traveler temporarily unavailable to fulfill his/her family-related roles (Roehling & Bultman, 2002), business trips can increase work-family conflict and strain between partners. This sequence of events, in which the family suffering from the frequent absence of the traveler exhibits strain, which, in turn, acts as a stressor for the traveler, is in fact the core of the spillover and crossover processes that increase personal and family tension (Westman, 2001).

The consequences of the continual adjustments that business travelers have to make in switching between the family and traveling roles have been reported in the literature. Liese's (2000) findings demonstrated that the business traveler's experience of increased psychological disorders is mirrored in the family. In the context of business travel, pressures within the family, such as the spouse's maladjustment to additional household and family responsibilities during the traveler's absence, or stressful job demands at the traveler's destination, can affect the business traveler and, accordingly, the balance within his/her family and create inter-role conflict.

Positive Impact. Apart from DeFrank et al. (2000), who devoted a few sentences to the possible positive outcomes of short business trips (p. 62), business trip research has focused on negative outcomes, with very little reflection on positive effects. The positive impact of short business trips, such as exposure to new places and cultures, insight into new business practices and product ideas, individual growth, career enhancing, and challenging has rarely been studied.

However, the growth in recent years of positive psychology, with its emphasis on the importance of studying human strengths and optimal functioning and its focus on the positive rather than the negative impact of various human conditions (Seligman, 2001, 2005), is demonstrating very promising findings. In line with this approach, we believe that, alongside the negative feelings caused by overload and other trip demands, business trips are also likely to evoke positive emotions through the opportunities to learn new things, the sense of accomplishment and the experience of time off that they present.

Westman and Etzion (2002) were the first to treat business trips as a special kind of respite and to demonstrate their positive effects. A possible mechanism that operates during respite is psychological detachment from work. Etzion et al. (1998) showed that even a respite that is not a time of leisure has the same impact as a vacation. Thus, though business travelers are in constant contact with the home office, the temporary respite from the work site may enable a gain of resources, as the trip allows for a sense of detachment from the workplace. In terms of conservation of resources theory (COR), such detachment prevents the loss of resources resulting from the chronic job demands.

The conservation of resources (COR) theory (Hobfoll, 1989) appears to be a good theoretical basis for the understanding of the positive effect of business trips on the well-being of the individual, and the connection between resources and well-being has long been established. According to COR theory spirals of loss or gain of resources are the result of the fact that initial gain creates further gain and initial loss creates further loss. The best way to resist stress, according to COR theory, is to interrupt loss spirals and create gain spirals. Business trips can create just that effect. By leaving the regular working atmosphere and distancing oneself from the daily demands (of work and home), the traveler might not only stop the loss of resources, which is the result of job pressure and family demands, but also gain new resources (new friends, better sense of self efficacy, new cultural experiences, rest, pleasant experiences etc.). In this way the total resource balance might turn-out more positive due to business trips. As Hobfoll and Shirom suggested (1993), a relaxation period between stress episodes allow for resource gain, and the time away from work, even on a business trip, can be taken as such a period.

An important issue raised by Liese (2000) among others is that of the impact of traveling on the family. Crossover research (Westman & Etzion, 1995; Westman & Vinokur, 1998; Westman et al., 2004b) indicates that burnout and job-related strain are transmitted in the family between spouses. By the same token, one can hypothesize that job-related positive experiences cross over between spouses too.

Business trips may also have positive effects on the spouses. Indeed, there is some evidence of gains of these trips to the spouses. Stewart and Donald (2006), investigating the effects of absence due to frequent business trips, found both negative and positive outcomes among the spouses at home. However, they found that respondents did not find their partners' absence to be inherently stressful. Among the positive outcomes, they emphasized independence, space, enhanced marital relations, and time for other activities, enhanced parent-child activities, sharing in positive experiences, financial rewards, and reduced role pressure. In sum, business trips have the potential for causing both negative and positive consequences to the travelers and their spouses and crossover of these experiences from travelers to spouses and vice versa.

THE CROSSOVER PROCESS

The process that occurs when a psychological strain experienced by one person affects the level of strain of another person in the same social environment is referred to as crossover (Bolger, Delongis, Kessler, & Wethington, 1989; Westman & Etzion, 1995) or transmission (Jones & Fletcher, 1993; Rook, Dooley, & Catalano, 1991). Crossover is a dyadic, inter-individual transmission of stress or strain. Findings suggest that one partner's strain affects the well-being of the other partner so that one's strain is a stressor to the other (Burke, Weir, & DuWors, 1980; Jones & Fletcher, 1993).

Westman and Vinokur (1998) specify three main mechanisms that can account for the apparent effects of a crossover process. These mechanisms include common stressors, empathetic reactions, and an indirect mediating interaction process. *Common stressors* affecting both partners will impact the strain of both partners and the similarity in the strain will appear as crossover. *Indirect crossover of strain* is a transmission mediated by interpersonal exchange. Thus, an increase in the strain of one partner is likely to trigger a provocative behavior or exacerbate a negative interaction sequence with the other partner which increases the partner's strain. In sum, job and family stressors raise demands for adaptation, which may lead to tension. These tensions may then lead to negative interactions in the family. *Direct empathetic crossover* implies that stress and strain are transmitted from one partner to another directly as a result of empathetic reactions. The basis for this view is the finding that crossover effects appear between closely related partners who care for each other and share the greater part of their lives together.

Accordingly, strain in one partner produces an empathetic reaction in the other that increases his or her strain.

Most studies have investigated the crossover of psychological strains, such as anxiety (Westman, Etzion, & Horovitz, 2004a), burnout (e.g., Bakker & Schaufeli, 2000), distress (Barnett et al., 1995), depression (Howe, Levy, & Caplan , 2004), maladjustment (Takeuchi, Yun, & Teslu, 2002), work-family conflict (Hammer et al., 1997), marital dissatisfaction (Westman, Vinokur, Hamilton, & Roziner, 2004b) and physical and mental health complaints (Gorgievski-Duijvesteijin, Giesen, & Bakker, 2000). Thus, till very recently, only negative outcomes have been the focus of crossover studies.

CROSSOVER OF POSITIVE EXPERIENCES

Westman (2001) suggested broadening the definition of crossover into contagion of positive as well as negative events. One possible reason for the neglect of the possibility of positive effects crossing over is that stress research relies heavily on medical models, with their emphasis on negative effects, just as negative affectivity was investigated for many years before researchers broadened their interest to positive affectivity.

The empathy definitions mentioned before allow for the sharing of both positive and negative emotions. If the crossover process operates via empathy, one would expect to find not only crossover of negative experiences, but positive experiences as well. Thus, empathy could just as easily involve the sharing of another's positive emotions and the conditions that bring them about. Positive experiences and feelings are not merely the absence of stress; they are qualitatively different experiences (Fredrickson, 2001; Fredrickson & Joiner, 2002). Thus, positive events and emotions may also cross over to the partner and have a positive impact on his or her well-being.

The core relational theme for empathy involves the sharing of another person's emotional state, distressed or otherwise. Thus, as strain in one partner may produce an empathetic reaction in the other, which increases the recipient's strain, the work engagement expressed by one partner may fuel the other partner's engagement. This process happens because one's thoughts are focused on the positive aspects of work that make him/her enthusiastic. One can think of many positive instances, such as enjoyable experiences at one's job leading to the crossover of job satisfaction and engagement, eliciting a good mood in the partner at home. Similarly, supportive family relationships and attitudes can create positive attitudes crossing over to the work setting. Altogether, crossover of positive affects appears to be fertile ground for enhancing theoretical thinking and making practical contributions to the literature.

Investigating the issue of positive crossover, Etzion and Westman (2001) examined the effect of a two-week organized tour abroad on crossover of burnout between spouses. Though they did not study crossover of positive emotions, they did find an ameliorating impact of the vacation on the crossover of burnout: they demonstrated a crossover of burnout before the vacation, but no significant crossover effect after the vacation. These findings indicate that positive events such as vacations, or a change from a stressful environment to a tranquil one, may stop the vicious circle of crossover of strain from one spouse to another.

CROSSOVER OF WORK ENGAGEMENT

Recently, researchers have begun to investigate the crossover of work engagement, which may be seen as a sense of energetic and effective connection with work activities, and the perception of being able to handle the demands of the job satisfactorily. Schaufeli and Bakker (2004) defined *work engagement* as a positive and fulfilling work-related state of mind characterized by vigor, dedication, and absorption. Vigor is characterized by high levels of energy and mental resilience while working, willingness to invest effort in work, and persistence in the face of difficulties. People who are vigorous usually take the initiative, generate their own positive feedback, and also want to invest their energies in other things besides working (Schaufeli et al., 2001). Dedication refers to being strongly involved in one's work and experiencing a sense of significance, enthusiasm, inspiration, pride, and challenge. The third dimension, absorption, is characterized by being fully concentrated and happily engrossed in one's work, such that time passes quickly and one has difficulty detaching oneself from work. In the present study we focused on the crossover of one dimension of engagement—vigor.

Hobfoll's COR theory (1989) may provide insights into understanding the experience of engagement. In COR theory terms, work engagement can be conceptualized as a result of continuous resource gain experienced by individuals in the workplace. Resources are functional in achieving work goals, reduce job demands and their associated costs, and stimulate personal growth, learning, and development. Thus, resources are not only necessary to deal with job demands; they are also important in their own right (Demerouti, Bakker, Nachreiner, & Schaufeli, 2001). Individuals who possess strong resource pools often experience spirals of resource gain because initial gain begets further gain and resource surpluses promote engagement. Demerouti et al., (2001) found that job resources were positively related to work engagement.

We found only three studies that detected crossover of positive experiences (Bakker, Demerouti, & Schaufeli, 2005; Demerouti, Bakker, & Schaufeli,

2005). Bakker, Demerouti and Schaufeli (2005) demonstrated crossover of work engagement among 323 couples working in a variety of occupations. The crossover of work engagement was significant, even after controlling for characteristics of the work and home environments of both partners. Demerouti, Bakker and Schaufeli (2005) detected crossover of life satisfaction from husbands to wives but not from wives to husbands. These findings were the first to demonstrate crossover of positive experiences. Bakker and Demerouti (forthcoming) investigated the crossover of engagement from working wives to their husbands. Their results from moderated structural equation modeling analyses showed that work engagement crossed over between partners. Furthermore, they found that empathy moderated the crossover effect. Men who were perspective takers were more strongly influenced by their partners' work engagement than their counterparts who were not perspective takers.

Thus, the finding that work engagement crosses over between partners replicated a previous study among working couples (Bakker et al., 2005). This strengthens our belief that positive experiences may cross over just as well as negative experiences. These findings offer partial support for the "direct-empathy" explanation for the crossover process (Westman, 2001).

HYPOTHESES

Hypothesis 1: *There is a negative relationship between demands (number of trips) and vigor. The higher the demands, the lower the vigor.*

Hypothesis 2: *There is a positive relationship between resources (trip control) and vigor: the higher the level of resources, the higher the level of vigor.*

Hypothesis 3: *There is a positive relationship between satisfaction from the business trip and vigor: the greater the satisfaction from the business trip, the higher the level of vigor.*

Hypothesis 4: *There is a relationship between work-family conflict and vigor*

Hypothesis 5: *Vigor crosses over from the travelers to their spouses and vice versa*

METHOD

The sample consisted of 275 couples, business travelers and their working spouses. The respondents (21.1% of them females) were required to travel abroad several times a year within the framework of their jobs. Most of the couples had children (88.7%). The mean number of trips per year was 9.11 and the average length of a trip was 6.79 days.

Procedure. Questionnaires were distributed by the travel coordinators of the participating organizations to the travelers and their spouses, who were asked to fill them out separately and return them in a pre-paid envelope to the university.

The questionnaire included a short introduction explaining the research objectives and guaranteeing full confidentiality followed by questions relating to characteristics of the traveler, the trip itself, the family and the organization.

Demographic variables: years of marriage, having children, age of children.

Characteristics of the trip: number of trips per year, length of trip.

Vigor, a component of engagement, was measured by five items of the engagement scale (Schaufeli & Bakker, 2001). The items were rated on a 7-point scale ranging from 0 (never) to 6 (always). A sample item is: "At my job, I feel strong and vigorous." Cronbach's α for the vigor scale was .83 for the travelers and .87 for the spouses.

Travelers' Business Trip Satisfaction (BTS) and Spouses Perception of Traveler's Business Trip Satisfaction was measured by seven items (Chia, 1999). Sample items (words in parentheses are for the spouse) are: "I (my spouse) see (sees) these trips as a necessary part of my (his/her) work", "I (my spouse) enjoy(s) my (his/her) business trips". Responses were made on a 7-point scale. The higher the score, the higher the BTS. Cronbach's α was .84 for the travelers and .87 for the spouses.

Work-family conflict was measured using two items from a scale developed by Vinokur, Pierce and Buck (1999). Sample items are: "How often does your job or career keep you from spending the amount of time you would like to spend with your family?" and "How often does your home life keep you from spending the amount of time you would like to spend on job- or career-related activities?" Responses were given on a 5-point scale ranging from Almost never/Never (1) to Almost always/Always (5). Cronbach's α was 83. for the travelers and .73 for the spouses.

Travelers' Trip Control and Spouses' Perception of Travelers' Trip Control. The extent to which respondents had control over their travel schedules was measured using two items (words in parentheses are for the spouse): "I have (my spouse has) control over my (his/her) travel schedule" and "It is not a problem if I (he/she) cannot go on a scheduled trip because of personal reasons". Responses were on a 7-point scale (1 = Strongly agree and 7 = Strongly disagree). A third question, "How flexible is your (your spouse's) company when deciding on your (his/her) travel agenda?" was answered on a 7 point scale (1 = Extremely inflexible and 7 = Extremely flexible). The spouses reported their perception of the travelers' trip control. Cronbach's α of the scale was .79 for the travelers and .87 for the spouses.

It should be clear that the business travelers' answers related to their job whereas the spouses' answers related to their perception of the travelers' job. Thus, the demands (number of trips), resources (control over trip) and business trip satisfaction the spouses reported, were their perception of what the travelers job characteristics and attitudes are. The correlations between travelers' demands, resources and BTS and the spouses' perceptions of travelers' demands, resources and BTS were quite high (.95, .63, .75), respectively.

RESULTS

Means and standard deviations of study variables for travelers and spouses are presented in Table 2.1. The mean levels of number of trips and business trip satisfaction reported by the travelers and their spouses were identical. The travelers reported higher mean levels of control than their spouses ($t(275) = 4.70$, $p < .001$, paired samples t-test) and also higher mean levels of vigor ($t(275) = 5.25$, $p < .001$) and WFC (t $(275) = 6.41$, $p < .001$).

Overview of the Model

The adequacy of the hypothesized relations between the variables was tested using structural equation modeling with the EQS program (Bentler, 2006). Following Hu and Bentler (1999), we report fit indices of two types, the Non-Normed Fit Index (NNFI, also known as TLI) and the Comparative Fit Index (CFI), and two indices of misfit, the Root Mean-Square Error

TABLE 2.1 Means and Standard Deviations among Study Variables among Travelers and Their Spouses (N = 275 couples)

Variable	Travelers		Spouses	
	M	**SD**	**M**	**SD**
Control	4.53	1.43	4.14	1.48
BTS[a]	4.33	1.15	4.13	1.16
Vigor	4.48	0.80	4.07	1.05
WFC[a]	2.99	0.98	2.45	0.95
Number of trips	9.11	6.42	9.11	6.42

[a] BTS = Business trips satisfaction; WFC = Work Family conflict

of Approximation (RMSEA) and the Standardized Root Mean-Square Residual (SRMR). NNFI and CFI close to or above 0.95 combined with RMSEA below .06 and SRMR below .09 are considered indicative of acceptable fit.

In the model we estimated, number of trips was computed as the mean of traveler's and spouse's reports and specified as an observed variable (the correlation between these two scores was $r = .97$). Using the accepted approach of parceling (Little, Cunningham, Shahar, & Widaman, 2002), trip control, business trip satisfaction, and vigor were each indicated for each respondent by a random third of the items that make up the scale, and work-family conflict was indicated by its two items. The data for the model came from the two sources (the travelers and their spouses), each employing the same methods of data collection. In order to account for the common methods effect, the corresponding factors and the residual errors of the corresponding indicators for the travelers and the spouses were allowed to correlate freely. To allow for meaningful comparisons of paths for the travelers and their spouses, factor loadings were constrained to be equal for both spouses.

In the first step, we tested the measurement model, which was found to fit the data well: χ^2 (177, $N = 258$) = 316.05, $p < .001$, NNFI = .940, CFI = .954, RMSEA = .055 and SRMR = .053. Next, we estimated the model of crossover of vigor specified in Figure 2.1. The estimated model with standardized regression coefficients is shown in Figure 2.2. This model fits the data well, with χ^2 (216, $N = 258$) = 409.09, $p < .001$, NNFI = .992, CFI = .994, RMSEA = .059, and SRMR = .080.

Tests of the Hypotheses

Hypothesis 1 predicted a negative relationship between number of trips and vigor for both travelers and their spouses. As can be seen from Figure 2.1, this hypothesis was not supported. The number of trips was positively related to vigor for travelers and was not related to vigor for their spouses. Hypothesis 2, suggesting a positive relationship between perceived trip control and vigor was supported for both travelers and spouses. Hypothesis 3, suggesting a positive relationship between satisfaction from the trip and vigor, received only partial support. Business trip satisfaction had a strong significant effect upon the traveler's vigor but perception of travelers' business trip satisfaction had no significant effect upon the spouse's vigor. Hypothesis 4 predicted a relationship between WFC and vigor for travelers and spouses without specifying a direction (positive or negative). We found a positive relationship between WFC and vigor for both the travelers and their spouses. Hypothesis 5, predicting bi-directional direct crossover, received only partial support. We detected a uni-directional significant path

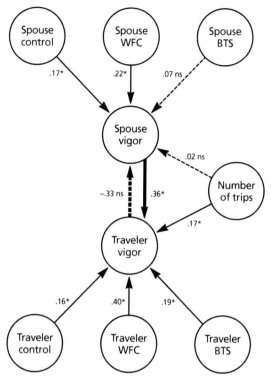

Figure 2.1 Structural equation model of vigor crossover from travelers to spouses.
Notes: BTS = Business trips satisfaction; WFC = Work and Family conflict; Spouses' BTS and
Trip control relate to their perception of the travelers' BTS and trip control.
* $p < .05$ χ^2 (177, N = 258) = 316.05, $p < .001$
NNFI = .940
CFI = .954
RMSEA = .055; SRMR = .053.

from the spouse's vigor (β = .36; $p < .05$) to the traveler's vigor. The path
from the traveler's vigor to the spouse's vigor was not significant.

DISCUSSION

This study attempted to integrate literature from the crossover domain and
the business trips domain. Thus our main aims were to test the impact of
demands, resources, WFC, and work attitudes on vigor and to test the crossover of vigor between business travelers and their spouses.

So far, most crossover researchers have focused on negative experiences
at work such as job stress and burnout (for a review, see Westman, 2001).

The current study is one of the first attempts to examine the crossover of positive work-related feelings and attitudes, specifically, vigor at work. Results of our study reveal that positive feelings and energy (vigor) expressed by the partner are indeed transmitted to the business traveler.

Based on the Job Demands-Resources model (Bakker & Demerouti, 2007) we examined possible correlates of vigor and tested the crossover effects after controlling for potential demands and resources at work and at the work-home interface. The results of the structural equation modeling (SEM) demonstrated a uni-directional crossover of vigor from spouses to their traveling partners.

Several crossover studies have found a uni-directional crossover of stress and strain, mainly from husbands to wives. However, the current study did not investigate crossover of negative experiences and the crossover phenomenon of the positive experience (vigor) did not occur between husbands and wives but between men and women business travelers and their spouses. Though most of the travelers in the current study were men and only 21.1% of them were females, it can not be considered a study of crossover from husbands to wives.

The asymmetric crossover we detected in this study from the spouses to the travelers indicates that travelers and spouses have different roles in their relationship. Furthermore, business trips are unique phenomena affecting the whole family. It seems that in families of this kind, spouses take the role of supporting and encouraging the travelers by transmitting vigor to them. Thus, we demonstrated a uni-directional crossover of vigor from spouses to travelers, via one of the mechanisms – empathy, as suggested by Westman and Vinokur (1998). Vigor crossed over by a direct process of empathy whereby one partner who feels vigorous as a result of the resources at work and in the environment, expresses this vigor towards the other partner. The partner, in turn, via this process of empathy feels vigorous too. Unfortunately, we focused only on the business traveler's job demands and resources and do not have data on spouse's job demands and resources. However, as some of the business trip literature reports positive effects of these trips for the spouses too, we suggest that when travelers are on trips, spouses may have more time and opportunity for social meetings with friends and family and more responsibility for the children. These activities give them more energy, which is felt as vigor at work and is transmitted to their traveling spouses.

The crossover of vigor from spouses to travelers might have intensified as a consequence of their interaction style. The intensity and openness of the information exchange between spouses is also a specific kind of coping which affects the crossover process. The high correlations between travelers' demands, resources and BTS and their spouses' perceptions of these variables indicates that spouses had information about the travelers' experiences. Jones and Fletcher (1993b) have addressed the nature of information communicated between the partners as mediating the crossover process, suggesting that the communication may mediate the relationship between the partners' moods. They found that the woman's mood was affected by her partner's communication pattern: it was more positive when her husband offloaded worries and frustrations. Jones & Fletcher (1996) suggested that the frequency and nature of couples' work-related discussion is likely to be a mediator in the transmission process. Crossfield, Kinman and Jones (2005) analyzed the impact of frequency of discussion and communication on the crossover process. They found that for women, the perception that communication with their partner is based on mutual understanding and helpfulness was related to higher levels of psychological well-being. Thus, it may be that the partners' involvement in the travelers' business trips experiences as evident from our findings also contributed to their vigor, which they transmitted to the travelers.

Another aim of the current research was to look for the antecedents of vigor. Following the JD-R model we hypothesized that demands will have a negative impact on vigor while resources will have positive impact. We further hypothesized that business trip satisfaction (BTS) will be positively related to vigor.

The hypothesis that the demand—number of trips—in the past year is negatively related to vigor was not confirmed. We found a positive relationship between number of trips and vigor among the travelers. Though number of trips may indicate overload, such trips may also have positive features. The trips supply new experiences, challenges, international knowledge, enhanced networks, and growth and therefore increase the vigor of the traveler in his/her work. We did not find any relationship between number of trips and spouse's vigor. Number of trips may affect other experiences among spouses, not measured in the current study.

As for resources, travelers' trip control and spouses' perception of travelers' trip control were both positively related to travelers' and spouses' vigor. The positive relationship between travelers' trip control and vigor corroborates previous findings of relationships between job autonomy and engagement (Bakker, Demerouti, & Schaufeli, 2005; Demerouti, Bakker & Schaufeli, 2005); indeed, the research literature has consistently demonstrated positive effects of perceived control for people facing a threatening situation (Karasek, 1979). The travelers benefited not only in terms of control but also in terms of increased energy. As hypothesized, control as a resource contributed to increasing vigor.

The positive relationship between the spouses' perception of the travelers' trip control and vigor can be explained as a consequence of the fact that their traveling partners have more flexibility in their trip schedules. This may be helpful to the working spouses at home in that they are able to invest more time and energy in their jobs; hence the impact on their vigor. Another possible explanation maybe that the experience of having control crosses over from the travelers to their spouses.

To the best of our knowledge, no study has looked at the relationship between WFC and vigor or engagement. Therefore, we did not specify a direction concerning the nature of the relationship between these two variables for both the travelers and their spouses. We found that the WFC of both partners was positively related to vigor. As families headed by business travelers are a particular career group, we have to relate to this finding within its own framework. Some researchers have related to difficulties concerning business travelers and their spouses in the family domain but did not relate specifically to WFC.

The literature on balancing work and family exhibits two contrary hypotheses: the role-strain hypothesis, which states that multiple roles create stressful conflict, and the expansion hypothesis, which claims that the multiple roles can serve as a buffer against stress. Thus, the conflict/depletion perspective implies an inverse relationship between work-role and family-role engagement, while the facilitation/enrichment perspective suggests that a positive relationship is possible (Marks, 1977; Grzywacz, 2000; Rothbard, 2001). In line with tenets of positive psychology (Seligman & Csikszentmihalti, 2000; Seligman, Steen, Park, & Peterson, 2005), the argument centers on the possibility that engagement in one context (e.g., family) can generate feelings of well-being that may spill over to the other context (e.g., work). For example, business travelers who are energized by vigor (i.e., engaged) in the family role can obtain more personal resources in terms of energy and motivation to allocate to the work role. Similarly, those who are engaged in the work role are likely to have more energy and commitment in the family role. Rothbard (2001) found support for both depletion (negative spillover) and enrichment (positive spillover) between work-role and family-role engagement in the same study.

The positive relationships that we found between WFC and vigor for both partners show that even if WFC is considered a liability and has been found to be correlated positively with stress and burnout in many previous studies, it can at the same time be a source of vigor. Furthermore, according to the principles of COR theory (Hobfoll, 1989, 2001), resource loss is more salient than resource gain, though resource gain may help buffer the effects of resource loss. Therefore under stressful circumstances, resource gain cycles are most likely to emerge as people seek to identify and mobilize resources. This implies that resource loss and resource gain can occur simultaneously.

FUTURE RESEARCH

Our findings suggest several directions of future research. The methodology of future research should be improved by employing longitudinal designs, collecting data at three points of time: before, during and after the business trip (see Westman, Etzion & Gurtler, 2004c; Westman, Etzion, & Gattenio, in press). Incorporating time into the research design is important as some demands and resources change during the trip. One of the assumptions of COR theory (Hobfoll, 2002) is that different resources reinforce each other in the sense that possession of resources leads to possession of other resources. Resources are said to "co-travel in resource caravans" (Hobfoll, 2002, p. 318); key resources facilitate the development and use of other resources. Drawing on these ideas, it is possible that over time resources enhance each other both within and across the work and the family domains and create a resource-gain spiral. Three or more occasions may help reveal the change in resource levels and their impact during business trips.

Vigorous feelings at work possibly allow employees to effectively cope with work-related demands, and more importantly are likely to have a positive impact on their well-being (Shirom, 2004). Future research—on crossover of positive feelings in general and on the impact of business trips on the process of crossover in particular—should focus on additional positive outcomes such as well-being, self-confidence, enrichment or growth.

In addition to their theoretical and methodological implications, our findings also have practical implications for work organizations which rely on business trips as an integral part of their employees' jobs. The findings emphasize the value of understanding the implications of business trips for the employees and their families, and the importance of coping with the difficulties and vagaries of business travel. Understanding the impact of business trips and dealing with it may reduce stress and increase engagement. HR managers and other organizational stakeholders may find in these studies useful tools to alleviate the negative effects of business travel and accentuate its positive aspects, thus safeguarding the organization's most important resource—the human resource.

It seems that according employees control over their trip schedule may keep them and their spouses vigorous even if they have to take many trips during the year. The happiness of their employees' spouses should also be a concern of the organization's trip planners, as we found that spouses' vigor crosses over to the traveling employee.

Interventions should target not only the travelers but also their spouses; to quote one of the travelers who was interviewed in our study: *"My organization is extremely sensitive and understanding about personal needs and issues. If I can't take a trip because I have an important family event that will be understood."*

Since business travel is beneficial to the organization, and since the stress of traveling can hinder the traveler's efficiency and ability to cope with organizational goals, it is important for the organization to take care of the traveler's well being connected to the trip. This can be done in two ways: minimizing the potential stressors and maximizing the positive effects of the trip. Our recommendation is to integrate these two ways for the benefit of the traveler, the family and the organization.

REFERENCES

Bakker, A. B., & Demerouti, E. 2007. The Job Demands-Resources model: State of the art. *Journal of Managerial Psychology, 22,* 309–328.

Bakker, A., Demerouti, E. (forthcoming). The crossover of work engagement between working couples: A closer look at the role of empathy.

Bakker, A. B., & Schaufeli, W. B. (2000). Burnout contagion process among teachers. *Journal of Applied Social Psychology, 30,* 2289–2308

Bakker, A. B., Le Blanc, P. M., & Schaufeli, W. B. (2005). Burnout contagion among nurses who work at intensive care units. *Journal of Advanced Nursing, 51,* 276–287.

Barnett, R. C., Raudenbush, S. W., Brennan, R. T., Pleck, J. H., & Marshall, N. L. (1995). Changes in job and marital experience and change in psychological distress: A longitudinal study of dual-earner couples. *Journal of Personality and Social Psychology, 69,* 839–850.

Bentler, P. M. (2006). *EQS 6 Structural Equations Program Manual.* Encino, CA: Multivariate Software, Inc.

Bolger, N., DeLongis, A., Kessler, R., & Wethington, E. (1989). The contagion of stress across multiple roles. *Journal of Marriage and the Family, 51,* 175–183.

Burke, R. J., Weir, T., & DuWors, R. E. (1980). Work demands on administrators and spouse well-being. *Human Relations, 33,* 253–278.

Chia, A., & Yeo, W.L. (1999). *Globalization and the experience of frequent business travelers: The case of Singapore.* Paper presented in the 14th Employment Research Unit Conference, Cardiff, Wales, UK.

Crossfield, S., Kinman, G., & Jones (2005). Crossover of occupational stress in dual-career couples. *Community, Work & Family, 8,* 211–232.

DeFrank R.S., Konopaske R. & Ivancevich J.M. (2000). Executive travel stress: perils of the road warrior. *Academy of Management Executive, 14*(2), 58–71.

Demerouti, E., Bakker, A. B., Nachreiner, F., & Schaufeli, W. B. (2001). The job demands-resources model of burnout. *Journal of Applied Psychology, 86,* 499–512.

Demerouti, E., Bakker, A., & Schaufeli, W. (2005). Spillover and crossover of exhaustion and life satisfaction among dual-earner parents. *Journal of Vocational Behavior, 67,* 266–289.

Dimberg, L. A., Striker, J., Nordanlycke-Yoo, C., Nagy, L., Mundt, K. A., & Sulsky, S. I. (2002). Mental health insurance claims among spouses of frequent business travelers. *Occupational and Environmental Medicine, 59,* 175–181.

Espino, C. M., Sundstorm, S. M., Frick, H. L., Jacobs, M., & Peters, M (2002). International business travel: Impact on families and travelers. *Occupational and Environmental Medicine, 59,* 309–322

Etzion D., & Bailyn, L. (1994). Patterns of adjustment to the career/family conflict of technologically trained women in the U.S. and Israel. *Journal of Applied Social Psychology, 24*(17), 1520–1549.

Etizion, D., Eden, D., & Lapidot, Y. (1998). Relief from job stressors and burnout: Reserve service as a respite. Journal of Applied Psychology, *83*(5), 577–585.

Etzion, D., & Westman, M. (2001). Vacation and the crossover of strain between spouses—Stopping the vicious cycle. *Man and Work, 11,* 106–118.

Fredrickson, B. L. (2001). The role of positive emotions in the positive psychology: The broaden-and-build theory of positive emotions. *American Psychologist, 56,* 218–226.

Fredrickson, B. L., & Joiner, T. (2002). Positive emotions trigger upward spirals toward emotional well-being. *Psychology Science, 13,* 172–175.

Gorgievski-Duijvesteijin, M. J., Giesen, C, W., & Bakker, A, B.(2000). Financial problems and health complaints among farm couples: Results of a 10-yr follow-up study. *Journal of Occupational Health Psychology. 5,* 359–373.

Greenhaus, J. H., & Beutell, N. J. (1985). Sources of conflict between work and family roles. *Academy of Management Review, 10,* 76–88.

Hammer, L. B., Allen, E., & Grigsby, T. D. (1997). Work-family conflict in dual-earner couples: Within-individual and crossover effects of work and family. *Journal of Vocational Behavior, 50,* 185–203.

Hobfoll, S.E. (1989). Conservation of resources: A new attempt at conceptualizing stress. *American Psychologist, 44,* 513–524.

Hobfoll, S.E. (1998). *Stress, culture and community: The psychology and philosophy of stress.* New York: Plenum.

Hobfoll, S.E. (2001). The influence of culture community and the nested-self in the stress process: Advancing conservation of resources theory. *Applied Psychology: An International Journal, 50,* 337–421.

Hobfoll, S.E. (2002). Social and psychological resources and adaptation. *Review of General Psychology, 6,* 307–324.

Hobfoll, S. E., & Shirom, A. (1993). Stress and burnout in the workplace: Conservation of resources. In T. Golombiewski (Ed.), *Handbook of organizational behavior* (pp. 41–61). New York: Marcel Dekker.

Howe, G., Levy, M., & Caplan, R. (2004). Job loss and depressive symptoms in couples: Common stressors, stress transmission, or relationship disruption? *Journal of Family Psychology, 18,* 639–650.

Hu, L.-t., & Bentler, P.M. (1999). Cutoff criteria for fit indexes in covariance structure analysis: conventional criteria versus new alternatives. *Structural Equations Modeling, 6,* 1–55.

Jones, F., & Fletcher, B. (1993). An empirical study of occupational stress transmission in working couples. *Human Relations, 46,* 881–902.

Karasek, R.A., (1979). Job demands, job decision latitude and mental strain: Implications for job redesign. *Administrative Science Quarterly, 24,* 285–307.

Leider, R.J. (1991). Till travel do us part. (stress caused by family separation resulting from business travel). *Training and Development, 45,* 46–51.

Liese, B. (April, 2000). International business travel and stress: Common ground for the individual and the organization. Paper presented at the International Travel health Symposium on Stress, the Business Traveler and Corporate Health. The World Bank, Washington DC.

Little, T. D., Cunningham, W. A., Shahar, G., & Widaman, K. F. (2002). To parcel or not to parcel: Exploring the question, weighing the merits. *Structural Equation Modeling, 9*, 151–173.

Marks, S. (1977). Multiple roles and role strain: Some notes on human energy, time and commitment. *American Sociological Review, 42*, 921–936.

Roehling, P. V., & Bultman, M. (2002). Does absence make the hearts grow fonder? Work related travel and marital satisfaction. *Sex Roles, 46*, 279–293.

Rogers, H.L. (1998). A survey of the travel health experiences of international business travelers. *A thesis submitted to the faculty of graduate studies of nursing*, Calgary, Alberta.

Rook, S. K., Dooley, D., & Catalano, R. (1991). Stress transmission: The effects of husbands' job stressors on emotional health of their wives. *Journal of Marriage and the Family, 53*, 165–177.

Rothbard, N. P. 2001. Enriching or depleting? The dynamics of engagement in work and family roles. *Administrative Science Quarterly, 46*, 655–684.

Schaufeli, W.B. & Bakker, A.B., (2004). Job Demand, Job Resources, and their Relationship with Burnout and Engagement: A Multi-Sample Study. *Journal of organizational Behavior, 25*, 293–315.

Seligman, M. E. P., & Csikszentmihalyi, M. (2000). Positive psychology: An Introduction. *American Psychologist, 55*, 5–14.

Seligman, M.E.P., Steen, T., Park, N., & Peterson C., (2005). Positive psychology progress: Empirical validation of interventions. *American Psychologist. 60*, 410–421.

Shirom, A. (2004). Feeling vigorous at work? The sonstruct of vigor and the study of positive affect in organizations. In P. Perrewe & D, Ganster. D. (Eds.). *Research in Occupational health* (volume 3) pp. 135–164).

Stewart, M., & Donald, F. (2006). Spouses experience of their partners' absence due to frequent business travel. *South African Journal of Psychology, 36*,103–123.

Striker, J., Luippold, R. S., Nagy, L., Liese, B., Bigelow, C., & Mundt, K. A. (1999). Risk factors for psychological stress among international business travelers. *Occupational and Environmental Medicine, 56*, 245–252.

Takeuchi, R., Yun, S., & Teslu, P. T. (2002). An examination of crossover and spillover effects of spouse and expatriate cross-cultural adjustment on expatriate outcomes. *Journal of Applied Psychology, 85*, 655–666.

Vinokur, A., Pierce, P., & Buck, C. (1999). Work-family conflicts of women in the Air Force: Their influence on mental health and functioning. *Journal of Organizational Behavior, 20*, 865–878.

Westman, M. (2001). Stress and strain crossover. *Human Relations, 54*, 717–752.

Westman, M., & Etzion, D. (1995). The crossover of stress, strain and resources from one spouse to another. *Journal of Organizational Behavior, 16*, 169–181.

Westman, M., & Etzion D. (2002). The impact of short overseas business trips on job stress and burnout. *Applied Psychology: An International Review, 51*, 582–592.

Westman, M., Etzion, D., & Horovitz, S. (2004a). The toll of unemployment does not stop with the unemployed. *Human Relations, 57*, 823–844.

Westman, M., Etzion, D., & Gattenio, E. (forthcoming). Business travels and the work-family interface: A longitudinal study. *Journal of Organizational and Occupational Psychology.*

Westman, M., Etzion, D., & Gurtler, E. (2004c). The work-family interface and burn-out. *International Journal of Stress Management, 11*, 413–428.

Westman, M., & Vinokur, A. (1998). Unraveling the relationship of distress levels within couples: Common stressors, emphatic reactions or crossover via social interaction? *Human Relations, 51*, 137–156.

Westman, M. Vinokur, A., Hamilton, M., & Roziner, I. (2004b). Crossover of marital dissatisfaction during military downsizing among Russian army officers and their spouses. *Journal of Applied Psychology, 89*, 769–779.

CHAPTER 3

OCCUPATIONAL STRESS AND WORKPLACE SLEEPINESS

Sarah DeArmond
University of Wisconsin–Oshkosh

Peter Y. Chen
Colorado State University

I'll sleep when I'm dead.
—Warren Zevon (1947–2003)

Snow and adolescence are the only problems that disappear
if you ignore them long enough.
—Earl Wilson (1907–1987)

PREVALENCE OF WORKPLACE SLEEPINESS

The 2008 National Sleep Foundation Poll revealed that nearly a third of a targeted, random sample of American adults reported getting a good night's sleep only a few nights per month and 65% of this sample reported experiencing sleep problems (e.g., difficulty falling asleep, waking during

Stress and Quality of Working Life, pages 41–65
Copyright © 2009 by Information Age Publishing
All rights of reproduction in any form reserved.

the night) at least a few nights each week. Additionally, the poll revealed that 29% of this sample had reported becoming very sleepy or actually falling asleep at work in the past month. This poses obvious problems for organizations. After all, sleepiness or one's closeness to sleep at work has been tied to decrements in job performance (e.g., Bonnet & Arand, 2005; Engle-Friedman et al., 2003; Gillberg, Kecklund, & Akerstedt, 1994; Rosa & Colligan, 1988) and has been noted as a risk factor for occupational accidents and injuries (Akerstedt, Fredlund, Gilberg, & Jansson, 2002; Gabel & Geberich, 2002; Lilley, Feyer, Kirk, & Gander, 2002; Melamed & Oksenberg, 2002; Nakata et al, 2005; Simpson, Wadsworth, Moss, & Smith, 2005). This makes it all the more startling that a majority (84%) of the 2008 NSF poll respondents reported coping with their sleepiness by accepting it and moving on. This seems to suggest that great numbers of adults are having problems with sleep and sleepiness and most are choosing to ignore the issue.

While some may believe that sleep and sleepiness are primarily under the control of individuals, the 2008 NSF poll tells a somewhat different story. The findings suggest that aspects of work and organizational life itself (e.g., long work hours) contribute to sleep problems. Given that workplace sleepiness can lead to negative consequences for organizations, it seems imperative for organizations to begin to identify organizational antecedents of workplace sleepiness. In 2003, Krauss, Chen, DeArmond, and Moorcroft noted that there has been a lack of systematic research and definitive findings in the realm of workplace sleepiness. They completed a facet analysis of the topic which suggested that occupational stressors might contribute to workplace sleepiness. In the current chapter, we summarize the findings of existing research on occupational stressors and workplace sleepiness and present a model to help guide future research in this area.

WORKPLACE SLEEPINESS AND SLEEP

Workplace sleepiness refers to how close someone is to sleep at work (DeArmond & Chen, 2008). Sleep is controlled by the brain (Culebras, 2002). The brain assesses whether the body needs sleep by evaluating two important factors: one's sleep quota and one's internal 24-hour biological clock/circadian rhythm. A sleep quota or the amount of sleep one needs is determined by one's amount of previous sleep and the amount of time that person has spent awake. A sleep quota increases by roughly one hour for every two hours spent awake and decreases by each hour spent sleeping (Carskadon & Dement, 2000). Our internal 24-hour biological clocks act like special alarm clocks. They indicate what time to get up and what time to go to bed. Most of our alarm clocks function somewhat similarly in that they generally indicate that the hours between 10 PM and 6 AM are for sleeping (Culebras, 2002). Further, this clock usually also indicates a period of secondary sleepiness from 2 PM to 4 PM. While the alarm may go off during this two-hour block in the afternoon, it is generally easier to turn off than the one that goes off at night. Therefore, this period may just be experienced as intense drowsiness. When a person does not get enough sleep or has his/her biological clock disrupted, that person tends to feel sleepy (Webb & Cartwright, 1978).

OCCUPATIONAL STRESS

Occupational stress is a phenomenon that has received a great deal of attention in the occupational health research literature in recent decades. Occupational stress refers to a stimulus-response process. The stimuli are commonly referred to as stressors and negative responses as strain (Beehr & Franz, 1986; McGrath, 1976; Schuler, 1980). As has been noted, Krauss et al. (2003) suggested occupational stressors as possible antecedents of workplace sleepiness. The suggestion was based on the idea that "people who experience a lot of stressors on the job may find it difficult to fall asleep at night, which could result in feeling sleepy during the day at work" (pp. 89, 92). Despite the lack of research on connections between occupational stressors and workplace sleepiness there has been research completed which focuses on relationships between occupational stressors and variables that are presumably related to sleepiness or sleepiness surrogates (DeArmond, 2004).

SLEEPINESS SURROGATES

Sleepiness surrogates include variables such as sleep quality, sleep quantity, fatigue, and sleep-related psychosomatic symptoms. Sleep quality is thought of as a surrogate due to evidence that indicates that there is a relationship between this variable and sleepiness (Pilcher, Schoeling, & Prosansky, 2000, Pilcher, Ginter, & Sadowsky, 1997, Gundel, Drescher, Maass, Samel, & Vejvoda, 1995). The most notable of the evidence, was a recent study by Pilcher et al. (2000) which showed that sleep quality proved to be a significant predictor of sleepiness. There has also been evidence to support sleep quantity as a sleepiness surrogate. After all, it has already been noted that for the average person it takes roughly one hour of sleep to compensate for two hours of wakefulness. Further, there is empirical evidence which supports a connection. A study by Rogers, Caruso, and Aldrich (1993) showed that decreases in sleep quantity lead to sleepiness (Rogers, Caruso, & Aldrich, 1993). Fatigue and sleepiness-related psychosomatic symptoms are also viewed as surrogates due to sleepiness-related content. Measures of these variables include items such as "I get tired very quickly" (Michielsen, DeVries, & Van Heck, 2003), "Have you had trouble sleeping?" (Spector & Jex, 1998), "Have you felt tired or fatigued?" (Spector & Jex, 1998).

RELATIONSHIPS BETWEEN OCCUPATIONAL STRESSORS AND WORKPLACE SLEEPINESS

In effort to summarize the existing research literature which investigates relationships between occupational stressors and workplace sleepiness or sleepiness surrogates, we will rely on the meta-analytic results reported by DeArmond (2004) in conjunction with other related research findings. The meta-analysis focused on the relationships between six of the most commonly discussed stressors in the occupational stress literature and the sleepiness surrogates previously mentioned. The stressors included role ambiguity, role conflict, workload, interpersonal conflict, situational constraints, and perceived control. Table 3.1 contains a complete listing of the correlations included in the analysis and the relevant data associated with these correlations.

The meta-analytic results are summarized in Table 3.2. Table 3.2 displays sample sizes (n), numbers of correlations (k), sample-size weighted mean correlations ($\bar{r}$), sample-size weighted variance (s_r^2), heterogeneous and homogeneous confidence intervals for these correlations, correlations (ρ) corrected for unreliability of the predictor, the variance of the corrected correlation coefficients (σ_ρ^2), credibility intervals, percentage of variance accounted for by sampling error (PVA_{SE}), and the chi-square test for homogeneity (χ^2). The results for each stressor are described in the subsequent section.

Role Ambiguity

Role ambiguity refers to "the degree to which required information is available to a given organizational position" (Kahn, Wolfe, Quinn, & Snoek, 1964, p. 25). Role ambiguity is dependent upon how clearly and consistently information regarding an employee's role requirements and position within an organization is communicated to that employee. There are many examples of situations in which role ambiguity might be experienced. For instance, role ambiguity could occur as a result of a simple miscommunication between a supervisor and a subordinate about what is expected of the latter. Role ambiguity could also be the result of a struggle to define the specific tasks which are part of a particular job. Consider the

TABLE 3.1 Data from Studies Included in the Meta-Analysis

Study	Rxx	Type of Sleepiness Measure[a]	n	r
Role ambiguity				
Spector & Jex (1991)		Symptoms*	232	0.27
Spector, Chen, & O'Connell, 2000	0.80	Symptoms*	110	0.02
Spector, Dwyer, & Jex, 1988	0.71	Symptoms*	156	0.06
Pollard, 2001	0.79	Symptoms*	198	0.28
Hellgren & Sverke, 2001	0.78	Symptoms*	569	0.23
Chen & Spector, 1991	0.82	Symptoms*	393	0.21
Jex, Burnfield, Grauer, Lax, Roelse, & Sroda, 2003[a]	0.80	Symptoms*	239	0.08
Jex, Burnfield, Grauer, Adams, & Morgan, 2003[a]	0.77	Symptoms*	197	0.18
Role conflict				
Chen & Spector, 1991	0.81	Symptoms*	391	0.19
Jex, Burnfield, Grauer, Adams, & Morgan, 2003[a]	0.82	Symptoms*	197	0.19
Spector, Chen & O'Connell, 2000	0.80	Symptoms*	110	0.02
Workload				
Landsbergis, 1988	0.71	Quality	239	0.20
Zohar, 1999	0.92	Fatigue and quantity	205	0.17
Spector, Fox & Van Katwyk, 1999		Symptoms*	111	0.20
Spector & Jex (1991)		Symptoms*	231	0.24
Spector, Chen & O'Connell, 2000	0.84	Symptoms*	110	0.16
Spector, Dwyer & Jex, 1988		Symptoms*	150	0.17
Beehr, Glaser, Canali & Wallwey, 2001	0.69	Symptoms*	108	0.24
DeCroon, Van Der Beek, Blonk, & Frings-Dersen, 2000	0.84	Symptoms*	514	0.43[b]
Widerszal-Bazyl, Cooper, Sparks, & Spector, 2000	0.83	Fatigue	248	0.10[b]

(continued)

TABLE 3.1 Data from Studies Included in the Meta-Analysis (continued)

Study	R_{xx}	Type of Sleepiness Measure[a]	n	r
De Croon, 2003[a]	0.88	Fatigue	1181	0.44[b]
Schreurs & Taris, 1998	0.78	Fatigue	179	0.16
Schreurs & Taris, 1998	0.78	Fatigue	302	0.31
Shirom, Westman, Shamai, & Carel, 1997	0.88	Fatigue	194	0.19
Kageyama, Nishikido, Kobayashi, & Kawagoe, 2001		Quantity	283	0.25
Samel, Wegmann, & Vejyoda, 1997		Fatigue	50	0.88[b]
Tummers, Landerweerd, & van Merode, 2002	0.87	Symptoms[*]	155	0.25
Tanz & Charrow, 1993		Quantity	1355	0.75[b]
Lee, 1992		Quantity	733	0.12[b]
Hellgren & Sverke, 2001	0.79	Symptoms[*]	569	0.23
Parkes, 2003	0.85	Symptoms[*] and quality	1440	0.09[b]
Chen & Spector, 1991	0.87	Symptoms[*]	390	0.10[b]
Jex, Burnfield, Grauer, Adams, & Morgan, 2003[a]		Symptoms[*]	197	0.18
Jex, Burnfield, Grauer, Lax, Roelse, & Sroda, 2003[a]	0.88	Symptoms[*]	238	0.21
Galambos & Walters, 1992		Quality	96	0.07[b]
Galambos & Walters, 1992		Quality	96	0.05[b]
Fortunato & Harsh, 2004[a]	0.83	Quality	467	0.10[b]
Interpersonal Conflict				
Spector, Fox, & Van Katwyk, 1999		Symptoms[*]	111	0.26
Spector, Chen, & O'Connell, 2000	0.72	Symptoms[*]	110	0.12
Spector, Dwyer, & Jex, 1988	0.81	Symptoms[*]	154	0.22
Chen & Spector, 1991	0.71	Symptoms[*]	388	0.18
Jex, Burnfield, Grauer, Adams, & Morgan, 2003[a]	0.88	Symptoms[*]	197	0.07
Jex, Burnfield, Grauer, Lax, Roelse, & Sroda, 2003[a]	0.86	Symptoms[*]	239	0.15
Fortunato & Harsh, 2004[a]	0.80	Quality	467	0.18

Situational Constraints

Study	R_{xx}	Measure	n	r
Zohar, 1999	0.86	Fatigue	205	0.21
Spector, Fox, & Van Katwyk, 1999	0.85	Symptoms*	113	0.22
Spector, Chen, & O'Connell, 2000	0.84	Symptoms*	110	0.08
Spector, Dwyer, & Jex, 1988	0.84	Symptoms*	156	0.24
Hellgren & Sverke, 2001	0.87	Symptoms*	569	0.15
Chen & Spector, 1991	0.88	Symptoms*	391	0.25
Jex, Burnfield, Grauer, Adams, & Morgan, 2003[a]	0.87	Symptoms*	197	0.16
Jex, Burnfield, Grauer, Lax, Roelse, & Sroda, 2003[a]		Symptoms*	238	0.20

Perceived Control

Study	R_{xx}	Measure	n	r
Landsbergis, 1988	0.80	Quality	239	-0.13
Spector, Fox, & Van Katwyk, 1999	0.77	Symptoms*	112	0.07[b]
Spector & Jex (1991)	0.87	Symptoms*	231	-0.004
Spector, Chen, & O'Connell, 2000	0.80	Symptoms*	110	0.02
Spector, Dwyer, & Jex, 1988	0.70	Symptoms*	156	-0.09
Beehr, Glaser, Canali, & Wallwey, 2001	0.81	Symptoms*	115	0.06
DeCroon, Van Der Beek, Blonk, & Frings-Dresen, 2000	0.72	Symptoms*	514	-0.22[b]
De Croon, 2003[a]	0.89	Fatigue and quality	673	-0.29
Schreurs & Taris, 1998	0.70	Fatigue	179	0.01
Schreurs & Taris, 1998	0.70	Fatigue	302	0.03[b]
Edwards & Rothbard, 1999		Symptoms*	1655	-0.09
Tummers, Landeweerd, & vanMerode, 2002	0.84	Symptoms*	155	-0.17
Parkes, 2003	0.70	Symptoms* and quality	1440	-0.13

Note: Symptoms = Psychosomatic symptoms, Quantity = Sleep quantity, Quality = Sleep quality, R_{xx} = Reliability of the stressor measure; all reliability coefficients are alpha coefficients, r = correlation coefficient, n = sample size

* Author calculated correlation between the stressor and the sleep related symptoms

[a] Unpublished work

[b] Data point was identified as an outlier

TABLE 3.2 Meta-Analysis of the Relationships between Occupational Stressors and Workplace Sleepiness

Predictor	n	k	$\bar{r}$	s_r^2	Confidence Interval		ρ	σ_ρ^2	Credibility Interval	PVA_{SE}	χ^2 (df)
					Heterogeneous	Homogeneous			Interval		
Role ambiguity	2,094	8	.19	.006	.13 to .24	.15 to .23	.21	.004	.10 to .33	57%	14.20 (7)[*]
Role conflict	698	3	.16	.004	.09 to .24	.09 to .24	.18	.000	.18 to .18	100%[a]	2.97 (2)
Workload	9,841	26	.29	.050	.20 to .38	.27 to .31	.34	.066	−.16 to .84	4%	587.55 (25)[*]
Interpersonal conflict	1,666	7	.17	.000	.12 to .21	.12 to .21	.23	.000	.23 to .23	100%[a]	4.21 (6)
Situational constraints	1,979	8	.19	.000	.15 to .23	.15 to .23	.21	.000	.21 to .21	100%[a]	4.77 (7)
Perceived control	5,881	13	−.09	.009	−.14 to −.03	−.11 to −.06	−.10	.009	−.29 to .09	23%	56.36 (12)[*]

Note: n = total number of participants, k = total number of correlations, $\bar{r}$ = sample-size-weighted correlation, s_r^2 = sample-weighted variance, ρ = correlation corrected for unreliability in the predictor, σ_ρ^2 = Variance of rho, PVA_{SE} = percentage of variance accounted for by sampling error, χ^2 = chi-square tests for homogeneity for uncorrected correlations

[a] Actual percentage of variance accounted for by sampling error was greater than 100% but was set to 100% as suggested by Hunter & Schmidt (1990)

[*] significant at $p < .05$

job of computer programmer. Computer programmers might be responsible for developing software that is new and unique. Therefore, there might not be clear, well-defined behaviors in which a computer programmer must engage. In fact, it could be argued that clarity would inhibit the creative process necessary in this job. Another thing that might result in role ambiguity is change. It is well-documented that the nature of work has and is continuing to change drastically (Cascio, 2003). For instance, with the advent of computers, the job of librarian changed dramatically. With this change, a librarian's required knowledge and skills were not only different but also unknown in some cases. When a job changes like this, new recruits could be given misleading job descriptions which might increase role ambiguity.

Kahn et al. (1964) suggested that the confusion and uncertainty induced when information is communicated unclearly and/or inconsistently is associated with strain such as tension and anxiety. Since 1964, there have been numerous studies connecting role ambiguity with different indices of strain, employee well-being, and organizational outcomes. Role ambiguity has been linked to negative affect and somatic symptoms (Frone, Russell, & Cooper, 1995; Gavin & Axelrod, 1977; Kemery, Mossholder, Bedeian, 1987; Spector, Dwyer, & Jex, 1988; Spector & O'Connell, 1994; Van Dijkhuizen & Reiche, 1980). Jackson and Schuler (1985) did a meta-analysis in which they found average corrected correlations between role ambiguity and job satisfaction of $-.46$, tension/anxiety of $.47$, organizational commitment of $-.41$, absence of $.13$, propensity to leave of $.29$, and self-ratings of job performance of $-.12$.

Table 3.2 demonstrates that there is support for a positive relationship between role ambiguity and sleepiness surrogates. The sample size weighted mean correlation between role ambiguity and sleepiness surrogates was $\bar{r} = .19$ and the estimated population correlation was $\rho = .21$. The sample-size weighted variance shows that the individual correlation coefficients do not deviate much from the sample-size weighted mean correlations. The confidence intervals did not contain zero which indicates that even after taking into account sampling error, one can be relatively confident that there is a positive relationship between these variables. The PVA_{SE} value which was less than 75% and the statistically significant χ^2 test indicate that there are likely moderators of this relationship.

Role Conflict

Kahn et al. (1964, p. 19) defined role conflict as "the simultaneous occurrence of two (or more) sets of pressures such that compliance with one would make more difficult compliance with the other". Role conflict can be exhibited in one of three forms: intra-sender conflict, inter-sender conflict, and inter-role conflict. Intra-sender conflict occurs when an employee is given conflicting instructions by one particular person. This person who gives role-relevant information is considered a role-sender (Kahn et al., 1964).

An example of this type of conflict would be an employee being told by a supervisor to complete a particular task by the end of the day, but being told by the same supervisor to do the task alone. The conflict would occur, if this person could complete the task alone but not by the end of the day. The supervisor is asking the employee to complete the task on a timeline that calls for teamwork, but is asking that the employee not solicit the help of others.

The second form of role conflict is inter-sender conflict. This type of conflict occurs when two role senders are putting pressure on someone to do two things that are in conflict with one another. For instance, one supervisor might ask a subordinate to complete a task by the end of the day and another supervisor could ask the subordinate to do the task alone. Here conflict emerges when the requests of both supervisors cannot be met.

The last form of role conflict, inter-role conflict, refers to a situation in which pressures from one role clash with pressures from another (Kahn et al., 1964). This type of conflict occurs when someone holds more than one role within an organization. For instance, an employee might have a formal role as a machinist and also serve as union representative. This employee could face increasing pressure from the union to carry out specific duties; yet, those duties could come in direct conflict with required parts of this person's formal job.

The common vein running through all of the above types of role conflict is pressures to do things differently. It is suggested that these conflicting pressures upset an existing equilibrium that leads to strain (Kahn et al., 1964). Role conflict has proven to be related to a variety of both individual well-being and organizational consequence variables. It has been a consistent finding that role conflict is positively correlated with somatic symptoms (Fusilier, Ganster, & Mayes, 1987; Ganster & Schaubroeck, 1991; Kemery et al., 1987, Spector et al., 1988; Spector & O'Connel, 1994). Based on meta-analytic results, Jackson and Schuler (1985) reported corrected average correlations between role conflict and the following consequences: job satisfaction (−.48), tension/anxiety (.43), organizational commitment (−.36), propensity to leave (.34), and job performance (as rated by others, −.11). The findings in Table 3.2 suggest that role conflict is also related to sleepiness surrogates ($\bar{r} = .16$, $\rho = .18$). The confidence intervals do not include zero adding further credence to this claim. There was no indication that moderators were operating on this relationship.

Workload

Workload refers to the amount and complexity of the work that employees have to do. Researchers have conceptualized workload in a variety of ways such as number of projects completed, number of hours worked, or speed of production. One concept similar to workload is role overload. Role overload deals specifically with an excess of role specific demands. Workload deals with demands that are not necessarily specific to one's role(s). Role overload deals with excessive amounts or complexity of role specific work, while workload deals with a range of work quantities and complexities (Jex, 1998). Given their similarity, for the purposes of the current chapter we will consider role overload as a type of workload.

The consequences of workload have received a great deal of attention in the occupational health literature. There have been studies finding that this stressor is significantly related to everything from general well-being (Van den Berg & Schalk, 1997) to coronary heart disease (Haynes, Feinleib, & Kannel, 1980; McCann, Benjamin, Wilkinson, Retzlaff, Russo, & Knopp, 1999). Research has shown workload to be correlated with psychological symptoms including tension, nervousness, irritability, unusual tiredness, and difficulties concentrating (Kirmeyer & Dougherty,1988; Kivimaeki, & Lindstrom, 1995). Further workload has proven to be positively related to physical health complaints such as headaches, stiffness in the neck and shoulders, and burning eyes (Carayon, 1993; Repetti, 1993). Spector et al. (1988) did a study in which they attempted to take more objective measures of occupational stressors by having supervisors report on the matter. They found a significant positive correlation between the number of hours worked as reported by supervisors and the number of health symptoms reported by workers.

Other research has provided evidence that workload has a negative effect on sleep quality (Martens et al., 1999), weekday sleep debt (Kageyama, Nishikido, Kobayashi, and Kawagoe, 2001), and both physical and psychological health (Kirkcaldy, Levine, & Shephard, 2000; McCann et al., 1999; Schulz, Kirschbaum, Pruesner, & Hellhammer, 1998). McCann et al. for instance, found that increases in workload were associated with increases in the concentration of triglycerides in the bloodstream. Elevated levels of triglycerides have been linked to cardiovascular disease. Schulz et al. (1998) revealed that those experiencing chronically high levels of workload tend to experience high cortisol secretions upon awakening in the morning. The authors note that increases in cortisol increase arousal levels and suggest that a possible consequence of enhanced morning arousal might be early exhaustion later in the day.

As evidenced by the sample-size weighted mean correlation and the estimated population correlation ($\bar{r} = .29$ and $\rho = .34$) in Table 3.2, workload has the strongest relationship with sleepiness surrogates of any of the occupational stressors included DeArmond (2004) meta-analysis. It is also noted that neither the homogeneous nor the heterogeneous confidence intervals included zero, and the low end of the heterogeneous confidence interval was .20 which is still a relatively sizeable correlation. The credibility intervals (included zero), percentage of variance accounted for by sampling error, and chi square tests all indicated that this relationship is likely moderated by other variables.

Interpersonal Conflict

Interpersonal conflict can include anything from minor verbal disagreements to physical fights that take place at work. There are a variety of things which might contribute to interpersonal conflicts. These include interpersonal differences, perceptions of injustice, and competitive environments. Often researchers focus on overt forms of interpersonal conflict (i.e., physical fights, overt verbal attacks). However, covert forms (i.e., spreading rumors, talking about coworkers behind their backs, and sabotage) should not and will not be overlooked in this review. Over the years research has shown that interpersonal conflict is related to increases in negative mood (Fox, Spector, & Miles, 2001; Repetti, 1993), counterproductive work behaviors (Fox et al., 2001), job dissatisfaction (Sutton, 1984, Spector et al., 1988), burnout (Brondolo et al., 1998), and intention to quit (Spector et al., 1988).

More notably for the current research purposes, interpersonal conflict has been shown to be correlated with psychological symptoms including nervousness, irritability, unusual tiredness, difficulties concentrating (Kivimaeki & Lindstrom, 1995) and physical symptoms including trouble sleeping, tiredness, and fatigue (Spector & Jex, 1998; Spector et al., 1988). Spector et al. measured interpersonal conflict using self-report and supervisor-report measures. These authors found significant positive correlations between interpersonal conflict and anxiety and frustration. Finally, and perhaps most notably for the current purposes, Bergmann and Volkema (1994) found that "lost sleep" was the second most common consequence of an interpersonal conflict at work.

The findings in Table 3.2 show that interpersonal conflict is also positively related to sleepiness surrogates ($\bar{r}$ = .17 and ρ = .23). Neither the homogeneous nor the heterogeneous confidence intervals included zero which indicates that even after taking into account sampling error, we can be relatively confident that there is a positive relationship between these variables. There was no indication that moderators were operating.

Situational Constraints

Situational constraints refer to organizational conditions that hinder job performance. For instance when one has a task that requires financial resources for successful completion and those resources are lacking, frustration as well as negative experiences may result (Peters & O'Conner, 1980). Two common measures of situational constraints are the Organizational Constraints Measure (Mathieu, Tannenbaum, & Salas, 1992) and the Organizational Constraints Scale (Spector & Jex, 1998). Scales such as these contain about how often one's job becomes difficult as a result of poor equipment, inadequate training, or organizational rules and procedures (Spector & Jex, 1998). Through the years, research has shown that situational constraints are related to counterproductive work behaviors (Fox et al., 2001), negative emotions (Fox et al., 2001), frustration (Jex & Gudanowski, 1992, Spector et al., 1988, O'Conner, Pooyan, Weekley, Peters, Frank, & Erenkrantz, 1984, Peters, O'Connor, Eulberg, & Watson, 1988), anxiety (Jex & Gudanowski, 1992; Spector et al., 1988), intent to quit (Jex & Gudanowski, 1992; Spector et al., 1988), turnover (O'Conner et al., 1984; Peters et al., 1988), and job dissatisfaction (Jex & Gudanowski, 1992, O'Conner et al., 1984, Peters et al., 1988, & Spector et al., 1988). The existing evidence which links situational constraints most closely to sleepiness is that which reports significant positive correlations between this variable and somatic symptom inventories (that include sleepiness related items). Spector et al. (1988) and Spector and O'Connell (1994) have both found positive correlations between these two variables. More notably, in a meta-analysis, Spector and Jex (1998) reported a positive mean correlation between situational constraints and somatic symptoms.

The findings of in Table 3.2 suggest that situational constraints are also likely related to workplace sleepiness. After all, the sample-size weighted mean correlation between situational constraints and sleepiness surrogates was .19 and the estimated population correlation was .21. Neither type of confidence interval contained zero adding further credence to this conclusion. There was no indication that moderators were operating.

Perceived Control

Perceived control (also referred to as decision latitude by Karasek, 1979) refers to how much discretion an employee has in how he/she goes about completing tasks and the role one is allowed in making decisions at work. Perceived control has been reported to be negatively associated with negative emotions (Fox et al., 2001), counterproductive work behavior (Fox et al., 2001), and job related depression (Haynes, Wall, Bolden,

Stride, & Rick, 1999). Perceived control has also been shown to have a significant positive correlation with job satisfaction (Haynes et al., 1999). Carayon (1992) found that perceptions of greater control were related to decreased boredom, tension/anxiety, depression, and anger. Further, research has demonstrated that there is a negative correlation between perceived control and both physical health complaints (Carayon, 1993) and psychological symptoms (Kivimaeki & Lindstrom, 1995). A meta-analysis conducted by Spector (1986) also revealed that high levels of perceived control were associated with low levels of physical symptoms such as sleep decrements.

The findings in Table 3.2 suggest that perceived control is related to sleepiness surrogates. The sample-size weighted mean correlation between perceived control and sleepiness surrogates was –.09 and the estimated population correlation was –.10. By looking at the confidence intervals one can see that even after taking into account sampling error, it seems likely that there is a negative relationship between these variables. All three tests for moderators indicated that they were likely to exist.

PROPOSED MODEL

The preceding review suggests that there are likely relationships between occupational stressors and workplace sleepiness. Since there is a dearth of research which explores connections between occupational stressors and workplace sleepiness specifically, the occupational health community would benefit from future studies focusing on relationships between these variables. It is suggested that this research explore reasons why these variables are related. Krauss et al. (2003) proposed that stressors could lead to sleep disturbances which could then lead to workplace sleepiness. However, Krauss et al. did not suggest mechanisms that might underlie the relationship between stressors and sleep disturbances. Therefore, we offer the model depicted in Figure 3.1 as a possible explanation for these relationships and hope that it offers avenues for future research.

The model depicted in Figure 3.1 suggests coping method choice as one factor which could determine whether sleep disturbances occur as a result of exposure to occupational stressors. It further suggests that coping method choice will vary as a function of how an individual appraises a stressor. Finally, the model suggests that the outcome of the appraisal process is going to be somewhat contingent on individual differences. In the subsequent sections we give explanations for the different parts of this theoretical model.

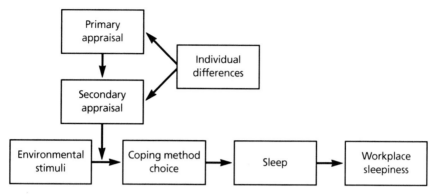

Figure 3.1 Proposed model.

OCCUPATIONAL STRESSORS AND COPING METHOD CHOICE: THE ROLE OF APPRAISAL

The transactional model of stress suggests that strain is experienced as a result of an interaction between a person and his/her environment (Lazarus, 1966; Lazarus & Folkman, 1984). According to the model, whether a person experiences strain in response to a stressor is dependent on how that person appraises the stressor. The first part of that appraisal process, primary appraisal involves determining whether the stimulus is stressful, benign-positive, or irrelevant. If the person determines that the stimulus is in fact stressful, the model suggests that he/she will then make a secondary appraisal. This step of the appraisal process involves evaluating what can be done to cope with the situation. It is thought that these two appraisal processes help to determine coping method choice which will likely in turn have an impact on the strain that a person experiences (Perrewé & Zellars, 1999; Sonnentag & Frese, 2003).

There are a number of researchers to date which have suggested that attribution might be involved in this appraisal process (Perrewé & Zellars, 1999; Peeters, Schaufeli, & Buunk, 1995), and that different types of attributions might lead to different consequences. Attribution refers to "a perception of inference or cause" (Kelley & Michela, 1980), and there are a variety of different types of attributions. Weiner's (1985) attribution theory suggests that causes can be classified along three different dimensions: locus, controllability, and stability. The first dimension, locus refers to whether an event or situation is the result of internal (factors within a person such as ability or effort) or external factors (factors within the environment). The second dimension, stability refers to whether a cause is likely to fluctuate or remain constant. The third dimension, controllability refers to whether or not a cause is under volitional control.

An employee might believe that having a workload which is too heavy is the result of something within himself such as his aptitude, the effort that he puts into his job, or his level of fatigue. That employee could alternatively believe that his heavy workload resulted from a factor external to him such as his supervisor's unreasonable expectations, downsizing due to an economic downturn, or an equipment failure. These same causes could then be classified on the dimension of controllability. The employee's aptitude and fatigue are likely outside of his volitional control. Similarly, the downsizing or the equipment failure would likely be considered to be outside of management's control. However, this employee's effort is likely within his control and the supervisor's expectations are also likely within her control. Finally, the causes could be classified on the dimension of stability. The employee's aptitude and the downsizing would likely be thought of as fairly stable. An employee's effort and fatigue, his supervisor's expectations, and the equipment failure would likely be considered unstable.

It is possible that an occupational stressor might have a different impact on workplace sleepiness dependent on how an attribution for this stressor is classified along these three dimensions. This is likely due to the different emotional reactions people have in response to different attributions and then how these different emotional reactions impact coping method choices. Perrewé and Zellars (1999) have offered a theory for how attributions made about stressors impact emotional reactions and in turn choices of coping methods. Coping methods can play a role in additional consequences for individuals and organizations. One such consequence could be workplace sleepiness.

Perrewé and Zellars suggested that stressors which are attributed to internal controllable factors (e.g., a lack of effort) will lead to feelings of guilt and those that are attributed to internal, uncontrollable factors (e.g., aptitude) will lead to feelings of shame. They suggested that those stressors that are attributed to external, controllable factors (e.g., unreasonable supervisor expectations) will lead to anger and that those stressors attributed to external, uncontrollable factors (e.g., equipment failure) will lead to frustration. According to Perrewé and Zellars, feelings of guilt will lead to problem-focused coping but all of the other feelings will lead to emotion-focused coping.

INDIVIDUAL DIFFERENCES AND APPRAISAL

It is likely that appraisal will be somewhat dependent on the characteristics of the individual doing the appraising. One characteristic that could influence the appraisal process is locus of control. Locus of control is an individual difference variable which refers to one's tendency to believe that the outcomes of his/her behavior are the result of that behavior or some aspect of his/her person or a tendency to believe that the outcomes are the results of chance, luck, fate, or something under the control of others (Rotter, 1990). Someone with an internal locus of control by definition would likely be more apt to attribute his/her experience with an occupational stressor to internal and controllable factors than someone who has an external locus of control who might be more apt to attribute the same stressor to external and uncontrollable factors. This could lead to different coping method choices and in turn different experiences with sleep. There is already empirical research which supports a connection between locus of control and coping method choice (Gianakos, 2002), locus of control and well-being (Spector, 1982). Further, there is research which indicates that locus of control can act as a moderator of stressor-strain relationships (Rahim, 1996) and that those who have an internal locus of control are more apt to make internal attributions (Levy, 1993).

There are other individual difference variables that could also have an impact on occupational stressor-workplace sleepiness relationships. Self-efficacy and neuroticism are two such variables. Each has been previously connected to the occupational stress process (Sonnentag and Frese, 2003). For instance, some studies have suggested that those who are more efficacious are less apt to experience strain as a result of exposure to stressors (Jex & Bliese, 1999). Other empirical work has shown that those who are more neurotic have a tendency to choose less effective coping methods (Gunthert, Cohen, & Armeli, 1999).

COPING METHODS AND SLEEP

Workplace sleepiness is conceptualized in this study as a form of strain. There is research which suggests that problem-focused coping decreases strain where as emotion-focused coping increases strain (Mitchell, Cronkite, and Moos, 1983). Therefore, it is possible that emotion-focused coping might lead to more workplace sleepiness than problem-focused coping. In addition, there may be certain types of emotion-focused coping that lend themselves to workplace sleepiness more than others. For instance, rumination and worry have both been identified as types of emotion-focused coping (Hong, 2007), which are linked to increases in sleep disturbances. However, other types of emotion-focused coping such as positive reappraisal (emphasizing the positive aspects of a situation and minimizing the negative) have not been associated with increases in sleep disturbances.

Rumination and worry are cognitive processes which involve passively and repetitively focusing on problematic situations, events, or symptoms of distress. Rumination involves thoughts about the past and worry involves thoughts about the future. There is substantial research to date which suggests that worry can have a negative impact on sleep quality by delaying sleep onset (Harvey, Tang, & Browning; 2005, Gross & Borkovec, 1982; Harvey, 2000). While less research has explored the relationship between rumination and sleep quality, there is still some evidence which suggests that this cognitive process is also related to sleep quality decrements (Thomsen et al., 2003). Thomsen et al. (2003) found that rumination was related to decrements in sleep quality, and more specifically this study showed that rumination was associated with both delayed sleep onset and more sleep disturbances.

CONCLUSION

The 2008 NSF poll suggests that many adults have problems with sleep and sleepiness during waking hours and more specifically during work hours. These problems pose a variety of concerns for organizations (e.g., job performance, occupational safety). This NSF poll, previous reviews of the workplace sleepiness research literature (Krauss et al., 2003), and the current review suggest that individuals, organizations, and researchers alike might be paying too little attention to this topic. The current chapter illustrates a need to better understand how occupational stressors might be linked to workplace sleepiness and offers a variety of potential avenues for future research. It is hoped that through future research in this area, that individuals and organizations can move beyond accepting workplace sleepiness as a fact of work life.

REFERENCES

* Indicates that this study was included in the meta-analysis

Akerstedt, T., Fredlund, P., Gillberg, M., & Jansson, B. (2002). A prospective study of fatal occupational accidents—Relationship to sleeping difficulties and occupational factors. *Journal of Sleep Research, 11*, 69–71.

Beehr, T. A., & Franz, T. M. (1986). The current debate about the meaning of job stress. *Journal of Organizational Behavior Management, 8*, 5–18.

*Beehr, T. A., Glaser, K. M., Canali, K. G. & Wallwey, D. A. (2001). Back to basics: Reexamination of demand-control theory of occupational stress. *Work & Stress, 15*, 115–130.

Bergmann, T. J. & Volkema, R. J. (1994). Issues, behavioral responses and consequences in interpersonal conflicts. *Journal of Organizational Behavior, 15*, 467–471.

Bonnet, M.H., & Arand, D.L. (2005). Performance and cardiovascular measures in normal adults with extreme MSLT scores and subjective sleepiness levels. *Sleep, 28*, 685–693.

Brondolo, E., Masheb, R., Stores, J., Stockhammer, T., Tunick, W., Melhado, E., Karlin, W. A., Schwartz, J., Harburg, E. & Contrada, R. J. (1998). Anger-related traits and response to interpersonal conflict among New York City traffic agents. *Journal of Applied Social Psychology, 28*, 2089–2118.

Carayon, P. (1992). A longitudinal study of job design and worker strain: Preliminary results. In J. C. Quick, L. R. Murphy, & J. J. Hurrell, Jr. (Eds.). *Stress and well-being at work: Assessments and interventions for occupational mental health* (pp. 19–32). Washington, DC: American Psychological Association.

Carayon, P. (1993). A longitudinal test of Karasek's job strain model among office workers. *Work & Stress, 7*, 299–314.

Carskadon, M.A., & Dement, W.C. (2000). Normal human sleep: An overview. In M.H. Kryger, T. Roth, & W.C. Dement (Eds.), *Principles and Practice of Sleep Medicine* (3rd ed., pp. 15–25). Philadelphia: Saunders.

Cascio, W.F. (2003). Changes in workers, work and organizations. In W.C. Borman, D.R. Ilgen, & R.J. Klimoski (Eds.) *Handbook of Psychology: Vol. 12. Industrial and Organizational Psychology* (pp. 453–491). Hoboken, NJ: Wiley.

*Chen, P.Y., & Spector, P.E. (1991). Negative affectivity as the underlying cause of correlations between stressors and strains. *Journal of Applied Psychology, 76*, 398–407.

Culebras, A. (2002). Normal sleep. In T.L. Lee-Chiong, Jr, M.J. Sateia, & M.A. Carskadon (Eds.), *Sleep Medicine* (pp. 1–6). Philadelphia: Hanley & Belfus.

*De Croon, E. M. (2003). *Stressful work sickness absence and turnover in truck drivers: From etiology to prevention.* Unpublished thesis, University of Amsterdam, Amsterdam.

*De Croon, E. M., Van Der Beek, A. J., Blonk, R. W. B. & Frings-Dresen, M. H. W. (2000). Job stress and psychosomatic health complaints among Dutch truck drivers: A re-evaluation of Karasek's interactive job demand-control model. *Stress Medicine, 16*, 101–107.

DeArmond, S. (2004). *The effects of job stressors on workplace sleepiness: A meta-analysis.* Unpublished master's thesis, Colorado State University, Fort Collins, Colorado.

DeArmond, S., & Chen, P.Y. (2008). *Aggression and workplace sleepiness: A longitudinal exploration.* Manuscript submitted for publication.

Dwyer, D.J., & Ganster, D.C. (1991). The effects of job demands and control on employee attendance and satisfaction. *Journal of Organizational Behavior, 12*, 595–608.

*Edwards, J. R. & Rothbard, N. P. (1999). Work and family stress and well-being: An examination of person-environment fit in the work and family domains. *Organizational Behavior and Human Decision Processes, 77*, 85–129.

Engle-Friedman, M., Riela, S., Golan, R., Ventuneac, A.M., Davis, C.M., Jefferson, A.D., et al. (2003). The effect of sleep loss on next day effort. *Journal of Sleep Research, 12*, 113–124.

*Fortunato, V. J., & Harsh, J. (2004). *Stress and sleep quality: The moderating role of negative affectivity.* Manuscript under review.

Fox, S., Spector, P. E. & Miles, D. (2001). Counterproductive work behavior (CWB) in response to job stressors and organizational justice: Some mediator and moderator tests for autonomy and emotions. *Journal of Vocational Behavior, 59,* 291–309.

Frone, M. R., Russell, M. &Cooper, M. L. (1995). Job stressors, job involvement and employee health: A test of identity theory. *Journal of Occupational & Organizational Psychology, 68,* 1–11.

Fusilier, M. R., Ganster, D. C. & Mayes, B. T. (1987). Effects of social support, role stress, and locus of control on health. *Journal of Management, 13,* 517–528.

Gabel, C.L., & Gerberich, S.G., (2002). Risk factors for injury among veterinarians. *Epidemiology, 13,* 80–86.

*Galambos, N. L. & Walters, B. J. (1992). Work hours, schedule inflexibility, and stress in dual-earner spouses. *Canadian Journal of Behavioural Science, 24,* 290–302.

Ganster, D. C. & Shaubroeck, J. (1991). Role stress and worker health: An extension of the plasticity hypothesis of self-esteem. *Journal of Social Behavior & Personality, 6,* 349–360.

Gavin, J. F. & Axelrod, W. L. (1977). Managerial stress and strain in a mining organization. *Journal of Vocational Behavior, 11,* 66–74.

Gianakos, I. (2002). Predictors of coping with work stress: The influences of sex, gender role, social desirability, and locus of control. *Sex Roles, 46,* 149–158.

Gillberg, M., Kecklund, G., & Akerstedt, T. (1994). Relations between performance and subjective ratings of sleepiness during a night awake. *Sleep: Journal of Sleep Research & Sleep Medicine,* 17, 236–241.

Gray, E. K. & Watson, D. (2002). General and specific traits of personality and their relation to sleep and academic performance. *Journal of Personality, 70,* 177–206.

Gross, R.J., & Borkovec, T.D. (1982). Effects of a cognitive intrusion manipulation on the sleep-onset latency of good sleepers. *Behavior Therapy, 13,* 112–116.

Gundel, A., Drescher, J., Maass, H., Samel, A., & Vejvoda, M. (1995). Sleepiness of civil airline pilots during two consecutive night flights of extended duration. *Biological Psychology, 40,* 131–141.

Gunthert, K.C., Cohen, L.H., & Armeli, S. (1999). The role of neuroticism in daily stress and coping. *Journal of Personality and Social Psychology, 77,* 1087–1100.

Harvey, A.G. (2000). Pre-sleep cognitive activity: a comparison of sleep-onset insomniacs and good sleepers. *British Journal of Clinical Psychology, 39,* 275–286.

Harvey, A.G., Tang, N.K.Y., & Browning, L. (2005). Cognitive approaches to insomnia. *Clinical Psychology Review, 25,* 593–611.

Haynes, S. G., Feinleib, M., & Kannel, W. B. (1980). The relationship of psychosocial factors to coronary heart disease in the Framingham study: III. Eight-year incidence of coronary heart disease. *American Journal of Epidemiology, 111,* 37–58.

Haynes, C. E., Wall, T. D., Bolden, R. I., Stride, C., & Rick, J. E. (1999). Measures of perceived work characteristics for health services research: Test of a measurement model and normative data. *British Journal of Health Psychology, 4,* 257–275.

*Hellgren, J. & Sverke, M. (2001). Unionized employees' perceptions of role stress and fairness during organizational downsizing: Consequences for job satisfaction, union satisfaction and well-being. *Economic and Industrial Democracy, 22*, 543–567.

Hong, R.Y. (2007). Worry and rumination: differential associations with anxious and depressive symptoms and coping behavior. *Behavior Research and Therapy, 45*, 277–290.

Hunter, J. E. & Schmidt, F. L. (1990). *Methods of meta-analysis: Correcting error and bias in research findings.* Newbury Park: Sage Publications.

Jackson, S. E. & Schuler, R. S. (1985). A meta-analysis and conceptual critique of research on role ambiguity and role conflict in work settings. *Organizational Behavior & Human Decision Processes, 36*, 16–78.

Jex, S. M. (1998). *Stress and job performance: Theory, research, and implications for managerial practice.* Thousand Oaks, Calif.; London; New Delhi: Sage Publications.

Jex, S.M., & Bliese, P.D. (1999). Efficacy beliefs as a moderator of the impact of work-related stressors: A multilevel study. *Journal of Applied Psychology, 84*, 349–361.

*Jex, S. M., Burnfield, J. L., Grauer, E., Adams, G., & Morgan, E. (2003). *The Role of Proactive Personality in Occupational Stress*, Poster presented at the 18th annual Conference of the Society for Industrial and Organizational Psychology, Orlando, FL.

*Jex, S. M., Burnfield, J. L., Grauer, E., Lax, G., Roelse, P., & Sroda, M. (2003). *The Interaction Between Stressors, Self-Efficacy, and Coping in Predicting Employee Health*, Presented at the 18th annual Conference of the Society for Industrial and Organizational Psychology, Orlando, FL.

Jex, S. M., & Gudanowski, D. M. (1992). Efficacy beliefs and work stress: An exploratory study. *Journal of Organizational Behavior, 13*, 509–517.

*Kageyama, T., Nishikido, N., Kobayashi, T. & Kawagoe, H. (2001). Estimated sleep debt and work stress in Japanese white-collar workers. *Psychiatry & Clinical Neurosciences, 55*, 217–219.

Kahn, R.L., Wolfe, D.M., Quinn, R.P., & Snoek, J.D. (1964). *Organizational Stress: Studies in Role Conflict and Ambiguity.* New York: John Wiley & Sons, Inc.

Karasek, R. A. (1979). Job demands, job decision latitude, and mental strain: Implications for job redesign. *Administrative Science Quarterly, 24*, 285–308.

Kelley, H.H., & Michela, J.L. (1980). Attribution theory and research. *Annual Review of Psychology, 31*, 457–501.

Kemery, E. R., Mossholder, K. W. & Bedeian, A. G. (1987). Role stress, physical symptomatology, and turnover intentions: A causal analysis of three alternative specifications. *Journal of Occupational Behavior, 8*, 11–23.

Kirkcaldy, B. D., Levine, R. & Shephard, R. J. (2000). The impact of working hours on physical and psychological health of German managers. *European Review of Applied Psychology/Revue Européenne de Psychologie Appliquée, 50*, 443–449.

Kirmeyer, S. L. & Dougherty, T. W. (1988). Work load, tension, and coping: Moderating effects of supervisor support. *Personnel Psychology, 41*, 125–139.

Kivimaeki, M. & Lindstroem, K. (1995). Effects of private self-consciousness and control on the occupational stress-strain relationship. *Stress Medicine, 11*, 7–16.

Krauss, A.D., Chen, P.Y., DeArmond, S., & Moorcroft, B. (2003). Sleepiness in the workplace: Causes, consequences, and countermeasures. In C.L. Cooper & I.T. Robertson (Eds.), *International Review of Industrial and Organizational Psychology* (Vol. 18, pp. 81–129). West Sussex, England: Wiley.

Kumar, A. & Vaidya, A. K. (1982). Neuroticism in short and long sleepers. *Perceptual & Motor Skills, 54,* 962.

*Landsbergis, P. A. (1988). Occupational stress among health care workers: A test of the job demands-control model. *Journal of Organizational Behavior, 9,* 217–239.

Lazarus, R.S. (1966). *Psychological Stress and the Coping Process.* New York: McGraw-Hill.

Lazarus, R.S., & Folkman, S. (1984). *Stress, Appraisal, and Coping.* New York: Springer.

*Lee, K. A. (1992). Self-reported sleep disturbances in employed women. *Sleep, 15,* 493–498.

Levy, P.E. (1993). Self-appraisal and attributions: A test of a model. *Journal of Management, 19,* 51–62.

Lilley, R., Feyer, A.M., Kirk, P., & Gander, P. (2002). A survey of forest workers in New Zealand: Do hours of work, rest, and recovery play a role in accidents and injury? *Journal of Safety Research, 33,* 53–71.

Martens, M.F.J., Nijhuis, F.J.N., Van Boxtel, M.P.J., & Knottnerus, J.A. (1999). Flexible work schedules and mental and physical health. A study of a working population with non-traditional working hours. *Journal of Organizational Behavior, 20,* 35–46.

Mathieu, J. E., Tannenbaum, S. I., & Salas, E. (1992). Influences of individual and situational characteristics on measures of training effectiveness. *Academy of Management Journal, 35,* 828–847.

McCann, B. S., Benjamin, G. A. H., Wilkinson, C. W., Retzlaff, B. M., Russo, J., & Knopp, R. H. (1999). Plasma lipid concentrations during episodic occupational stress. *Annals of Behavioral Medicine, 21,* 103–110.

McCann, S. J. & Stewin, L. L. (1988). Worry, anxiety, and preferred length of sleep. *Journal of Genetic Psychology, 149,* 413–418.

McGrath, J.E. (1976). Stress and behavior in organizations. In M.D. Dunnette (Ed.), *Handbook of industrial and organizational psychology* (pp. 1351–1395). Chicago: Rand McNally.

Melamed, S., & Oksenberg, A. (2002). Excessive Daytime Sleepiness and Risk of Occupational Injuries in Non-Shift Daytime Workers. *Sleep: Journal of Sleep and Sleep Disorders Research, 25,* 315–321.

Michielsen, H. J., De Vries, J. & Van Heck, G. L. (2003). Psychometric qualities of a brief self-rated fatigue measure: The fatigue assessment scale. *Journal of Psychosomatic Research, 54,* 345–352.

Mitchell, R.E., Cronkite, R.C., & Moos, R.H. (1983). Stress, coping, and depression among married couples. *Journal of Abnormal Psychology, 92,* 433–448.

Moorcroft, W.M. (1993). *Sleep, Dreaming, and Sleep Disorders: An Introduction* (2nd ed.). Lanham, MD: University Press of America.

Nakata, A., Ikeda, T., Takahashi, M., Haratani, T., Fujioka, Y., Fukui, S., et al. (2005). Sleep-related risk of occupational injuries in Japanese small and medium-scale enterprises. *Industrial Health, 43,* 89–97.

National Sleep Foundation (2008). Sleep in America Poll: Summary of Findings. [On-line]. Available: http://www.sleepfoundation.org/site/c.huIXKjM0IxF/b.3933533/.

O'Connor, E. J., Pooyan, A., Weekley,J., Peters, L.H., Frank, B., Erenkrantz, B. (1984). Situational constraint effects on performance, affective reactions, and turnover: A field replication and extension. *Journal of Applied Psychology, 69*, 663–672.

*Parkes, K. (2003). Shiftwork and environment as interactive predictors of work perceptions. *Journal of Occupational Health Psychology, 8*, 266–281.

Peeters, M.C.W., Schaufeli, W.B., & Buunk, B.P. (1995). The role of attributions in the cognitive appraisal of work-related stressful events: an event-recording approach. *Work & Stress, 1995*, 463–474.

Perrewé, P.L., & Zellars, K.L. (1999). An examination of attributions and emotions in the transactional approach to the organizational stress process. *Journal of Organizational Behavior, 20*, 739–752.

Peters, L.H., & O'Conner, E.J. (1980). Situational constraints and work outcomes: The influences of a frequently overlooked construct. *Academy of Management Review, 5*, 391–397.

Peters, L. H., O'Connor, E. J., Eulberg, J. R. & Watson, T. W. (1988). An examination of situational constraints in air force work settings. *Human Performance, 1*, 133–144.

Pilcher,J. J., Ginter, D. R. & Sadowsky, B. (1997). Sleep quality versus sleep quantity: Relationships between sleep and measures of health, well-being and sleepiness in college students. *Journal of Psychosomatic Research, 42*, 583–596.

Pilcher, J. J., Schoeling, S. E. & Prosansky, C. M. (2000). Self-report sleep habits as predictors of subjective sleepiness. *Behavioral Medicine, 25*, 161–168.

*Pollard, T. M. (2001). Changes in mental well-being, blood pressure and total cholesterol levels during workplace reorganization: The impact of uncertainty. *Work and Stress, 15*, 14–28.

Rahim, A. (1996). Stress, strain, and their moderators: An empirical comparison of entrepreneurs and managers. *Journal of Small Business Management, 34*, 46–58.

Repetti, R. L. (1993). Short-term effects of occupational stressors on daily mood and health complaints. *Health Psychology, 12*, 125–131.

Rogers, A. E., Caruso, C. C. & Aldrich, M. S. (1993). Reliability of sleep diaries for assessment of sleep/wake patterns. *Nursing Research, 42*, 368–372.

Rosa, R.R., & Colligan, M.J. (1988). Long workdays versus restdays: Assessing fatigue and alertness with a portable performance battery. *Human Factors, 30*, 305–317.

Rotter, J.B. (1990). Internal versus external control of reinforcement: A case history of a variable. *American Psychologist, 45*, 489–493.

*Samel, A., Wegmann, H. M. & Vejvoda, M. (1997). Aircrew fatigue in long-haul operations. *Accident Analysis & Prevention, 29*, 439–52.

*Schreurs, P. J. G. & Taris, T. W. (1998). Construct validity of the demand-control model: A double cross-validation approach. *Work & Stress, 12*, 66–84.

Schuler, R. S. (1980). Definition and conceptualization of stress in organizations. *Organizational Behavior & Human Decision Processes, 25*, 184–215.

Schulz, P., Kirschbaum, C., Pruesner, J. & Hellhammer, D. (1998). Increased free cortisol secretion after awakening in chronically stressed individuals due to work overload. *Stress Medicine, 14*, 91–97.

*Shirom, A., Westman, M., Shamai, O. & Carel, R. S. (1997). Effects of work overload and burnout on cholesterol and triglycerides levels: The moderating effects of emotional reactivity among male and female employees. *Journal of Occupational Health Psychology, 2,* 275–288.

Simpson, S.A., Wadsworth, E.J.K., Moss, S.C., & Smith, A.P. (2005). Minor injuries, cognitive failures and accidents at work: Incidence and associated features. *Occupational Medicine, 55,* 99–108.

Sonnentag, S., & Frese, M. (2003). Stress in organizations. In W.C. Borman, D.R. Ilgen, & R.J. Klimoski (Eds.) *Handbook of Psychology: Vol. 12. Industrial and Organizational Psychology* (pp. 453–491). Hoboken, NJ: Wiley.

Spector, P.E. (1982). Behavior in organizations as a function of employee's locus of control. *Psychological Bulletin, 91,* 482–497.

Spector, P. E. (1986). Perceived control by employees: A meta-analysis of studies concerning autonomy and participation at work. *Human Relations, 39,* 1005–1016.

*Spector, P. E., Chen, P. Y. & O'Connell, B. J. (2000). A longitudinal study of relations between job stressors and job strains while controlling for prior negative affectivity and strains. *Journal of Applied Psychology, 85,* 211–218.

*Spector, P. E., Dwyer, D. J. & Jex, S. M. (1988). Relation of job stressors to affective, health, and performance outcomes: A comparison of multiple data sources. *Journal of Applied Psychology, 73,* 11–19.

*Spector, P. E., Fox, S. & Van Katwyk, P. T. (1999). The role of negative affectivity in employee reactions to job characteristics: Bias effect or substantive effect? *Journal of Occupational and Organizational Psychology, 72,* 205–218.

*Spector, P. E. & Jex, S. M. (1991). Relations of job characteristics from multiple data sources with employee affect, absence, turnover intentions, and health. *Journal of Applied Psychology, 76,* 46–53.

Spector, P. E., & Jex, S. M. (1998). Development of four self-report measures of job stressors and strain: Interpersonal conflict at work scale, organizational constraints scale, quantitative workload inventory, and physical symptoms inventory. *Journal of Occupational Health Psychology, 3,* 356–367.

Spector, P. E. & O'Connell, B. J. (1994). The contribution of personality traits, negative affectivity, locus of control and type a to the subsequent reports of job stressors and job strains. *Journal of Occupational & Organizational Psychology, 67,* 1–12.

Sutton, R. I. (1984). Job stress among primary and secondary schoolteachers: Its relationship to ill-being. *Work & Occupations, 11,* 7–28.

*Tanz, R. R. & Charrow, J. (1993). Black clouds–work load, sleep, and resident reputation. *American Journal of Diseases of Children, 147,* 579–584.

Thomsen, D.K., Mehlsen, M.Y., Christensen, S., & Zachariae, R. (2003). Rumination—relationship with negative mood and sleep quality. *Personality and Individual Differences, 34,* 1293–1301.

*Tummers, G. E. R., Landeweerd, J. A. & van Merode, G. G. (2002). Organization, work and work reactions: A study of the relationship between organizational aspects of nursing and nurses' work characteristics and work reactions. *Scandinavian Journal of Caring Sciences, 16,* 52–58.

Van Dijkhuizen, N. & Reiche, H. (1980). Psychosocial stress in industry: A heartache for middle management? *Psychotherapy & Psychosomatics, 34*, 124–134.

Van den Berg, P. T. & Schalk, R. (1997). Type A behavior, well-being, work overload, and role-related stress in information work. *Journal of Social Behavior & Personality, 12*, 175–187.

Ware, J. C. (1988). Sleep and anxiety. In R.L. Williams, I. Karacan, & C.A. Moore (Eds.). *Sleep disorders: Diagnosis and treatment* (2nd ed., pp. 189–214). New York: Wiley.

Webb, W.B., & Cartwright, R.D. (1978). Sleep and dreams. *Annual Review of Psychology, 29*, 223–252.

Weiner, B. (1985). An attributional theory of achievement motivation and emotion. *Psychological Review, 92*, 548–573.

*Widerszal-Bazyl, M., Cooper, C. L., Sparks, K. & Spector, P. E. (2000). Managerial stress in private and state organisations in Poland. *Stress Medicine, 16*, 299–314.

*Zohar, D. (1999). When things go wrong: The effect of daily work hassles on effort, exertion and negative mood. *Journal of Occupational & Organizational Psychology, 72*, 265–283.

CHAPTER 4

THE EXPERIENCE
OF WORK-RELATED STRESS
ACROSS OCCUPATIONS

Sheena Johnson
University of Liverpool

Cary Cooper
Lancaster University

Sue Cartwright
UMIST

Ian Donald and Paul Taylor
University of Liverpool

Clare Cook
Robertson Cooper Ltd, Manchester, UK

ABSTRACT

Purpose: To compare the experience of occupational stress across a large and diverse set of occupations. Three stress related variables (psychological well

Stress and Quality of Working Life, pages 67–77

being, physical health and job satisfaction) are discussed and comparisons are made between 26 different occupations on each of these measures. The relationship between physical and psychological stress and job satisfaction at an occupational level is also explored.

Design/methodology/approach: The measurement tool used is a short stress evaluation tool which provides information on a number of work related stressors and stress outcomes. Out of the full ASSET database 26 occupations were selected for inclusion in this paper. Findings Six occupations are reporting worse than average scores on each of the factors physical health, psychological well being and job satisfaction (ambulance workers, teachers, social services, customer services call centres, prison officers and police). Differences across and within occupational groups, for example, teaching and policing, are detailed. The high emotional labour associated with the high stress jobs is discussed as a potential causal factor.

Research limitations/implications: This is not an exhaustive list of occupations and only concerns employees working within the UK. Originality/value There is little information available that shows the relative values of stress across different occupations, which would enable the direct comparison of stress levels. This paper reports the rank order of 26 different occupations on stress and job satisfaction levels

INTRODUCTION

This chapter outlines research into the experience of occupational stress within a large and diverse set of occupations. The measurement tool used in the research is a short stress evaluation tool (Robertson Cooper, 2002a) which has been described as measuring a number of work related stressors and stress outcomes (Faragher et al., 2004). Three of these stress outcomes (psychological well-being, physical health and job satisfaction) are discussed and comparisons made between different occupations on each of these measures.

The experience of workplace stress has been subject to a large amount of research and interest in the topic shows no sign of waning. It is now generally accepted that prolonged or intense stress can have a negative impact on an individual's mental and physical health (Health and Safety Executive, 2001; Cooper et al., 2001). The Health and Safety Executive (2004) state that around half a million people in the UK experience work-related stress at a level that they believe is making them ill, up to five million people feel "very" or "extremely" stressed by their work and work-related stress costs society about £3.7 billion every year. Significant health implications have also been reported, for example, the HSE (2001) describes how ill health can result if stress is prolonged or intense, with the negative effects including heart disease, back pain, gastrointestinal disturbances, anxiety and depression. In addition to this they outline how stress can lead to other behaviors such as more tobacco smoking, excessive alcohol or caffeine consumption and skipping meals, which can also contribute to health problems.

The stress experienced by different occupation types and job roles has been discussed in many papers with a number of different occupations being described as experiencing above average levels of stress, for example, teachers (Travers and Cooper, 1993) healthcare (Cooper et al., 1999), nurses and social workers (Kahn, 1993), and the ambulance service (Young and Cooper, 1999) to name but a few. There are a number of work related stressors which have been linked to an increased likelihood of an individual experiencing negative stress outcomes. Cooper and Marshall's (1976) original model of work related stress included five sources of stress at work, each of which are represented in the revised model of stress on which ASSET is based (Robertson Cooper, 2002b).

Cooper and Marshall's five sources of stress, with examples of the components of these sources given for each, are:

1. Intrinsic to the job, including factors such as poor physical working conditions, work overload or time pressures;
2. role in the organization, including role ambiguity and role conflict;
3. career development, including lack of job security and under/over promotion;
4. relationships at work, including poor relationships with your boss or colleagues, an extreme component of which is bullying in the workplace (Rayner and Hoel, 1997); and
5. organizational structure and climate, including little involvement in decision-making and office politics.

Additional sources of stress also represented in the ASSET model are the impact a persons working life has on their life outside of work (work-life balance), the amount of satisfaction people derive from their work, the amount of control and autonomy people have in the workplace, and levels of commitment in the workplace both from the employee to the organization and from the organization to the employee.

The amount of stress a person experiences at work is likely to be a result of the interaction of a number of factors such as the type of work they are doing (their occupation), the presence of work stressors, the amount of support they receive both at work and at home and the coping mechanisms they use to deal with stress. Different occupations will have different basic stressors, for example, the threat of violence, lack of control over work decisions or long working hours. However, people working in the same occupation will experience different levels of stress due to the interplay of many other factors, for example, their personality type and the support mechanisms they have available to them. It is not possible therefore, to say that all people working in a certain occupation will experience the same amount of stress. It is however, reasonable to state that employees working in high-risk occupations will have an increased likelihood of experiencing negative stress outcomes.

An extreme or advanced form of stress that is increasingly studied within occupations that have been termed as in the "human service" arena is burnout (Maslach and Jackson, 1981; Cordes and Dougherty, 1993). Burnout has been described as comprising three elements, emotional exhaustion—characterised by a lack of energy and a feeling that one's emotional resources are used up, depersonalisation—marked by the treatment of clients as objects rather than people, and personal accomplishment—characterised by a tendency to evaluate oneself negatively. The specific role and influence of emotions in the workplace have been subject to further (and ongoing) research and emotion work has been described as possessing the following characteristics; it is a significant component of jobs that require either face to face or voice to voice interaction with clients; the emotions displayed in these jobs are intended to influence other people's attitudes and behaviors; and the display of emotions has to follow certain rules (Zapf et al., 1999). Subsequent research described how emotional dissonance can be experienced by employees if they are required to express emotions that they do not genuinely feel, which can result in feelings of hypocrisy and may ultimately lead to lowered self esteem and depression (Zapf, 2002). Fox and Spector (2002) reported that emotion work and the experience of emotional exhaustion are related and emotional dissonance is negatively correlated with job satisfaction.

Certain occupations are more likely to involve an emotional element of work suggesting that employees in these occupations are likely to be more vulnerable to stress than occupations that do not require emotional displays. For example, Kahn's (1993) work suggests that caregivers (for example, nurses and social workers) are more likely to suffer from emotional exhaustion because they are required to display intense emotions within their jobs. Other stressors are also evident in many occupations, for example, the threat of violence (e.g., social work, police), lack of control over the job (e.g., call centres) or work overload (e.g., teachers). It is therefore, unsurprising that much of the research into workplace stress focuses on these "high risk" occupations. However, there is little information available that shows the relative values of stress across different occupations, which would enable the direct comparison of stress levels. For this reason the current paper aims to provide information on physical health, psychological well-being and job satisfaction across 26 different occupation types.

METHODOLOGY

The occupational scores on physical and mental ill health and job satisfaction are taken from research into occupational stress using the ASSET stress questionnaire. The factor structure, reliability and validity of ASSET are discussed elsewhere (Faragher et al., 2004; Johnson and Cooper, 2003) and therefore, are not covered in depth here. However, a brief overview of the measurement tool is necessary to provide the context in which the occupational data has been gathered. ASSET was devised as a short stress evaluation tool which can be completed quickly and easily by all employees in an organization and as such is designed to be used in the first phase of a two-phase stress risk assessment (the second stage taking the form of a more detailed examination of the "problem areas" of an organization as identified by high stress scores on ASSET). Since ASSET is a copyrighted questionnaire it is not possible to reproduce it in its entirety. However, Table 4.1 outlines the 12 factors measured by the questionnaire. The factors of interest in this paper are:

1. "Your Job" which correlates highly with the Warr (1990) job satisfaction scale (Faragher et al., 2004) and as such is reported here as a useful indication of levels of job satisfaction.
2. "Physical Health"; and
3. "Psychological Well-being" which has been shown to have good convergent validity with the GHQ12 (Johnson and Cooper, 2003).

The GHQ and GHQ12 are accepted measure of minor psychiatric disorders (Goldberg et al., 1997).

ASSET has been used as a stress measurement tool in over 26 organizations resulting in a large dataset of over 25,000 individuals encompassing many different occupation types. This enables the direct comparison of reported stress levels at an occupational level. Twenty-six different occupations were selected for this paper, each of which are ranked on their physical health, psychological well-being and job satisfaction scores. This enables the occupations to be compared, providing information on which occupations are reporting the highest levels of stress and the lowest levels of job satisfaction.

TABLE 4.1   ASSET Factor Structure

Factor	Description
Work relationships	Sources of stress relating to the contacts people have at work with their colleagues/managers.
Your job	Sources of stress relating to the fundamental nature of the job itself
Overload	Sources of stress relating to workload and time pressures
Control	Sources of stress relating to the amount of control people have over their work
Job security	Sources of stress relating to the level of job security perceived by people
Resources and communication	Sources of stress relating to the equipment/resources available at work and the effectiveness of communication in the workplace
Work–life balance	Sources of stress relating to the extent to which the demands of work interfere with people's personal and home life
Pay and benefits	Sources of stress relating to pay and benefits
Commitment of the organization to the employee	The extent to which people feel their organization is committed to them
Commitment of the employee to the organization	The extent to which people are loyal and dedicated to their organization
Physical health	Physical symptoms associated with stress
Psychological well-being	Clinical symptoms indicative of stress induced mental ill-health

RESULTS

Table 4.2 reports the sample size and mean score for each occupation on the measures of physical health, psychological well-being and job satisfaction. Table 4.3 displays these occupations in rank order with the rank of one indicating the highest score on the scale. Occupations appearing in italics are those that report scores above the norm for the ASSET database suggesting that these occupations are experiencing worse than average physical health and psychological well-being and lower than average job satisfaction.

Physical Health

This factor includes questions about the physical symptoms often associated with stress. Higher scores on this scale indicate worsening physical health.

TABLE 4.2   Sample Size and Mean Scores for Occupations on Physical Health, Psychological Well-Being, and Job Satisfaction

Occupation	n	Physical health	Psychological well-being	Job satisfaction
Accountant	111	12.66	17.47	18.74
Allied health professionals	334	12.76	18.61	25.50
Ambulance	52	15.13	20.22	30.37
Analyst	210	12.26	16.79	17.94
Bar staff	71	14.35	18.43	24.60
Clerical and admin	1,433	14.23	19.49	22.93
Customer services—call center	278	14.45	18.90	28.74
Director (public sector)	144	12.39	18.78	21.10
Director/MD (private sector)	11	10.00	15.18	13.82
Fire brigade	269	12.55	20.56	24.25
Head teachers	295	13.53	17.48	22.50
Lecturers	1,051	13.18	19.66	22.71
Medical/dental	166	12.67	17.82	25.66
Management (private sector)	36	14.24	19.33	24.59
Management (public sector)	686	12.80	17.47	22.87
Nursing	1,539	12.83	18.33	27.14
Prison officer	118	14.34	19.26	33.89
Police	1,027	14.09	19.03	29.24
Senior police	406	13.16	17.79	20.81
Research—academic	337	13.43	19.15	21.06
School lunchtime supervisors	165	12.13	15.43	20.09
Secretarial/business support	105	13.52	17.65	21.70
Social services providing care	535	14.85	24.35	28.14
Teachers	916	14.98	21.54	27.44
Teaching assistant	444	13.58	17.37	22.14
Vets	262	12.40	19.75	23.89
Norm score for ASSET	**25,352**	**13.83**	**18.81**	**25.28**

Psychological Well-Being

This factor includes questions relating to the clinical symptoms indicative of stress induced mental ill-health. It has been shown to correlate highly with the GHQ12. Higher scores indicate worsening psychological well-being.

Discussion

Of the 26 occupations included in the research, six (ambulance, teachers, social services, customer services—call centres, prison officers and police) were identified as having worse than average scores on each of the three factors. These are the occupations that were reported as being the most stressful regarding physical and psychological well-being and as having the lowest levels of job satisfaction. This is not an entirely surprising finding as most of these have been identified previously as being stressful occupations (Travers and Cooper, 1993; Kahn, 1993; Young and Cooper, 1999).

Each of the above occupations involve emotional labour, an element of work which has been described as relevant to the experience of work related stress (Zapf et al., 1999; Zapf, 2002) in that all these job roles require either face to face or voice to voice interaction with clients and in each of these occupations the emotions that the employees are required to display as part of their job have to follow strict rules. Think of for example, the emotional labour that teachers have when working with unruly or unwilling to learn children without letting a child see their frustration or the demands on police officers when facing potentially dangerous and volatile situations whilst through necessity having to be outwardly calm and appear to be fully in control of a situation.

Although the emotional component of work is almost certainly relevant to the experience of work stress it cannot be the only explanation for high stress levels as the lower than average scores on psychological well-being and physical health reported by nurses (a job with high emotional content) are anomalous to this theory. Other stressors, for example, the threat of violence in the workplace (a risk factor in social services, prison officers and police), lack of control over work issues (often discussed in relation to call centre work, for example, see Holman and Fernie (2000)) and work overload (nurses, teachers and social services) to name but a few will undoubtedly all play an important role in the experience of work stress. The identification of the causes of stress for any particular occupation would require analysis of the presence and intensity of workplace stressors, which is beyond the scope of the current paper.

The least stressed and most satisfied occupations are analysts, school lunchtime supervisors and directors/MDs within the private sector. Interestingly directors in the public sector score higher on all three factors than directors/MDs in the private sector although this finding is reversed when looking at management rather than director level. Here, management in the private sector score higher than management in the public sector on all three factors. However, given the low numbers of directors/MDs from the private sector (n 11) these scores should be interpreted with caution.

The rank order of these occupations provides information on the relative stress and job satisfaction scores between occupations. Of equal interest however, is the comparison of scores across occupations within the same occupational group, for example, within teaching and policing.

It is generally recognized that teaching is a stressful occupation and past research has supported this (Travers and Cooper, 1993). This is reflected in the positioning of teachers at above average levels on physical and psychological health and lower than average levels of job satisfaction. However, the ASSET scores also reveal that teachers are experiencing higher stress levels and lower job satisfaction levels than both head teachers and teaching assistants, neither of whom score above the norm on any of the factors. One possible reason for this is that teachers are working in close contact with children every working day and therefore, will be experiencing high levels of emotional labour. Head teachers and teaching assistants do not generally take charge of the classroom or if they do it is for short periods of time or whilst under supervision. It is also possible that the differences between teachers and head teachers are due to their very different roles, with head teachers being in a more managerial position. The difference between teachers and teaching assistants could be the result of teachers being more accountable for the day-to-day running of the classroom and levels of performance (both their own and their students) reflecting on their ability as a teacher. Additionally, many teachers are concerned about the amount of paperwork they are now required to complete, often it has been argued at the detriment of time teaching or preparing lessons for the children. Teaching assistants do not have this level of paperwork. Finally, if teaching assistants are trainee teachers they will have entered the profession relatively recently and therefore, are not able to compare the "old" way of teaching with the "new." A comparison that any teacher who has been in the profession for more than ten years will have an opinion on. The changes within the teaching profession within the last ten years or so have been blamed for the high levels of stress reported by teachers (Moriarty et al., 2001). Of course much of this is speculative and in order to tease out the reasons behind these differences a full study on stress within our schools would be required.

Another interesting area for discussion is the differences found within different levels of the police. Police officers were one of the top six occupations experiencing the most stress and least job satisfaction. However, in comparison, senior police officers are scoring much lower scores revealing them to be less stressed and more satisfied. Again it is not possible to be sure why these differences are occurring but the fact that on the whole police officers will spend more time "on the beat" and interacting with the public than senior police officers who will spend at least a proportion of their time behind the scenes suggests that the experience of emotional labour may again prove to be salient.

Occupations from within the medical profession reveal that although nurses, medical dental and allied health professionals are all scoring lower than average levels of job satisfaction they are not reporting high scores on the stress factors. This is contrary to previous findings that suggest nurses in particular experience higher than average stress levels (Kahn, 1993).

On the whole the rank order of the occupations is consistent with existing research and general belief about how stressful these different occupations are. However, as detailed above there are some interesting differences between roles within the same occupational setting, for example, teachers and head teachers, and police and senior police. The premise that emotional labour is an important facet of the experience of occupational stress is supported in that all of the high stress occupations revealed above involve high levels of emotional labour. However, the identification of specific stressors for individual occupations requires more in-depth analysis of the interaction between stressors and stress outcomes.

The finding that physical health, psychological well-being and job satisfaction are linked was expected and supports existing research in this area (Dewe, 1991). It is therefore, not surprising that many of the occupations that are reporting high stress levels are also reporting low levels of job satisfaction.

Work Related Stress

This chapter provides information on the rank order of occupations in relation to job satisfaction and the experience of negative stress outcomes, and as such allows the identification of "high" and "low" stress occupations. Although some suggestions have been made to explain the findings, a full analysis of the relevant stressors for any particular occupation is not attempted. Past research into high-risk occupations is on the whole supported with occupations previously described as reporting high stress levels also indicating high stress levels here. Further work on the ASSET database, including the analysis of the particular stressors most relevant to individual occupations, is underway and will be reported in subsequent papers.

REFERENCES

Cooper, C. L., & Marshall, J. (1976). Occupational sources of stress: a review of the literature relating to coronary heart disease and mental ill health. *Journal of Occupational Psychology, 49,* 11–28.

Cooper, C. L., Clarke, S., & Rowbottom, A. M. (1999). Occupational stress, job satisfaction and well being in anaesthetists. *Stress Medicine, 15,* 115–126.

Cooper, C. L., Dewe, P. J., & O'Driscoll, M. P. (2001). *Organizational stress: A review and critique of theory, research and applications.* Sage Publications, CA.

Cordes, C. L., & Dougherty, T. W. (1993). A review and an integration of research on job burnout. *Academy of Management Review, 18*(4), 621–656.

Dewe, P. (1991). Primary appraisal, secondary appraisal and coping: Their role in stressful work encounters. *Journal of Occupational Psychology, 64,* 331–351.

Faragher, E. B., Cooper, C. L., & Cartwright, S. (2004). A shortened stress evaluation tool (ASSET). *Stress and Health, 20*(4), 189–201.

Fox, S., & Spector, P. E. (2002). Emotions in the workplace: The neglected side of organizational life introduction. *Human Resource Management Review, 12,* 1–5.

Goldberg, D. P., Gater, R., Sartorius, N., & Ustun, T. B. (1997). The validity of two versions of the GHQ in the WHO study of mental illness in general health care. *Psychological Medicine, 27,* 191–197.

Health and Safety Executive. (2001). *Tackling work related stress.* London: HSE Books.

Health and Safety Executive (2004). *Work related stress.* Retrieved May 7, 2004, from www.hse.gov.uk/stress/ index.htm.

Holman, D., & Fernie, S. (2000). "Can I help you?" Call centres and job satisfaction. *Centrepiece: The Magazine of Economic Performance, 5*(1), 2–5.

Johnson, S., & Cooper, C. (2003). The construct validity of the ASSET stress measure. *Stress and Health, 19,* 181–185.

Kahn, W. A. (1993). Caring for the caregivers: patterns of organizational caregiving. *Administrative Science Quarterly, 38*(4), 539–564.

Maslach, C., & Jackson, S. E. (1981). The measurement of experienced burnout. *Journal of Occupational Behavior, 2,* 99–113.

Moriarty, V., Edmonds, S., Blatchford, P., & Martin, C. (2001). Teaching young children: Perceived satisfaction and stress. *Educational Research, 43*(1), 33–46.

Rayner, C., & Hoel, H. (1997). Workplace bullying: A concise review of literature. *Journal of Community and Applied Social Psychology, 7,* 181–189.

Robertson Cooper (2002a), *ASSET.* Manchester, UK: Robertson Cooper Ltd.

Robertson Cooper (2002b), *ASSET technical manual.* Manchester, UK: Robertson Cooper Ltd.

Travers, C. J., & Cooper, C. L. (1993). Mental health, job satisfaction and occupational stress among UK teachers. *Work and Stress, 7*(3), 203–219.

Warr, P. (1990). The measurement of well being and other aspects of mental health. *Journal of Occupational Psychology, 63,* 193–210.

Young, K. M., & Cooper, C. L. (1999). Change in stress outcomes following an industrial dispute in the ambulance service: A longitudinal study. *Health Services Management Review, 12,* 51–62.

Zapf, D. (2002). Emotion work and psychological well being: A review of the literature and some conceptual considerations. *Human Resource Management Review, 12,* 1–32.

Zapf, D., Vogt, C., Seifert, C., Mertini, H., & Isic, A. (1999). Emotion work as a source of stress: The concept and development of an instrument. *European Journal of Work and Organizational Psychology, 8*(3), 371–400.

CHAPTER 5

WORK-RELATED MENTAL DISORDERS

A Perspective of the Brazilian Occupational Medicine and Psychiatry

Duílio Antero de Camargo

INTRODUCTION

The field called Mental Health and Work is designed mainly to study the work dynamics, organization and processes in order to promote workers' mental health through effective diagnostic, preventive and treatment actions, in addition to helping to find the cause of the work-related mental disorders (Guimarães, 1998).

The knowledge acquired in this field support the new approaches in Occupational Medicine and Psychiatry to understand and mitigate the psychological distress at work. Today, due to a number of changes in workers' health promotion and protection, work-related mental disorders have been given special attention due to its high prevalence in work environments and to recent regulations related to the theme.

A new medical specialty was added to the field of Mental Health and Work, the Occupational (or Labor) Psychiatry, which in Brazil became

Stress and Quality of Working Life, pages 79–91
Copyright © 2009 by Information Age Publishing
All rights of reproduction in any form reserved.

more important after the publication of the new list of work-related diseases (Ministry of Health, 1999) which is an significant milestone regarding prevention, surveillance and workers' health.

This new list deals, among other occupational diseases, with work-related mental disorders, among them depressive disorders, post-traumatic stress, sleep disorders, the burnout syndrome, (work-related) alcoholism and some dementia states (triggered by occupation neurointoxications).

For a better understanding of these diseases, elements related to the interface between Occupational Medicine and Psychiatry are described.

OCCUPATIONAL MEDICINE

Occupational Medicine is aimed mainly at working on the harmful impacts of the work environment on workers' health, with actions based on specific regulations by the Ministry of Labor called **Regulatory Norms** (RN Ministry of Labor, 2003) related to Safety and Occupational Medicine. These norms are divided into 33 specific items and serve as a foundation for organizations to manage the potential risk to their workers' health. Norms NR-7 and NR-9 stand out among these norms.

One of its main instruments is the Program for the Medical Control of Occupational Health (Ministry of Labor, 2004. PCMSO/ NR7), which consists in promoting and protecting workers' health, reducing injuries and work-related diseases through primary and secondary actions. In this program, we find some items such as medical examinations (admissional, regular, position change, return to work and dismissal examinations) that are mandatory and aimed at the early detection of potential diseases.

In contrast, the Environmental Risk Prevention Program (Ministry of Labor, 2003. PPRA/NR9) is concerned with recognizing, reducing and eliminating the environmental risk sources, described in Table 5.1.

PSYCHIATRY

Psychiatry studies mental and behavioral disorders that affect individuals, being divided into several specialties such as Child Psychiatry, Forensic Psychiatry and others, with the current reemergence of Occupational Psychiatry (or Labor Psychiatry), a term that has been used since 1927 (Selligman-Silva, 1994) and *currently recommended by the World Psychiatric Association* (WPA, 2003). This is the field of psychiatry that examines work-related mental disorders from the preventive, diagnostic and therapeutic point of view aiming at promoting and protecting workers' mental health.

TABLE 5.1   Environmental Risks

Environmental Risks	Caused by
Chemical risks	Dusts, fumes, mists, gases, vapors and substances, compounds and chemicals in general.
Physical risks	Noise, vibration, ionizing and non-ionizing radiation, cold, heat, abnormal pressure and moisture. Special attention is given to the psychosocial impacts of hearing loss induced by noise.
Biological risks	Viruses, bacteria, protozoa, fungi, parasites and bacilli. Special attention is given to the psychosocial impact of the disease caused by the Human Immunodeficiency Virus (HIV).
Ergonomic risks	Intense physical exertion; lifting and movement of weights by hand; inadequate postures; rigid control of productivity; shift and night work; and other situations of physical and/psychological stress. Special attention is given to the psychosocial impacts of work-related musculoskeletal disorders.
Accident or mechanical risks	Unguarded machines and equipment; inadequate or defective tools; probability of fire or explosion and other risk situations (that may contribute to accidents). Special attention is given to the psychosocial impacts of occupational accidents.

Due to the increasing incidence of work-related mental disorders today, Occupational Psychiatry started to become more visible particularly after the publication of the new list of work-related occupational diseases where, among many other occupational diseases, the following mental disorders are listed, coded according to CID–10 (OMS, 1997):

- Dementia in other specific diseases classified elsewhere (F02.8);
- *Delirium*, not overlapping dementia (F05.0);
- Mild cognitive disorder (F06.7);
- Organic personality disorder (F07.0);
- Non-specified organic or symptomatic disorder (F09);
- Work-related chronic alcoholism (F10.2);
- Depressive episodes (F32);
- Post-traumatic stress state (F43.1);
- Neurasthenia (includes the "Fatigue Syndrome") (F 48.0);
- Other specified neurotic disorders, including "Professional Neurosis" (F48.8);
- Disorder of the wakefulness-sleep cycle, caused by non-organic factors (F51. 2);
- Feeling of being burned out "Burnout Syndrome", professional exhaustion syndrome) (Z73.0).

Table 5.2 summarizes some of these disorders and their etiological agents or work-related risk factors, according to the List of Work-Related Diseases.

TABLE 5.2 List of Occupational Risk Agents or Factors with the Respective Work-Related Mental and Behavioral Disorders

Mental Disorders	Etiological Agents or Occupational Risk Factors
1. Dementia and other specific diseases classified elsewhere F.02.8	Manganese; Asphyxiating substances; Carbon Sulfide.
2. *Delirium*, not overlapping dementia F.05.0	Methyl Bromide; Carbon Sulfide.
3. Other mental disorders resulting from brain injury and dysfunction and from physical disease (F.06); Mild Cognitive Disorder (F.06.7)	Toluene and other neurotoxic aromatic solvents; Lead and its toxic compounds; Trichlorethylene, Tetrachlorethylene, and other toxic halogenated organic compounds; Methyl Bromide; Manganese and its toxic compounds; Mercury and its toxic compounds; Carbon Sulfide
4. Personality and behavioral disorder resulting from brain disease, injury and dysfunction (F.07); Organic Personality Disorder (F.07.0); Other personality and behavioral disorders resulting from brain disease, injury and dysfunction (F.07.8)	Toluene and other neurotoxic aromatic solvents; Trichlorethylene, Tetrachlorethylene, Triclorethane and other toxic halogenated organic compounds; Methyl Bromide; Manganese and its toxic compounds; Mercury and its toxic compounds; Carbon Sulfide
5. Non-specified Organic or Symptomatic Mental Disorder F.09	Toluene and other neurotoxic aromatic solvents; Trichlorethylene, Tetrachlorethylene, and other toxic halogenated organic compounds; Methyl Bromide; Manganese and its toxic compounds; Mercury and its toxic compounds; Carbon Sulfide
6. Mental and behavioral disorder caused by alcohol use: chronic alcoholism (work-related) F.10.2	Problems related to the job and unemployment: difficult work conditions; circumstance related to the work conditions.
7 Depressive episodes F.32	Toluene and other neurotoxic aromatic solvents Trichlorethylene, Tetrachlorethylene, Triclorethane and other toxic halogenated organic compounds; Methyl Bromide; Manganese and its toxic compounds; Mercury and its toxic compounds; Carbon Sulfide
8. Reactions to severe stress and adaptation disorders (F.43); Post-traumatic stress state F.43.1	Other physical and mental problems related to work: reaction after severe or catastrophic occupational accident or assault at the workplace (Z.56.6); Circumstance related to work conditions (Y.96).

Mental Disorders	Etiological Agents or Occupational Risk Factors
9. Neurasthenia (includes the "Fatigue Syndrome") F.48.0	Toluene and other neurotoxic aromatic solvents; Trichlorethylene, Tetrachlorethylene, Triclorethane and other toxic halogenated organic compounds; Methyl Bromide; Manganese and its toxic compounds; Mercury and its toxic compounds; Carbon Sulfide
10. Other specified neurotic disorders (includes "professional neurosis" F.48.8	Problems related to the job and to unemployment (Z.56.5); Unemployment (Z.56.0); Job change (Z.56.1); Threat of losing the job (Z.56.2); Strenuous work pace (Z.56.3); Disagreement with the supervisor and coworkers (Z.56.5); Other work-related physical and mental difficulties (Z.56.6).
11. Disorder of the wakefulness-sleep cycle caused by non-organic factors F.51.2	Problems related to the job and to unemployment (Z 56).(-): Poor fit to the organization of work hours (Work in shifts or night work) (Z.56.6); Circumstance related to the work conditions (Y.96).
12. Feeling of being burned out ("Burnout Syndrome, Professional exhaustion syndrome) Z.73.0	Strenuous work pace (Z.56.3); Other work-related physical and mental difficulties (Z.56.6).

Source: List of Work-Related Diseases (MS, 1999).

The interest of professionals working with mental health at the workplace in the study of these disorders today is warranted by its medical, administrative, healthcare and legal implications.

Occupational Psychiatry proposes some contributions for a better understanding and standardization of medical-administrative actions. It classifies disorders within the following Psychiatric Syndromes:

- Work-related Organic Syndromes;
- Work-related Non-Organic Syndromes;
- Psychiatric Syndromes related to Accidents at the Workplace, to Occupational Diseases and to Psychosocial Factor at the Workplace (Camargo, 2005).

Work-Related Organic Psychiatric Syndromes

Caused by agents that produce direct injury on the brain (chemicals) and chronic alcoholism, the main symptoms and neuropsychiatric signs are: cognitive changes; changes compromising fine and gross motor coordination; sensorial changes that alter visual, hearing, tactile perception among others; d) visual-spatial changes that include apraxias; personality changes, with changes in behavior; and changes that influence the mood (Jardim & Glina, 2000).

The main mental disorders and risk factors attributed to these syndromes are shown on Table 5.1, numbers 1 to 8.

Next is a summary of some of these syndromes.

Dementia (F02.8)

According to the CID-10, dementia is characterized by changes in memory, thought, orientation, comprehension, calculation, ability to learn, language, judgment, in a state of conscience clarity (WHO, 1997).

Taking manganese as an example, the risk factors are present for individuals working the following areas: steel milling, manufacturing of dry batteries (and accumulators), of dyes, paints and fertilizers (Dias, 1995).

Delirium (F05.0)

According to the CID-10, delirium is characterized by disorders of consciousness, attention, delusion, of thought (with or without delusions), of memory, psychomotor behavior (hypo- or hyperactivity) (WHO, 1997).

Taking carbon sulfide as an example, workers at the viscose (rayon) industry; working in the production of varnishes, resins and textiles are exposed to risk factors (Dias, 1995).

Chronic Alcoholism (work-related)–F.10.2

The main feature of the dependence syndrome is the frequently irresistible desire to consume alcoholic beverages and in its etiology lie biological, psychological and social causes. It can be attributed to work-related conditions being represented by the following risk psychosocial factors: disregarded activities such as garbage collectors and gravediggers; hazardous activities such as mining and civil construction and in boring jobs such as security guards. (Selligman-Silva, 1995).

Work-Related Non-Organic Psychiatric Syndromes

These syndromes differ from the above mentioned syndromes in that they present a non-organic etiology, being triggered by emotional conflicts related to work conditions and organization. Psychosocial and organizational factors play a key role in the emergence and worsening of these disorders.

Next, some of the main disorders included in the list of work-related conditions are described, such as: depressive disorders, post-traumatic stress disorder; burnout.

Depressive Disorders

According to CID-10, depressive disorders are clinically characterized by depressed mood, loss of interest and pleasure and low energy level, leading to increased fatigue and decreased activity level; decreased concentration and attention; decreased self-esteem and self-confidence; guilt thoughts; self-injuring or suicidal ideas or acts; disturbed sleep; decreased appetite; among others (WHO, 1997).

In the occupational setting, depression can show as somatic changes and can be connected to accidents, alcoholism and absenteeism (Selligman-Silva, 2005).

Among the epidemiological features of depressive disorders, the changes occurred in the labor force in industrialized economies associate stress and depression starting in the 1980's, with depression being a significant problem in some countries (ILO, 2000): in the USA it affects up to on tenth of adult workers; in Finland, over 50% of workers suffer from stress, anxiety, depression and sleeplessness; in Germany, depression causes more disability than physical diseases; in the United Kingdom, almost 3 out of 10 workers suffer annually from mental health problems, particularly depression.

The organic occupational risk factors can be associated to the following neurotoxic products: heavy metals (mercury, lead, manganese) and others (Jardim, 2000). On the other hand, there are the psychosocial risk factors, which can occur in the occupational setting, such as: successive disappointments in frustrating work situations; excessive performance demands generated by excessive competition; threats to lose a place at the organizational hierarchy; job losses; dismissal, prolonged unemployment (Brazilian Ministry of Health, 1999).

Post-Traumatic Stress Disorders

According to CID-10, post-traumatic stress disorders are characterized by a sensation of numbness (paralysis); emotional dullness; anhedonia; episodes of repeated re-experiencing of the trauma as intrusive memories (flashbacks); fear and avoidance of situations that recall the trauma; hyper vigilance; these symptoms can be associated with anxiety and depressive symptoms and alcohol use (WHO, 1997).

Epidemiologically, the following incidence if found under the following situations: victims of disasters and severe accidents; in people who witnessed the violent death of others; in people that have been victims of torture, terrorism, rape or other crime (Selligman-Silva, 2003).

In an analysis of occupational risk factors, post-traumatic stress disorder was found[1]: in military police officers seen at the psychiatry clinic at the Military Police Central Hospital in Rio de Janeiro (Maurat & Figueira, 2002); in victims of severe workplace accidents (life threatening, disfigurement, assaults and other violent crimes); in employees working at banks (and other places) who suffered an armed robbery; urban train drivers after episodes of people being run over by the trains where they worked (Selligman-Silva, 2003).

Burnout

Also known as "professional exhaustion" syndrome, burnout is linked to the continuous exposure to chronic emotional and interpersonal stressors at the workplace, being clinically characterized by the following signs: emotional exhaustion (*feelings of emotional exhaustion and affective emptiness*); depersonalization (*negative reaction, insensitivity or excessive withdrawal from the people who should be the targets of services or care*); decreased personal involvement at work—(*feelings of decreased competence and success at work*) (Jardim & Glina, 2000). The following symptoms can be found among non-specific symptoms: sleeplessness, fatigue, irritability, anguish, tremors, sadness, depression and anxiety symptoms. Additionally, people suffering from burnout have often shown great involvement with their work (role or enterprise) as if it were a *mission.*

Regarding its epidemiology, it can be found in teachers, in several countries, with the syndrome being attributed to factors such as professional devaluation, loss of the recognition of the profession and of the dignity as a result of institutional changes (Jardim & Glina, 2000); in Dutch dentists, related to gender (te Brake, Bloemendal, & Hoogstraten, 2003); in Japanese and (Shimizu, Mizoue, Kubota et al., 2003) American nurses (Vahey , Aiken, Sloane et al., 2004).

As for occupational risk factors, the occupational areas most affected by burnout are the following: the teaching profession; health professionals, such as nurses and physicians; police and prison officers; people subjected to organizational changes such as temporary dismissal and downsizing (Jardim, 2000).

PSYCHIATRIC SYNDROMES RELATED TO OCCUPATIONAL DISEASES, TO PSYCHOSOCIAL FACTORS AT THE WORKPLACE AND TO OCCUPATIONAL ACCIDENTS

Psychiatric Syndromes Related to Occupational Diseases

The occupational diseases that can have psychological consequences frequently found in our setting are the following: hearing loss caused by noise; neurological intoxication by heavy metals; disease caused by the Human Immunodeficiency virus (HIV); work-related musculoskeletal disorders (WMSDs), which is described below.

Work-Related Musculoskeletal Disorders (WMSDs)

This disorder is most frequently found in the upper limbs and can affect tendons, muscles and peripheral nerves, being associated to repetitive movements and/or dynamic or static muscle overload, giving rise to a number of clinical conditions such as tenosynovitis of the wrist and finger flexing muscles, neck strain syndrome and carpal tunnel syndrome, among others (Camargo, Fontes, & Oliveira, 2004).

Among the man psychological symptoms caused by these conditions are the following: anxiety, depression, irritability, frustration and hostility.

The activities at the greatest risk are typists, assemblers and cashiers (bank/stores).

PSYCHIATRIC SYNDROMES RELATED TO PSYCHOSOCIAL FACTORS AT THE WORKPLACE

Occupational stress occurs when work demands do not match workers' abilities, resources or needs and can trigger or worsen: smoking, caffeine consumption, drug addiction, sleep disorders and absenteeism according to the Encyclopedia of Occupational Health and Safety (ILO, 1998). Its chronic effects can trigger or worsen: cardiovascular and GI tract diseases; muscle-skeletal disorders. The following are among the main psychosocial and organizational stressors: too many activities, excessive time pressure and repetitive work; lack of social support by supervisors, colleagues and the family; physical stressors such as chemicals, noise, high temperatures; work in shifts among others (ILO, 1998).

Factors inherent in the workplace are the person-work environment fit, workload and work hours, ergonomic factors among others (ILO, 1998):

Individual factors include behavior patterns (hostility, competitiveness, impatience, restlessness) and coping styles translated as the "effort to reduce the negative effects of stress" (ILO, 1998).

Interpersonal factors include violence at the workplace (mobbing), bullying, intimidation, coercion, persecution, physical violence (homicide) and sexual harassment that can lead to avoidance, phobias, sleeplessness, depression, family conflicts and somatization (ILO, 1998).

Psychiatric Disorders Related to Occupational Accidents

The main consequences of (severe) occupational accidents are bodily changes, sensitivity loss, immobility, family dependence and social isolation (Osasco Metal Workers's Union, 2001).

Occupational accidents can trigger the following conditions: anxiety, phobic, depressive and adaptation disorders (post-traumatic stress disorder).

DIAGNOSTIC PRINCIPLES AND CAUSATION OF WORK-RELATED PSYCHIATRIC DISORDERS

Diagnostic Principles

The diagnostic criteria take into account worker's occupational, social and psychological factors and the assessment should include the following: complete history focused on occupational issues with detailed accounts of personal and familial background, examination of the mental status and complementary tests. It should include epidemiological factors and occupational risk factors to help reach a diagnosis and understand the causation.

Diagnosis is made after assessing the risks (occupational, social and psychological). Some guidelines that help establish a relationship between the damage and/or disease and work are: the nature of the exposure, the specificity of the causal relationship and the strength of the causal association, the type of causal relationship with the work, the degree or intensity of exposure, exposure time and latency, previous records regarding the worker's health status, epidemiological evidence (Brazilian Ministry of Health, 2001).

Causation Principles

In order to check causation, Schilling's Classification is used, which is described next (Mendes, 1995). Group I is characterized by the usual "professional diseases", which include occupational neurointoxications. In Group II, the work can be a contributing risk factor, including some cases of post-traumatic stress disorder. Finally, in Group III work is a trigger of a latent condition and may include depressive episodes (F32).

Next, factors related to occupational, social and psychological risks are assessed through a questionnaire (presented here as a summary as a suggestion of the "Protocol for the investigation of the cause of work-related mental disorders) and also the main indicators of mental health disorders related to these risks (Camargo, 2005).

TABLE 5.3   Summary of the Protocol for the Investigation of the Causes of Work-Related Mental Disorders

1. Occupational Risks *Based on the nomenclature of Occupational Medicine literature*	2. Social Risks *Based on the nomenclature described at CID-10: Factors influencing the health status and contact with healthcare services (Z.00–Z.99)*	3. Psychological Risks *Based on a) personality types at CID-10 (Personality Disorder F.60.0–F.60.7); b) the classification of Mental Disorders*
A) **Related to the company.** Describe *(NR, environmental risks, work station, others)*	A) Related to childhood and adolescence events (Z.61) Describe *Abuse/separation from the parents/affective losses* B) Related to housing and economic status (Z.59); *Inadequate housing / extreme poverty*	A) Pre-morbid personality *Used as a clinical description parameter to characterize the potential traits of the per-morbid personality the personality types of Personality Disorders at CID-10 (anxious, obsessive-compulsive, others)*
B) **Worker-related** Describe *(role, tasks performed, work relationships, previous jobs, others)*	C) Related to family circumstances. Describe Conflicts/death, divorce D) Relationships with the social environment *Living alone; be the target of persecution*	B) Mental disorders Describe *Current/Previous episodes of Mental Disorders.*

TABLE 5.4   Summary of the Main Indicators of Mental Health Disorders Related to the Risks (protocol conclusion)

Occupational Risks	Social Risks	Psychological Risks
1. the greater the environmental risks (chemical, physical, others); 2. lack of/ineffective protection measures (personal/collective); 3. difficulties in relationships with colleagues and supervisors; 4. greater degree of dissatisfaction and non-achievement at work.	1. events related to childhood/adolescence: occurrence of abuse, traumatic separation from the parents, death of close relatives; 2. family-related events: conflicts and death in the family, divorce/(traumatic) separation.	1. the more pathological the pre-morbid personality traits; 2. the more severe the mental disorder episodes before the assessment and also the current mental disorder episodes.

CONCLUSION

The purpose of this chapter was to present a brief summary of work-related mental disorders under the perspective of Mental Health and Work, Psychiatry and Occupational Medicine in order to better understand work-related psychiatric syndromes in terms of their concepts, diagnoses and causes.

These syndromes are characterized by their diagnostic complexity and require further theoretical-practical investigation and standardization of the management provided by the practitioners of occupational medicine, psychiatry, psychology and others.

REFERENCES

te Brake H., Bloemendal E., & Hoogstraten J. (2003). Gender differences in burnout among Dutch dentists. *Community Dent Oral Epidemiol.* Oct;31(5):321–7. Acessed February 04, 2004, >>>http://www.ncbi.nlm. nih.gov/ entrez/<<<

Camargo, D.A. (2005). *Psiquiatria Ocupacional: aspectos conceituais, diagnósticos e periciais dos transtornos mentais relacionados ao trabalho.* Dissertação de Mestrado. Faculdade de Ciências Médicas da UNICAMP – Campinas, SP. p.177–207.

Camargo D.A., Fontes A.P., & Oliveira J.I. (2004). Diagnóstico da LER-DORT em Saúde Mental e Trabalho. In: Guimarães L.A.M. & Grubits S. *Série Saúde Mental e Trabalho.* São Paulo: Casa do Psicólogo,. Vol. III, p. 131–144.

Dias, C.D. O manejo dos agravos à saúde relacionados com o trabalho (Lista das Doenças Profissionais ou do Trabalho Anexo II, Decreto 611. 1992) (1995). In: Mendes R. *Patologia do Trabalho,* Rio de Janeiro: Atheneu,. p. 59–85.

Guimarães, L.A.M. et al. (1998). *Projeto Matrix–"Saúde Mental, Qualidade de Vida e Trabalho, em Instituições de Ensino Superior–Diagnóstico, Prevenção e Tratamento".* Campinas: UNICAMP, mimeo.

Jardim S.R. & Glina, D.M.R. (2000). O diagnóstico dos transtornos mentais relacionados ao trabalho. In: Glina, D.M.R., & Rocha, L.M. *Saúde Mental no Trabalho: desafios e soluções.* São Paulo: V K, p. 17–52.

Jardim S.R. (2000). O diagnóstico dos transtornos mentais relacionados ao trabalho. Arquivos Brasileiros de Psiquiatria, Neurologia e Medicina Legal, ano 95, nº 74: jul-ago-set: Rio de Janeiro, p. 47–52.

Maurat, A.M. & Figueira, I. (2002). Transtorno de Stress Pós-Traumático (TEPT) e Transtorno Agudo de Stress (TAE) em policiais militares atendidos no Ambulatório de Psiquiatria do Hospital Central da Polícia Militar do Estado do Rio de Janeiro. *Rev. Bras. Psiquiatr.,* out., vol.24 supl.2, p.26–43. ISSN 1516-4446.

Mendes, R. (1995). Aspectos Conceituais da Patologia do Trabalho. In: Mendes R. *Patologia do Trabalho,* Rio de Janeiro: Atheneu, p. 33–47.

Ministério da Saúde (1999). *Portaria no 1.339/GM,* de 18 de novembro.

Ministério da Saúde. (2001). A investigação das relações saúde-trabalho, o estabelecimento do nexo causal da doença com o trabalho e as ações decorrentes (capítulo 2). In: *Doenças Relacionadas ao Trabalho–Manual de Procedimentos para os Serviços de Saúde,* org. Dias E.C. Brasília: M.S., p. 27- 36.

Ministério do Trabalho. (2003). Normas Regulamentadoras (NR, Portaria nº 3214) Brasília: acessed September 27, http://www.mte.gov.br/

Ministério do Trabalho. (2003). *Programa de Controle Médico de Saúde Ocupacional* (PCMSO, NR-7) Brasília: acessed September 27, http://www.mte.gov.br/

Ministério do Trabalho. (2003). *Programa de Prevenção dos Riscos Ambientais* (PPRA,NR-9) Brasília: acessed September 27, http://www.mte.gov.br/

Organización Internacional del Trabajo . (2000). *Aumentan los costos del estrés en el trabajo, y la incidencia de la depresión es cada vez mayor.* Un informe de la OIT estudia la salud mental en el trabajo en Alemania, Estados Unidos, Finlandia, Polonia y Reino Unido. Genebra: OIT, October. ISBN 92-2-112223-9.

Organización Internacional del Trabajo. (1998). *Enciclopedia de Salud y Seguridad en el Trabajo,* copyright da edição inglesa, Madrid.

Organização Mundial da Saúde. (1997). *Classificação de transtornos mentais e de comportamento da CID-10 (Classificação Internacional das Doenças): descrições clínicas e diretrizes diagnósticas.* Tradução de Dorgival Caetano. Porto Alegre: Artes Médicas.

Selligman-Silva, E. (1994). O Campo da Saúde Mental do Trabalho. In: Selligman-Silva E. *Desgaste Mental no Trabalho Dominado.* Rio de Janeiro: Cortez, p. 45–90.

Selligman-Silva, E. (1995). Psicopatologia e psicodinâmica do trabalho. In: Mendes R. *Patologia do Trabalho,* Rio de Janeiro: Atheneu, p. 287–310.

Selligman-Silva, E. (2003). Psicopatologia e Saúde Mental no Trabalho. In: Mendes R. *Patologia do Trabalho.* Rio de Janeiro: Atheneu, Vol II, p. 45–90.

Shimizu, T., Mizoue, T., Kubota, S., Mishimai, N., & Nagata, S. (2003) Relationship between burnout and communication skill training among Japanese hospital nurses: a pilot study. *J Occup Health.* May; 45(3):185–90. Acessed February 24, 2004. / 02/04, http://www.ncbi. nlm.nih.gov/entrez/.

Sindicato dos Metalúrgicos de Osasco. (2001). Vítimas dos ambientes de trabalho– Rompendo o Silêncio. São Paulo, maio. 6ª ed.

Vahey, D.C., Aiken, L.H., Sloane, D.M., Clarke, S.P., Vargas, D. (2004). Nurse burnout and patient satisfaction. *Med Care.* Feb;42(2 Suppl):II57–66. Acessed February 24, 2004, //www.ncbi.nlm.nih.gov/entrez/.

World Psychiatric Association (WPA). (2003). Scientific Section on Occupational Psychiatry. Acessed September 27, http: www.wpanet.org/home.html.

SECTION 2

MITIGATING THE NEGATIVE EFFECTS OF OCCUPATIONAL STRESS

CHAPTER 6

LEADERSHIP FROM A POSITIVE HEALTH PERSPECTIVE

A Qualitative Study

Marilyn Macik-Frey
Nicholls State University

James Campbell Quick
The University of Texas at Arlington and
Lancaster University Management School, UK

Phillip Shinoda, David A. Mack, David A. Gray
University of Texas at Arlington

Nathan Keller
United States Army

Cary L. Cooper
Lancaster University Management School, UK

INTRODUCTION

An explosion of interest in a new "positive" agenda, the basis for this special issue, has only emerged within the last 10 year. It views the study of human

Stress and Quality of Working Life, pages 95–121
Copyright © 2009 by Information Age Publishing
All rights of reproduction in any form reserved.

physical, social and psychological functioning from the positive, strength-based or exceptional functioning perspective and has spurred research in a variety of disciplines. Much work remains to be done to develop a framework and an understanding of how to conceptualize human functioning from this positive perspective. The predominant paradigm of the past with its emphasis on the abnormal, dysfunctional and negative deviations dominated the social sciences and stands in contrast to the positive agenda.

The "positive" agenda, although relatively new, appears to bridge academic disciplines. In medical science, a "positive" health philosophy has been proposed in which health is defined as more than just the absence of disease (Ruff and Singer, 1998). Psychology, lead by the ideas of Martin Seligman and others, is shifting toward increased study of the positive, strength-based, and functional aspects of human behavior, emotion and cognition (Seligman & Csikszentmihalyi, 2000) known as "positive" psychology. Seligman encouraged the American Psychological Association to move towards building "theoretical understanding and [to] use scientific methodology to discover and promote factors that allow individuals, groups, organizations and communities to thrive and prosper" (Luthans, 2002, p. 58; Seligman & Csikszentmihalyi, 2000). Finally, the study of organizational behavior has followed suit with its own "positive" agenda, positive organizational behavior (POB) (Luthans, 2002) and positive organizational scholarship (POS) (Cameron, Dutton & Quinn, 2003).

Within the "positive" agenda, leadership has been a target of study. The general theme emerging from the work is that building on strengths is potentially much more effective than working to eliminate weaknesses (Buckingham & Clifton, 2001; Luthans, 2002). Our study takes a look at leadership through a different but related positive lens, that of "positive" health. The premise of positive health is that health is much more than the absence of disease, the view that has dominated medicine for years.

"Positive" Health

Conceptualizing health from a positive perspective requires re-thinking what constitutes the components of a healthy individual. We created the case below to illustrate and explain the contrasting nature of the traditional or disease model of health and the emerging positive perspective.

Grace Smith was diagnosed with an aggressive form of cancer. Prior to this diagnosis, Grace had no negative health symptoms. All vital signs, including blood pressure, cholesterol, and lab tests were within normal limits. She essentially had no other health complaints. She worked as an assistant manager in a retail setting and had done essentially the same job for 20 years. She did not pursue more challenging roles at work and was not considered to be motivated to advance by her supervisors. She had never married, had few friends and no hobbies or interests outside of her work which she considered a necessary evil to put food on her plate and a roof over her head. As a result of this diagnosis, Grace underwent surgery, radiation therapy and finally an extended series of chemotherapy. After many months, her medical team declared that the treatment had been successful; Grace was cancer free, had no other negative health symptoms and could return to her normal life. She was left feeling weak, depressed and fearful of recurrence. She was questioning her role in life and her ability to handle any additional hardship. Her physical and mental abilities seemed to have declined. She resented that she had had to go through such and ordeal and that she would now have to worry about the cancer returning for the rest of her life. The question we propose is: Is Grace now "healthy"?

In the traditional approach to medicine and "health" the answer would be "yes" as long as all negative indicators of disease were back to baseline. However, within the positive movement that has surfaced in medicine (Ruff and Singer, 1998). Grace would be far from healthy. Ruff and Singer (1998) propose a much more comprehensive conceptualization of health; one that includes physical, mental, social and psychological components of well-being. They propose core elements of positive health that move beyond the medical perspective that deals with the body, biology and physiology to one which incorporates aspects of both the mind and the body. These core elements include:

1. Leading a Life of Purpose
2. Quality Connections to Others
3. Positive Self Regard and Mastery
4. Perception of Negative Events as Paths to Meaning and Purpose

These elements are proposed as those that define health and as ones that are common between cultures. Finally, they suggest that emotion is the critical link between mind and body. Life purpose and quality connections to others "engage the body because they are emotionally laden". (Ruff and Singer, 1998:p.10)

Grace, although free from sign or symptoms of physical disease, does not fit the "positive" definition of health. Her scenario creates a bleak picture of her long term recovery and ultimate subjective well-being. She lacks life purpose, quality connections, positive self regard and her reaction to her cancer and remission is negative vs. one of thankfulness, learning and strengthening her life purpose. Thus, these two very different perspectives of health illustrate the difficulty researchers are having merging the old negative or disease paradigm with the new "positive" paradigm. It also demonstrates the much more comprehensive view of health as vigor, vitality, thriving and strength, one that for most people is much more appealing than maintaining baseline functioning.

However, within the positive movement that has surfaced in medicine (Ruff & Singer, 1998), psychology and social science (Seligman & Csikszent-mihalyi, 2000) and organizational studies (Luthans, 2002; Spreitzer & Sonenshein, 2004), Graces's scenario demonstrates the absurdity of looking at health, well-being, success or performance only from this negatively skewed perspective. It eliminates the entire positive half of human functioning, the positively skewed dimensions or as Spreitzer and Sonenshein, (2004) term "positive deviance."

"Positive" Leadership

We began with a health example despite our qualitative study being directed towards leadership. We did this because of the interesting parallel we see between the core elements of "positive" health and the transformational nature of highly effective leadership.

> Jake Miller, a young employee of a large accounting firm, was selected to participate in a highly competitive leadership development training program created by the firm to enhance the leadership capabilities of their most promising talent. Jake participated in a year long program that began with extensive testing to determine the key areas for improvement. Jake then went through a series of training activities to target those key areas. Upon completion if the program, Jake had successfully improved these target skills. He was placed in a management position because of his stellar performance on post-testing of his target areas for improvement. He subsequently led through a similar process of identifying deviation from the norm and setting targets to correct those deficits. Was Jake's leadership development likely to result in highly effective or transformational outcomes?

Obviously, this scenario, like the health case of Grace, demonstrates the error of working on leadership by eliminating deficits. The ability to perform at an exceptional level as a leader requires more than the baseline skills, it requires a comprehensive approach that at minimum includes and optimally emphasizes the positive. We suggest that a "positive" health model is a reasonable model to explain highly effective leadership. The leader must strive for health and facilitate health in his/her followers. Health from this lens includes purpose, positive relationship, self mastery and learning from misfortune.

We looked to find evidence of core features of positive health within the leadership philosophies of business and community leaders. We performed a qualitative analysis of extensive interviews with these leaders on their perceptions of leadership. The purpose of this paper is to identify qualitative support for the positive health—leadership connection within the descriptions of these leaders' personal behavior and life patterns. More importantly, to substantiate that leaders also facilitate these core positive health dimensions in followers as a means of transforming their performance into the extraordinary. Our qualitative analysis suggests that a key component of highly effective leadership such as found within transformational leaders is their ability to promote positive health and vitality within their followers.

In the following sections, we provide the theoretical arguments that support the positive health—leadership connection. This review addresses the basis of quality connections with others and self mastery within attachment theory and the development of interdependence and autonomy, strength of purpose and the philosophical arguments around mind-body health.

THEORETICAL ARGUMENTS

Three underlying arguments, two of which are buttressed by decades of empirical research, can help us understand the link between positive human health and positive leadership strengths. How do strong, positive leaders develop? First we explore one positive theory of human development that is anchored in an ethological approach to personality development. Second we examine how this foundation of positive human development bridges into the adulthood years, in particular through the study of successful executives. Third we examine the emerging positive health framework, which contrasts with the more traditional disease and disorder oriented models of health both in medicine and in psychology.

Positive Human Development

Ainsworth and Bowlby (1991) pioneered an ethological approach to personality development by focusing their attention on development during the childhood years. They framed attachment theory and argued that attachment is one instinctual human drive, though not the only one. A second human drive that they acknowledge is exploration, which leads to understanding and mastery of the world. According to attachment theory, children grow to become self-reliant and securely interdependent when they have secure attachment figures in their lives to whom they may turn in times of threat, danger, stress, and need (Bowlby, 1988). When they are not threatened, do not experience danger or stress, and do not have a need for protection or reassurance, then children respond to their exploratory instinct and act autonomously in the world, learning to explore and develop mastery within their environment(s). Hence, the paradox of self-reliance is the capacity to act autonomously as well as to form secure attachments.

This positive, healthy theory of human development during the childhood years may be interrupted in such a way as to cause developmental delays or problems. This may result either from the experience of separation or of loss (Bowlby, 1973, 1980). For example, when a child experiences the instinctual need to attach under conditions of threat, danger, or stress and is unable to make connection with the attachment figure, the result is a problem of separation, which in degrees leads to the experience of separation anxiety and anger (Bowlby, 1973). This stands in contract to the experience of felt security resulting from connection with the attachment figure in time of need (Bowlby, 1982). In addition, the experience of loss of a significant, secure attachment figure may lead to developmental delays or problems (Bowlby, 1980). There is inevitable sadness and depression that results from significant loss and the question is one of alternative forms of secure attachment for the child.

These developmental issues may then lead to two alternatives other than the capacity for self-reliance and secure interdependent attachments. One alternative is dismissive attachment, which is an insecure form of attachment that discounts the importance of felt security in healthy human relationships (Ainsworth & Bowlby, 1991). The individual who forms dismissive attachments leaves an impression of bravado, strength, and a tough-guy or tough-gal façade. This façade masks the need for secure relationships that is characteristic of all people. A second alternative is preoccupied attachment, which is also an insecure form of attachment but in this case acknowledges the importance of felt security in healthy human relationships. However, those who form preoccupied attachments are fearful of letting go (Ainsworth & Bowlby, 1991). Those who form preoccupied attachments exhibit a disorganized pattern of connecting with and relating to other people. Both dismissive and preoccupied styles of attachment come from insecurity and stand in contrast to the secure style of self-reliant interdependence.

Positive, healthy human development forms a foundation for positive health during the adulthood years and as a foundation for healthy leadership development. If the childhood years are not ones in which secure attachment figures are present and self-reliance emerges, all is not lost. Because attachment and exploration are instinctual human drives, it is quite possible to catch up developmentally once an individual identifies dependable, reliable, secure attachment figures. Further, Lynch (2000) makes the clear case for the medical importance of healthy human relationships during the adulthood years along with exploring the medical consequences of loneliness for those who do not form and maintain heartfelt communication. Hence, the cry unheard is the cry of the heart for secure human connection.

Successful Executives—Pressure and Support

In-depth interviews and qualitative research with successful executives in a range of industries from health care to real estate and basic steel manufacturing to the admiralty found a strikingly similar pattern of secure attachments among both male and female senior leaders (Quick, Nelson & Quick, 1987, 1990). While American folklore values the notion of independence as embodied in the images of John Wayne, the reality of American icons such as Dwight David Eisenhower, Lee Iacocca, and even the war and western heroes played by John Wayne is really quite different. Specifically, these larger than life figures are securely anchored in a set of personal and professional relationships and thus better characterized as interdependent rather than independent. Certainly they have the capacity for autonomous action and activity yet they turn to a wide range of others for advise, counsel, information, expertise, and/or reassurance in the process of making key decisions or executing critical plans with consequences of import.

The original aim of this line of research was to understand the preventive stress management methods of these successful executives. Specifically, how did they maintain their health and well-being under demanding and stressful conditions? Planning and time management techniques, exercise programs, prayer and meditation, cognitive restructuring and transformational coping, leisure time activities, and relaxation were among the popular stress management approaches during the 1980s (Quick & Quick, 1984). However, not a single one of these approaches was common across all the executives studied, rather the only common denominator among the stress management methods for these men and women was self-reliance, secure attachments, and social supports (Nelson, Quick & Quick, 1989).

Joplin, Nelson and Quick (1999) go on to explore the role of secure attachments, interdependence, and social support in the health of managers and employees in a wider range of work settings. As with the successful executives, they found that relationships in the work environment and the home environment were both consequential for health and well-being. This line of research through the 1980s and 1990s builds on the attachment theory foundations of Bowlby (1982) and Ainsworth and Bowlby (1991) and provides evidence that secure attachments during the adulthood years help to combat job stress while enhancing an individual's health and well-being. Hence, the need for secure attachments continues to be important during adulthood.

A secondary aim of the "successful executive" research was to understand the causes of stress for these executives. More broadly in organizations, when we look at the causes of job and work stress, there are over 25 different measures aimed at identifying causes of stress, modifiers of the stress response, and/or consequences of stress at work (Quick, Quick, Nelson & Hurrell, 1997). One interesting emergent measure of job stress is the Job Stress Survey (JSS) by Spielberger, Reheiser, Reheiser, and Vagg (1999). The JSS is interesting because it isolates pressure and lack of organizational support as the two key, independent sources of stress on the job. The JSS also examines the frequency and the intensity of these sources of stress, which are two of the three important dimensions of any stressor or demand. The third dimension is duration. Why is it interesting that pressure and lack of organizational support emerge as two key, independent sources of stress? It is because these two factors parallel the instinctual drives of exploration and attachment originally discussed by Ainsworth and Bowlby (1991). That is, exploratory behavior leads to mastery of the world and pressure at work is the source of demand for performance and achievement, hence mastery, of the job environment. In a similar way, attachment behavior leads to the experience of felt security and organizational support is the basis for people at work to feel safe and secure.

In the same way that there is an intractability between exploration and attachment such that a balance in these competing drives must be struck, so too must there be a balance struck between the pressure generated for performance on the job and support provided to enable people to feel safe and secure. Too much pressure can be experienced as mean-spiritedness while too much support can lead to indolence and lack of motivation. Healthy stress on the job is challenging while excessive stress on the job interferes with performance. How do these lines of research by Ainsworth and Bowlby (1991) and by Nelson, Quick and Quick (1989) relate to positive health and leadership.

Positive Human Health

The dominant traditional models of health are anchored in disease and disorder frameworks practiced in much of medicine and psychology (Levi, 1979; Wallace, Doebbeling, & Last, 1998). Even the prevention models in occupational health psychology and preventive medicine aim to identify, minimize, and manage health risk factors (Quick & Tetrick, 2003). However, the seminal American psychologist and philosopher William James took a different perspective over a century ago (Bjork, 1997). James viewed health as the natural state for humans, not disease. Originally educated in medicine and physiology, James believed that disease should yield to the proper therapeutics and that it should not be simply accepted as a part of the human condition (Bjork, 1997). In his dialectic view, health was the standard and disease was the deviant condition to be removed. Thus, the dominant traditional models of health stand in contrast to James' perspective and the emerging positive definition of health.

It was for Ruff and Singer (1998) nearly 90 years after James to outline three principles for a positive definition of health and for Martin E.P. Seligman during his presidency of the American Psychological Association in 1999 to provide a framework for understanding disorders, prevention, and positive strengths. Seligman articulated the three missions of psychology as:

- To repair damage through psychotherapy and other therapeutics;
- To prevent mental health and behavior problems; and
- To build on strength factors and competency.

Ryff and Singer (1998) advance a more positive approach to the definition of health by breaking out of the traditional medical and psychotherapeutic models. Their three principles for what constitutes 'health' are:

1. It is a philosophical position pertaining to the meaning of the good life rather than strictly a medical [or psychological] question.
2. Health includes both the mind (mental) and the body (physical) and more importantly how they interact or influence each other.
3. Health is a 'multidimensional dynamic process rather than a discrete end state.'

Their positive approach to health does not deny the existence of negatives or negative events. As we noted earlier, negative events within this framework are possible pathways to deeper meaning and purpose in the life experience. Hence, they transform negatives and negative events into positive outcomes. While James aimed to eradicate the negative embodied in disease and disorder (Bjork, 1997), Ryff and Singer (1998) aim to transform the negative into something of positive or developmental value in life. This is very consistent with the third of their core features of positive health: positive self-regard and self-mastery. This is also consistent with Siegel's (1986) view of transforming the experience of having cancer into a pathway for deepening and broadening exceptional patients' understanding of the value and power of their lives.

In addition to positive self-regard and a life of purpose as two core features of positive health, Ryff and Singer (1998) propose quality connections to others as a core feature of positive health. This echoes the attachment behavior theory of Ainsworth and Bowlby (1991) and the successful executive finding of Nelson, Quick, and Quick (1989).

This suggests that it is not in isolation or in solitary achievement that fulfillment is found but it is rather in collaboration, in cooperation, and in connection to others that fulfillment is found. That is, we find ourselves in relationship to others, not apart from others in the world.

Our study interprets the remarks of executive leaders about leadership within the framework of positive health. We are looking for collaborating evidence that leaders in the field interpret the meaning of leadership using language that supports positive health.

METHOD

The study of the positive dimension of health, psychology, sociology and organizational behavior is in its early stages. The ability to change the dominant paradigm from one that emphasizes negative deviance to one that incorporates positive deviance has proven to be difficult. The understanding of a positive health view or a strength based view is often attempted within the existing health or organizational behavior models, for example, trying to measure positive health using existing parameters. We have clear guidelines for what constitutes disease or negative deviations such as blood pressure, cholesterol or blood level readings. However, we do not have a comparable set of positive ranges that identify health beyond just the absence of disease. The ability to re-conceptualize social and human sciences from a more positive deviance aspect requires preliminary work in the conceptualization of human thriving, excellence and strength. Our study uses a qualitative format as a means to identify positive identifiers of leadership from the perspective of executive level leaders.

Bartunek and Seo (2002) suggest that a qualitative approach can add meaning or value above that obtained through quantitative methods alone. They suggest that variables are often assumed to have a constant meaning in a quantitative study. However, constructs which are dynamic and are based on human perception (job insecurity in their article and leadership in ours), may benefit from being analyzed qualitatively, allowing for the individual differences in perspective to emerge. This form of analysis provides a richer, albeit more complex and varied, description of a concept. Within our sample, for example, there were 28 relatively independent definitions of leadership. Although there were common elements, no two definitions were considered identical, demonstrating the richness of such qualitative data.

Much of the work to date related to the emerging "positive" agenda is theoretical (Luthans, 2002; Ruff and Singer, 1998; Seligman & Csikszent-mihalyi, 2000). Attempts to validate these theories can include quantitative data analysis in which constructs are defined and measured by the researcher to test hypothetical relationships. We have chosen a richer format to explore the constructs, one that collects the "actors" perceptions of leadership. We then preformed an interpretive analysis of the language rich interview data to determine the level that the interviewees' comments match the conceptualization of "positive" health. Qualitative research is especially appropriate and powerful in the early stages of scientific inquiry of a new or emergent area of study. Qualitative research becomes the leading edge of inquiry to help better frame, refine, and conceptualize within a domain, thus setting the stage for subsequent empirical testing and more quantitatively rigorous means of scientific research.

In our case, we are looking to form a more comprehensive view of the positive dimensions of leadership using our positive health framework. We used the meanings of leadership generated by executive leaders as our source of data. This method is expected to "provide understanding of the underlying dynamics and meaning-making associated with [leadership] and how they are enacted and how they evolve" within numerous contexts (Bartunek and Seo, 2002, p. 240). Thus, rather than attempting to define the parameters of positive leadership and how it fits within the positive health core features (Ruff and Singer, 1998), qualitative research may offer "the possibility of stimulating the development of new understanding about the variety and depth with which organizational members experience important organizational phenomenon." (Bartunek and Seo 2002, p. 240). These diverse perspectives are sorely needed as we attempt this major shift toward the positive end of human functioning in our understanding of leadership.

Johnson, Buehring, Cassell and Symon (2006) outline a contingent criteriology for evaluating qualitative research that advocates differing evaluation criteria based on the philosophical position taken by the research. Using their classification, our study best fits neo-empiricism. These authors define this philosophical position as one that uses non-quantitative methods "to develop inductively thick descriptions of the pattern in the inter-subjective meanings that actors use to make sense of their everyday worlds." This philosophy assumes a "real and inter-subjective world which science can neutrally represent and explain". Lincoln & Guba (1985) recommend the use of credibility (authentic representations), dependability (minimization of researcher idiosyncrasies), confirmability (researcher self-criticism) and transferability (extent of applicability) as alternative criteria for evaluating the value of qualitative studies. Thus, we have addressed credibility through our selection of high level leaders within existing organizations, dependability through our method of data collection described below, confirmability through the use of multi-person analysis and transferability through the use of leaders within a broad range of industries.

We initiated an in-depth idiographic inquiry in an effort to understand how leaders define and understand leadership. We conducted 30 interviews of chairmen, CEO's, presidents, and other senior executives in banking, construction, education, advertising, financial services, oil field production, transportation, and a range of other basic industries. Participants were limited to executive level leaders with the assumption that this subject pool would have established ideas and experience in leadership as a function of achieving their current level within their respective organizations. Of the interviews, 28 completed transcriptions were available for analysis. The two interviews not included in the analysis were rejected in one case because the audio transcription was unintelligible and the other case it was incomplete.

A standard interview protocol was used for each of these interviews. A series of ten uniform questions were asked to structure each leadership interview. However, interviewees were encouraged to elaborate on areas outside of the specific question format relevant to the study of leadership and leadership development, thus their responses were not overly constrained by the standardized protocol. The interview questions are included in Appendix 1. The interviews were audio-recorded using a digital recorder and then transcribed. Interview time was initially set at one hour, but many of the interviews lasted considerably beyond the initial hour. Several individuals participated in the gathering of the interview data. Each interview was conducted with a team of 2 to 3 research team members, but few of the leaders interviewed had exactly the same interview team. We believe that this method of gathering the interviews decreases interviewer bias in the responses. All members of the research team that conducted interviews were instructed to use the ten questions as the basis for the interview and to encourage elaboration of any additional leadership relevant information that was elicited. The interview data were transcribed verbatim for further analysis.

ANALYSIS AND RESULTS

Each of the 28 transcripts was thoroughly reviewed by three judges and then a three-step process led to 25 conceptual themes. First, key words or phrases related to leadership or leadership development were drawn from the interview responses. Second, these key words were grouped by general concepts. Third, the pool of general concepts was examined for distinctiveness and 25 conceptual themes emerged from the groupings review. The frequency of each topic was summed across the 28 interviews to get a general idea of both the breadth of ideas and the consistency of response across the interviews. Table 6.1 contains the results. The conceptually similar key words and the number of interviews out of the 28 analyzed in which the theme emerged are presented.

Interpretive and qualitative analysis of these general dimensions was done using the four core features of positive human health as an organizing structure. The following subsections provide excerpts from interviews

TABLE 6.1   Frequency of General Conceptual Theses in Leaders' Interviews

Conceptual Theme	Frequency
Vision, objective, common goal, greater good	28
Communication and/or listening	24
Mentor and develop others; Get the best out of others	22
People skills, focus on people	21
Early parental influence	21
Integrity, character, ethics, respect, value driven	18
Emotional connection, relationship, accessibility, empathy	17
Self awareness, willingness to learn, lifelong learning	17
Allow risk taking, create trust, safety, learn from mistakes	17
Motivation and persuasion	16
Drive to lead, passion, a calling, ambition	16
Early life experience	15
Courage, take action, make decisions, confidence	15
Consistency and commitment	14
Mentor influence on leader	13
Comfort with change, flexibility, adaptable	11
Leaders are "chosen" by followers	10
People skills more important than technical skills	9
Patience, willingness to invest time, persistence	9
Work as hard as others, be example, servant leader	7
Assess and analyze	6
Sales skills, sell ideas	6
Compassion	4
Excellence	2
Give back to community, unselfish	2

relevant to each of Ruff and Singer's (1998) core elements of "positive" health: leading a life of purpose, quality connections to people, self regard and self mastery, and perceptions of negative events as paths to meaning and purpose. The samples of interview data are preceded in each section by a description and interpretation of the data within the "positive" leadership and health framework.

Leading a Life of Purpose

The first core element includes living a purposeful life and in our study also involved facilitating the adoption of purpose in followers. Ruff and

Singer (1998) provide a detailed review of philosophical, psychological, mental health, social science, and organizational health literature underscoring the importance of purposefulness in life, but they point out that most of this research is about illness or "how adverse work conditions or unemployment contribute to human dysfunction. Largely missing is a counterpoint literature on how work facilitates human purpose, meaning, self-realization, and enactment of one's unique abilities, and thereby enhances one's health. (p. 8)".

The interviews show that leaders believe in having purpose in their lives but also prevalent in the data is reference to the leaders' need to help others understand, accept and embrace a purpose and work toward the common good. It is interesting to note that 100% of our sample reported purpose, higher goals, common good and mission/vision as important components of leadership and/or characteristics of good leaders. This concept is the only one that was reported in some form by all leaders in our sample. We therefore consider this a fundamental concept of leadership based on the views of this group.

The following excerpts from leadership interviews relate to purpose and illustrate the richness of the data better than frequency counts alone. Creswell and Miller (2000) and Creswell (1998) suggest that one acceptable method to validate qualitative data is to provide "thick, rich description" to support the interpretation by the researchers. This method of reporting analysis provides the reader an opportunity to benefit from the richness of the information obtained as well as to judge the appropriateness of the analysis.

The following quotes demonstrate the leader's role in creating and accomplishing a mission or goals and in motivating others to focus and feel good about these goals from a personal standpoint.

> "... leadership is just about any form of behavior that one can demonstrate in any given situation to constructively contribute to moving a team of people or a person or an organization towards the achievement of strategic goals and objectives.... keeping people motivated and focused and feeling good about themselves."

> "You have to have the self confidence and courage to believe that you're doing what's right for the business and organization, not for yourself but it's for everybody."

In many of the comments related to purpose, leaders emphasized the importance of helping followers see the personal relevance of the mission or goals. Basically to connect at a personal or an emotional as well as a cognitive level with the purpose, followers must understand them and believe they are important and representative of their personal values.

"Yes, you have to have a goal. Sometimes part of leadership is helping them understand what the goals and objectives are and why and having people embrace those so that they become theirs. If they are only yours then other people haven't taken ownership over them and you're probably not going to get anywhere . . . it could also be personal goals and objectives, too."

". . . to acertain . . . the collective will of the group and to make sure that I am in fact leading them in directions that they want to go."

"I think you really have to be willing to allow all of the group that you lead to own the ultimate goals that you're trying to achieve. Then the goals become the group's goals, it's not just your goals. To me that is almost the fundamental starting point."

". . . getting people's hearts involved and understanding what that purpose is and buying into it and understanding how it helps the organization they work for and how it also aligns with their personal goals and values."

". . . leadership is an ability to connect the people with the mission . . . connect the core values that people share with the mission . . . they view you as someone that connects at a value level with them. They really need to understand their value and how they can express themselves in a manner and grow as a person and an individual and moving toward the goal."

"I think leadership distinguished from being a manager or management is the ability to draw a picture of a vision out there that people can relate to and understand and buy in to . . . understand how important it is that that vision be something that people can connect to personally."

". . . it's the ability to recognize the need to fulfill your own personal needs and desires but to also play a productive part in the world."

"A leader is someone who can gain consensus from a team of people that the mission is worth committing the energy and the effort and that there is a higher calling than just the mission. A higher calling is that there's some core values involved that a person really believes are important for how they live their life and what they stand for and what they achieve with their life, what's invested in their life."

"I think leaders connect people with something that's fundamental about them that they want to accomplish with their lives."

"Work for the common good, the mission, not for a personal agenda."

Quality Connections to People

The second core feature of positive health according to Ruff and Singer (1998) is quality connections to people and in the theoretical development of this paper we equate this dimension with the attachment pattern of interdependence (Ainsworth & Bowlby, 1991; Bowlby, 1982, 1988) defined as healthy personal attachment behavior that "appears paradoxical because the person seems independent while maintaining a host of supportive, interpersonal attachments that afford a secure base" (Quick, Joplin, Nelson, Mangelsdorff, & Fiedler, 1996, p. 281). This seemingly contradictory pattern provides the foundation for healthy relationships. Autonomy without the interpersonal dimensions is simply acting in isolation and interpersonal attachments without the ability to act autonomously is limiting. Interdependence provides the autonomous ability to act and the relational dimension to maintain long term healthy commitments to and support of others.

One dominant aspect of leadership development reported by the interviewees involved the influence of relationships through the lifespan. In particular, the presence of strong parental influence or in the absence of parental influence strong "other" mentors early in life that provided support, encouraged autonomy and self efficacy. These relationships suggest a basis for the development of healthy personal attachments. These leaders, having developed a healthy sense of autonomy based on healthy interpersonal attachments, report similar "role models" or "mentors" or friendships throughout their leadership development.

Strong parental influence was reported by 79% of the respondents. The comments involved reference to parents and family as foundational elements in their leadership development either through the instilling of values and principles or in some cases actual observation of parental leadership in their work and community. Here are a few examples:

"really goes back to how you grew up. I grew up in a close knit family where there are some values, where there was a strong commitment of the family members to each other, particularly as for my parents and that contributed to a sense of responsibility to the people around you. You don't live in isolation for yourself. You have a responsibility to others."

"I never consciously thought about how I learned [leadership]. I suppose from my father and mother, what I would call early mentoring."

"I always had parents that listened to me . . . they thought my point of view was important or made me feel that it was . . . that gives you confidence."

"My dad encouraged us to kind of challenge what it was or understand what was going on around us."

"I think strong parents were the whole key. Their deep respect towards others. My father is a very intelligent man and he has a very strong opinion but he has a very deep respect for all types of people. "

"Valuing people. That I learned from my father. I mean I was a smart young guy and I thought I had a lot of answers when I was in my twenties and back then what I really didn't have an appreciation for was the value of people. I thought I was just very smart. You can figure out stuff better than other people and then you win (independent). What I learned from [my father] is that you really have to value people and if you value people and make them feel appreciated they'll want to work for you and help build success."

"I don't think I ever figured out that I was a leader, it just happened....You know sometimes you grow up in an atmosphere that your family around you has led others and they have been successful and it's just something that you took to, because...you got good training in the beginning and good ethics. You're honest and you're straightforward and you're a conservative and you like to be successful, and that comes from doing a good job for people. I think for myself individually, it's mostly a lot of how I grew up and how I was raised by my parents."

In the absence of parental influence and in many cases along with such influence, 46% of the respondents reported examples of strong mentor or key non-family member influence on their own development.

"The nature of that mentoring relationship...was focused on the quality of my thoughts and actions.... The way in which you interact with people and the manner in which you build relationships."

"One leader I admired was a minister...he was very upbeat, a firm type person...[he] made you feel good because he affirmed you. [He] built your confidence and lifted you up."

"...they genuinely cared about me and my success...It's great to see that in an early point in your career and how powerful that human connection can be."

Along with the influence of significant others in the respondents lives, there was also unanimous agreement that leadership involved a vision or purpose that promoted a common goal and resulted in greater good for the group, organization or community. This common theme also relates to the idea of interdependence. The realization of leaders that they work not for themselves (autonomous goals) but rather for the common good to achieve a greater purpose or outcome for all which requires reliance on others, commitment to others, support from others and the reciprocal give and take of relationships, a key element in interdependence.

"Growing up in a small town...at the end of the day, all those people are connected. If the doctor leaves and all of a sudden there isn't going to be a doctor in town...interesting dynamic. It taught me a deep respect and high regard for the role of each person in the town."

Results relating to the paradox of interdependence are that over 80% of respondents reported the importance of "independent" or autonomous skills such as taking action, having courage to make difficult decisions, self confidence to act, technical skills, analytic skills, persistence, excellence and ambition. Specific comments included "having the courage and resolve to make difficult decisions over and over again", In contrast, a full 100% mentioned aspects of interpersonal interdependence such as emotional connection with followers, developing and maintaining relationships ("the whole essence of leadership is relationship"), being accessible, showing empathy, shared goals, mentoring and developing others and being mentored and coached by others, motivation, persuasion, showing respect for others, and being willing to "get hands dirty" by working side by side with others", "not expecting others to do what you wouldn't do", or being a servant leader. These seemingly contradictory characteristics imply a sense of independence and ability to act alone with the concurrent link to people and the realization that there is an essential connectedness that must occur in organizations and the leader is often an important component of developing that interdependence. Our results support that the leaders from our subject pool indirectly report the importance of this paradoxical construct and to promote this characteristic in their followers.

> "To have a winning team you have to have winning individuals that are good individually but they know what it takes to work together and create the winning team."

Self Regard and Self Mastery

The next core feature of positive health is self regard and self mastery. Ruff and Singer (1998) suggest that purposeful life and meaningful connection to others "likely builds and maintains positive self-regard, sense of self-realization, personal growth, and mastery". Thus, the elements of positive health are dynamic and interrelated.

The leader interviews show a link to this element through the reference to helping others succeed, develop their strengths and mastery as well as in comments about their own competence and mastery. Many of the leaders reported a strong sense of self efficacy, confidence and courage as critical elements of leadership. They discussed skills necessary to lead. The also expressed a need to achieve, a passion or a calling to excel and/or to lead. Specifically:

- 79% indicated the need to have communication and/or listening skills
- 75% reported a high need for people skills
- 64% mentioned the importance of integrity and ethics
- 61% emphasized willingness to learn on their part and self awareness
- 57% expressed a passion or drive to lead

- 54% specifically mentioned courage as a critical element of leadership. We interpret courage as the willingness to take the necessary risks to lead which we expect is linked to high self regard, self efficacy and self mastery.

Here are a few examples:

"So I'm always up for big changes, I love the challenges. I love to do things totally different."

"I always had a need for achievement. I always felt a calling to leadership."

"It all starts with vision and being able to communicate that to all the people that can help execute it."

"Leadership requires practice, a certain level of skill and it requires understanding your surroundings because you have to be able to adapt."

"Leaders must take responsibility for others, engage other people,... have positive relationships, strong communication skills and trust."

"Communication and self presentation skills are important... [helps to] gain confidence and courage."

"Probably the single most important skill is listening. To listen actively and perceptively to the people you are trying to lead. Humility is a real important dimension."

"Leadership is more of an internal set of principles and convictions and visions.... Must have confidence, dedication, persistence and conviction."

"Leadership can also... be confidence, when you are doing things well all the time, you are being confident and you are not afraid to lead. You have to have conviction of what you're doing, and you have to have a belief and passion."

"I have vision, I have confidence, I have conviction, I have dedication, and you know persistence."

"Leadership really comes down to first of all setting an example for behavior in all facets of your life... and having the courage and resolve to make difficult decisions over and over again."

"You have people that might just come to work everyday and their work day is fine, happy to get that job done and glad to go home at the end of the day but they don't volunteer for more work or care to get ahead. I was always one of those types of individuals who was willing to take on additional work just because, more for the enjoyment of it than I was trying to get ahead. Perhaps a lot of people want to get ahead but there's just some personal satisfaction, taking on a lot of projects and multi-tasking and you want to do those projects and just want to see the results at the end of the day."

"You must have courage. Courage to try something new, courage to accept that you're wrong. Courage to lead people down a path that is not defined, and courage to be able to go first . . . the number one is courage."

Leaders also expressed a belief that a critical component of leadership is helping others develop their strengths, develop self mastery and develop confidence. It is not just the role of the leader to have high self regard, but to instill high self regard in followers by helping them develop their abilities. Following are some examples that represent the leaders' commitment to the growth of others.

". . . there is something about always wanting to be the best that you can be and reach your potential and believing that your potential is always a little bit higher and maybe doesn't have any limits . . . you are failing if you are not reaching your potential even if you're doing better than average."

"Touching people on a regular basis and making sure you understand their needs and then supplying their needs.

(You were confident in your abilities?) "I think once you sort of know it or people tell you then you finally believe it . . . you have something that is constructive [abilities] and can be used for the good and you have to be very responsible about how you do that."

". . . so they can learn more about themselves and the things that are important to them, and really understand themselves from the inside out. And know how to be able to communicate that and how to be able to develop their own in themselves what they feel are their own leadership qualities."

"I look for . . . the willingness to learn. You can always teach them the skill, you can never teach them the attitude."

". . . it's a philosophy of getting the best out of people"

". . . leadership is being respected by other people . . . knowing that everyone has the potential to make a contribution and as a leader part of your role is to get the best out of them."

"I look for people that have a hunger to learn."

"I kind of enjoy the role of leadership because to tell you the truth an amount of self satisfaction comes from being the leader and helping others . . . channel them to that goal, helping them to see the goal, and making the right decisions."

"I think leadership is the ability to inspire and empower people to do the best job that they can . . . it involves setting the proper example and it involves work ethic. It involves a clear vision of what you're trying to accomplish. It involves a leader's responsibility to define the path towards the completion of those objectives. I think it involves walking the walk instead of talking the talk."

"I believe you got to empower people and you've got to give them the tools to do their job and kind of get out of the way."

"It is all about expanding the knowledge of the people that work with me so they can be more effective in their roles."

"I see my role as enabling all of the business partners, people I work with and the people I work for, to be as successful as possible."

"The best way to exhibit leadership is to not only be able to lead people and to be able to exhibit the qualities of a leader and be able to help people accomplish their goals but , it's also to grow leaders . . . the real work of a leader is to grow other leaders in order to perpetuate the process."

"To contribute as the supervisor of a whole bunch of people in a corporate setting is trying to figure out and then help each one of them figure out what they're best at and then use them in the most effective way in the organization based on what they are best at and then all that kind of works."

"I think you look for a broad thinker, someone who is curious, interesting and innovative and isn't afraid to think of something different . . . you can sense confidence, not arrogance, but confidence, someone who can communicate well."

Perception of Negative Events as Paths to Meaning and Purpose

Ruff and Singer (1998) do not advocate a model of health that ignores negative experience or negative emotion. "On the contrary, because positive health is ultimately about engagement in living, difficult experience, pain and struggle are inevitably parts [of life]" (Ruff and Singer, 1998). Rather, they suggest that in healthy individuals negative events often result in a constructive reaction and/or learning that can lead to a better understanding of life purpose, a closer connection to others and personal growth. The following examples illustrate the leaders' acknowledgement that meaning and growth can occur as a result of how you view and react to hardship.

". . . you have to learn that turmoil is just normal and you got to let it energize you and not let it slow you down."

". . . another big factor in my success has been just insecurity and anxiety of growing up poor and that gives you an inner drive at times to be successful."

". . . very often bad backgrounds lead to great leadership"

"I had some spectacular failures in my early life. . . . I got fired from my second job that I got out of college, primarily because of a smart-alecky attitude and insubordination but again that was lack of social skill that was also a lack of, and again over compensating probably in terms of behavior, but I learned a lot. I learned a lot in that process and in my next job I almost got fired there for similar things then it began to occur to me you know, that I've got to learn better how to relate to other people."

"You know you make mistakes and you get your teeth kicked in and that's a real hard way to learn but that's the way most of us learn"

"... work was just part of life ... I had three jobs when I was eleven and was obviously going to school all the time so they weren't full time jobs, but it was just a great little laboratory where you learn how people make their lives work and to respect different people in different social situations, different economic situations. To learn how they must love their families to do what they do."

"I was constantly in a state of being torn from one environment and being replanted in a new environment throughout high school. It was a constant series of relocations and dislocations. So when I was young I really focused my attention on how to make friends and how to try and fit in."

"I've had a lot more failures than I've had successes and I've tried to learn from my failures and I think failure is one of the best ways to learn."

"The most important lessons in life I think we learn directly and they usually involve a degree of pain. Pain is one of the best educators there is. Pain is a natural aspect of life and pain doesn't have to be stabbing yourself with the scissors you know pain can come in a whole lot of ways. I mean there's social, emotional, academic, I mean there are all kinds of measurements of pain ... I've experienced a lot of pain so I've learned a lot."

"I mean you can sit down with Tommy Franks and you know Tommy can tell all these great principles but Tommy is going to have a real hard time relaying to that person how he overcame the doubts ... It's not the bullet points of Tommy's life that are going to make a person understand, it's a true honest to God discussion about the tough times. How did he get through the tough times? ... He had to dig down into some internal strength, commitment, faith, confidence, he had some core values that he had to dig down and rely upon to get through those tough times."

"Another aspect of making mistakes that I'm tolerant of is [when] something is learned or shared with others so that we don't make that mistake again ... When we know we're doing something well I want that learning shared. When we make a mistake I want that learning shared."

"... he was a true inspiration the more I learned about him. He was a West Texas rancher, went broke three times, went broke in the depression with a sheep ranch. He went broke in the grocery business and got wiped out by a flood, again in the grocery business. He never declared bankruptcy. Every time he paid back every penny that he owed, started over, pulled himself up from the boot straps and was a true West Texas honorable gentleman whose word was his bond."

"I was kind of like a fish out of water. First of all the academic standards were about ten times what I was used to; two, the people were real different. My brother didn't acclimate to it too well, but at the end of the day it was a life changing experiences for me because it gave me an appreciation for academics, actually that I never had before and gave me a much better education than I would have otherwise had. That was a big event in my life."

CONCLUSION

The positive approach to the study of human functioning in medicine, sociology, psychology, and the organizational sciences is beginning to take a foothold but is still very much in its infancy. The theoretical arguments for this line of research are compelling as they suggest that a more efficient and effective way to move toward optimal human functioning may very likely be through the study of the positive or above average side of the curve that represents human functional possibilities. For many years the study of the negative deviations from the norm have dominated our research leading us to accept the end product as absence of the negative rather than presence of the positive. This dramatic positive shift in thinking requires very new ways of viewing behavior, emotion and cognition. It is not always possible to understand the positive from the predominant disease or dysfunction-based models. Thus, there are critics of the positive agenda that suggest it is simply a semantic difference that does not add substantively or significantly to our understanding of human functioning.

The purpose of our study was to look at leadership through this positive lens. Specifically, we chose positive health as defined by Ruff and Singer (1998) as a framework for analyzing the conceptualization of leadership from the perspective of executive leaders in the field. Since the study of positive health, thriving and vitality is relatively recent, a qualitative method provides rich detail of how "leadership" as a construct is conceptualized by established leaders. Using this language rich data, we analyzed the frequency and meanings of interview dialogue that supported the positive health model. The core elements of positive health, a life of purpose, quality connection to others, self mastery and self regard and creating deeper meaning and purpose from adversity, were used as the framework. The results of this qualitative interpretation show a strong emphasis by leaders in the field of those four elements. We suggest that a significant factor in leadership is positive health of the leader and more significantly the facilitation of positive health in followers.

The qualitative interview format provides rich, descriptive data that characterizes how functioning leaders view the meaning of leadership. It is interesting to note that in our interviews the predominant language was about promoting purpose, supporting followers, building healthy relationships and striving for excellence. This is very aligned with the human developmental perspective reflected in attachment theory and the exploratory drive. That is, mastery and achievement are as central to healthy human development as are secure, supportive relationships and attachments. Very little in comparison within the transcripts discussed how to overcome dysfunction or a desire to eliminate the negative. Leadership, in particular transformational leadership, promotes the performance of individuals, teams and organizations to achieve at levels that they might not otherwise have achieved, the very definition of positive deviance. Our study provided qualitative evidence to support that within this group of high level leaders, the meaning of leadership parallels the facilitation of positive health.

LIMITATIONS AND FUTURE RESEARCH

This qualitative study provides insight into the basis of leadership and is able to imply through interpretive analysis how the responses from these leader interviews fit within the realm of positive health. However, like most qualitative studies, the analysis does not fit the same rigorous standards as that found in quantitative studies.

The method of data collection is less controlled and the very nature of the study requires that unstructured responses and tangential thinking be encouraged so as to gather the most reliable information about leaders own views and not to be unduly influenced by preconceived ideas of the researchers. The result is a compilation of ideas that can be analyzed for key elements of leadership and leadership development.

This type of research provides the foundation for further studies. Qualitative research is often the leading edge of new directions and within new domains of inquiry. Subsequent research then employs other and often more quantitative means of investigation and testing. For example, a quantitative analysis using valid measures of interdependence would serve to test the proposed importance of this construct within a subject pool of high impact leaders. Additional areas of study might include examining the relationship of interdependence or strength of purpose in leaders and performance outcomes, as well as the relationship of these positive health elements to other established antecedents or potential antecedents of leadership such as emotional intelligence, hope, self efficacy and communication competence. The growing realization in the study of organizations is that leadership is not about a person (the leader), but about the relationship and interpersonal interaction that occurs between leaders, followers, peers, superiors and other stakeholders in the functioning of the organization. Our findings suggest an additional area of interest, as we continue the study of leadership, is to further explore the relationship of positive health or flourishing and leadership.

REFERENCES

Ainsworth, M. D. S., and Bowlby, J. (1991). An ethological approach to personality development. *American Psychologist*, 46, 333–341.

Adler, N.E., Boyce, W.T., Chesney, M.A., Folkman, S. and Symc, S.L (1993). Socioeconomic inequalities in health: No easy solution, *Journal of the American Medical Association*, 269, 3140–45.

Bartunek, J.M. and Seo, M. (2002). Qualitative research can add new meaning to quantitative research. *Journal of Organizational Behavior*, 23, 237–242.

Bjork, D.W. (1997). *William James: The Center of His Vision*. Washington, DC: American Psychological Association.

Bowlby, J. (1973). *Separation Anxiety and Anger, Vol. 2*. New York: Basic Books.

Bowlby, J. (1980). *Loss: Sadness and Depression, Vol. 3*. New York: Basic Books.

Bowlby, J. (1982). *Attachment, Second Edition*. New York: Basic Books.

Bowlby, J. (1988). *Secure Base: Parent-Child Attachment and Healthy Human Development*. New York: Basic Books.

Buckingham, M. and Clifton, D.O. (2001). *Now, Discover Your Strengths*. New York, NY: The Free Press.

Cameron, K., Dutton, J.E. and Quinn, R.E. (2003). *Positive organizational scholarship: Foundations of a New Discipline*. San Francisco: Berrett Koehler, Publishers.

Creswell, J. W. (1998). *Qualitative Inquiry and Research Design: Choosing Among Five Traditions*. Thousand Oaks, CA: Sage.

Creswell, J.W., and Miller, D.L. (2000) Determining validity in qualitative inquiry. *Theory Into Practice*, 39, 124–130.

Fredrickson, B.L. and Losada, M.F. (2005) Positive affect and complex dynamics of human flourishing. *American Psychologist*, 60 (7), 678–86.

Johnson, P., Buehring, A., Cassell, C. and Symon, G. (2006) Evaluating qualitative management research: Towards a contingent criteriology. *International Journal of Management Reviews*, 8 (3), 131–156.

Joplin, J.R.W., Nelson, D.L. and Quick, J.C. (1999) Attachment behavior and health: Relationships at work and home. *Journal of Organizational Behavior*, 20, 783–96.

Levi, L. (1979) Psychosocial factors in preventive medicine, in *Healthy People: The Surgeon General's Report on Health Promotion and Disease Prevention Background Papers* (pp. 207–52). Washington, DC: US Department of Health, Education, and Welfare.

Lincoln, Y.S. and Guba, E. (1985) *Naturalistic Enquiry*, Beverly Hill, CA: Sage.

Luthans, F. (2002) 'Positive organizational behavior: Developing and managing psychological strengths', *Academy of Management Executive*, 16, 57–75.

Lynch, J.J. (2000). *A Cry Unheard: New Insights into the Medical Consequences of Loneliness*. Baltimore, MD: Bancroft Press.

Macik-Frey, M., Quick, J.C. and Quick, J.D. (2005) 'Interpersonal communication: The key to social support for preventive stress management', In C.L. Cooper

(Ed.) *Handbook of Stress, Medicine, and Health, 2nd Edition* (pp. 265–92). Boca Raton, FL: CRC Press.

Mack, D.A., Shannon, C., Quick, J.D., and Quick, J.C. (1998) Chapter IV – Stress and the preventive management of workplace violence', in R.W. Griffin, A. O'Leary-Kelly and J. Collins (eds) *Dysfunctional Behavior in Organizations— Volume 1: Violent behavior in Organizations* (pp. 119–41). Greenwich, CT: JAI Press.

Nelson, D.L. and Quick, J.C. (2006) *Organizational Behavior: Foundations, Realities and Challenges, 5th Edition.* Mason, OH: South-Western/Thompson.

Nelson, D.L., Quick, J.C. and Joplin, J. (1991) 'Psychological contracting and newcomer socialization: An attachment theory foundation', *Journal of Social Behavior and Personality*, 6, 55–72.

Nelson, D.L., Quick, J.C., and Quick, J.D. (1989). Corporate warfare: Preventing combat stress and battle fatigue. *Organizational Dynamics*, 18(1), 65–79.

Quick, J. C., Joplin, J. R., Nelson, D. L., Mangelsforff, A. D., & Fiedler, E. 1996. Self-reliance and military service training outcomes. *Military Psychology*, 8: 279–293.

Quick, J.C., Nelson, D.L., and Quick, J.D. (1987). Successful executives: How independent? *Academy of Management Executive*, 1(2), 139–145.

Quick, J.C., Nelson, D.L., and Quick, J.D. (1990). *Success and Challenge at the Top: The Paradox of the Successful Executive.* Chichester, England: John Wiley.

Quick, J.C., Cooper, C.L., Quick, J.D. and Gavin, J.H. (2002) *The Financial Times Guide to Executive Health.* London and New York: FT/Prentice Hall.

Quick, J.C. and Quick, J.D. (1984). See Quick, Quick, Nelson, and Hurrell (1997).

Quick, J.C., Quick, J.D., Nelson, D.L. and Hurrell, J.J. Jr (1997) *Preventive Stress Management in Organizations,* Washington, DC: American Psychological Association. (Original work published in 1984 by J.C. Quick and J.D. Quick.)

Quick, J.C., Saleh, K.J., Sime, W.E., Martin, W., Cooper, C.L., Quick, J.D. and Mont, M.A. (2006) 'Stress management skills for strong leadership: Is it worth dying for', *Journal of Bone & Joint Surgery*, 88 (1), 217–25.

Quick, J.C. and Tetrick, L.E. (2003). *Handbook of occupational health psychology.* Washington, D.C.: American Psychological Association.

Quick, J.D., Quick, J.C. and Nelson, D.L. (1998) Chapter 12 The theory of preventive stress management in organizations. In Cooper, C.L. (ed.) *Theories of Organizational Stress*: 246–68. Oxford and New York: Oxford University Press.

Ryff, C.D. and Singer, B. (1998) 'The contours of positive human health', *Psychological Inquiry*, 9 (1), 1–28.

Seligman, M.E.P. (1990) *Learned optimism.* New York, NY: Knopf.

Seligman, M.E.P., and Csikszentmihalyi, M. (2000). Positive psychology: An introduction. *American Psychologist* , 55, 5–14.

Siegel, B.S. (1986). *Love, Medicine, & Miracles.* New York: HarperCollins Publishers.

Shirom A. (2003) 'Feeling vigorous at work? The construct of vigor and the study of positive affect in organizations', in D. Ganster and P.L. Perrewé (eds) *Research in Organizational Stress and Well-being*, 3, 135–165. Greenwich, CT: JAI Press.

Spielberger, C.D., Reheiser, E.C., Reheiser, J.E., and Vagg, P.R. (1999). Measuring stress in the workplace: The Job Stress Survey. In D.T. Kenny, J.G. Carlson, F.T. McGuigan, and J.L. Sheppard (Eds.) *Stress and Health: Research and Clinical*

Applications (pp. 481–496). Ryde, Australia: Gordon & Breach, Science Publisher/Harwood Academic Publishers.

Spreitzer, G.M. and Sonenshein, S. (2003) Becoming extraordinary: Positive deviance and extraordinary organizing. In K. Cameron, J. Dutton, & R. Quinn (eds.) *Positive Organizational Scholarship.* San Francisco: Berret Koehler Publishers, p. 207–224.

Wallace, R.B., Doebbeling, B.N. and Last, J.M. (1998) *Maxcy-Rosenau-Last Public Health and Preventive Medicine, 14th Edition.* Stamford, CT: Appleton & Lange.

APPENDIX
INTERVIEW QUESTION FORMAT

1. What is leadership? How do you define it?
2. Where did you get these ideas about leadership?
3. How do you get to be a leader?
4. To what would you attribute your success as a leader? Why do people follow you?
5. When did you realize that you were a leader? Describe the situation.
6. Are we producing as many good leaders now as in the past?
7. What do you think is the status of leadership potential in new graduates? What are their strengths in this area; where are they lacking?
8. Is leadership born or made?
9. Can you teach leadership? If not, why not? If so, how?
10. What have you done to develop your leadership skills?

CHAPTER 7

THE ROLE OF POLITICAL SKILL IN NEUTRALIZING THE DYSFUNCTIONAL IMPACT OF NEGATIVE AFFECTIVITY ON PSYCHOLOGICAL AND PHYSIOLOGICAL STRAINS[1]

Kelly L. Zellars
University of North Carolina–Charlotte

Pamela L. Perrewé
Florida State University

Ana Maria Rossi
Clinica De Stress E Biofeedback, Alegre, Brazil

Charles J. Kacmar
University of Alabama

Wayne A. Hochwarter and Gerald R. Ferris
Florida State University

123

ABSTRACT

We examined the neutralizing effects of political skill on the negative affectivity (NA)—job strain relationships. Strain was operationalized as job tension, job dissatisfaction, and muscle tension (e.g., measured by electromyography—EMG). Results supported the moderating or "neutralizing" effects of political skill such that greater political skill reduced the negative effects of NA on job tension and job dissatisfaction. Interestingly, political skill increased the EMG of those high in NA. We discuss implications of our findings and offer suggestions for future research.

Succeeding in stressful organizational environments is at least partially due to the exceptionally good political skill possessed by many executives (Perrewé, Ferris, Frink, & Anthony, 2000). Political skill is an interpersonal style that combines social astuteness with the capacity to adjust and calibrate behavior to different situational demands in a manner that appears to be sincere, inspires trust, and results in effective influence over others (Perrewé, Zellars, Ferris, Rossi, Kacmar, & Ralston, 2004).

Recent research in the area of job stress suggests that political skill may serve as a coping mechanism in the stressor–strain relationship (Perrewé, et al., 2004). Specifically, Perrewé et al. (2004) examined the neutralizing effects of political skill on perceived role conflict–strain relationships, where strain was operationalized as psychological anxiety, somatic complaints, and physiological strain (i.e., heart rate, systolic and diastolic blood pressure). Results supported the buffering effects of political skill such that greater political skill reduced the negative effects of role conflict on all types of strain.

The positive benefit of political skill in the stressor-strain relationship (Perrewé et al., in press) may come about through its influence on how individuals appraise the challenges occurring within their workplace environment. According to Lazarus' (1991) transactional theory, stress can be defined as a relationship between persons and their environments that is cognitively appraised (or evaluated) as being relevant to their well being, and in which the persons' resources are evaluated as being taxed or exceeding their ability. The essence of the transactional theory of stress is to consider how individuals appraise what is happening in order to understand their emotional and physiological reactions (Lazarus, 1991). In the present study, we investigate whether individuals with higher political skill react to their appraisals differently than individuals with lower political skill.

Because of the strong emphasis on appraisal in the Lazarus (1991) model, it is important to consider the large body of research that has examined the influence of individual predispositions on cognitive appraisals of stressors. Negative affectivity (NA) is the dispositional characteristic most often studied in job stress research (Chen & Spector, 1992; Fox & Spector, 1999;

Moyle, 1995; Watson, Pennebaker, & Folger, 1987). In the current study, we examine the potential neutralizing effects of political skill in the relationships between NA and strain outcomes.

Negative Affectivity

NA is an individual's predisposition to experience aversive emotional states across time and across situations (Watson & Clark, 1984; Watson & Pennebaker, 1989). Individuals high in NA "... tend to focus on the negative side of others and are less satisfied with themselves and their lives" (Watson & Pennebaker, 1989, p. 235). On the other hand, low NAs perceive their environment in a largely non-negative manner. NA has been a prominent variable in research concerning employee performance and well being (Chen & Spector, 1992). Empirical studies consistently report positive relationships between NA and dysfunctional outcomes such as job dissatisfaction, job tension, and somatic complaints (e.g., Spector & O'Connell, 1994).

Researchers examining well being have suggested a number of mechanisms through which NA plays a role in organizations (Moyle, 1995; Spector, Zapf, Chen, & Frese, 2000). Moyle (1995) tested and found evidence for three models in which NA plays a role in employee health and well being. Specifically, evidence suggested that NA was a direct cause of strains, that the relation of NA to strains was mediated by perceptions of job stressors, and that NA moderated the relation between job stressors and strains. This last model suggested that NA was a vulnerability factor in that high NA individuals will respond to job stressors with strains. Further, results indicated that little relation between job stressors and strains existed for low NA individuals. Thus, there appears to be sufficient empirical evidence to suggest that NA can be utilized as a substantive variable in organizational stress research.

In related research, Spector, Chen, and O'Connell (2000) proposed one of the most intriguing conceptual frameworks for the role of NA in organizational research. They suggested a number of plausible mechanisms that would explain why NA would relate to job stressors and/or strains. Two of these mechanisms, perception and hypersensitivity, are most directly related to the current study and are examined further.

Perception Mechanism

The perception mechanism suggests that NA affects individuals' tendencies to perceive job stressors. To the extent that job stressors lead to job strains, this should produce correlations between NA and strains as well. Theoretically, high NAs tend to view the world in a negative way, and view their environment as threatening. At issue is whether this tendency should be considered a bias or not. If one considers the self-report of job stressors to represent individual perceptions, NA would explain in part why some individuals would be more likely than others to perceive job stressors.

Specifically, NA only would be considered a bias if one considers self-report data to represent the objective environment. In that case, NA would introduce extraneous variance in that different individuals would report variable levels of job stressors when the situation was constant. However, self-reports generally are considered to represent perceptions rather than the objective environment, and thus NA would not produce bias (Perrewé & Spector, 2002).

Hyper-Responsivity Mechanism

The hyper-responsivity mechanism suggests that individuals who are high in NA have a heightened response to perceived stressors. Two forms of evidence support this view: NA relates to strains, and NA moderates the relationship between job stressors and strains. The former mechanism is more indirect as there are other means by which NA might relate to strains other than hyper-responsivity (Perrewé & Spector, 2002). As previously discussed, individuals high in NA perceive high levels of stressors. Assuming that stressors lead to strains, this would result in a relationship between NA and strain, although mediated by stressors.

There is considerable evidence linking NA to strains in the workplace. Spector and Jex (1998) showed, in a small meta-analysis, that NA related to physical symptoms and to symptoms requiring a doctor visit. NA also has been shown to relate to psychological strains of depression (Fortunato, Jex, & Heinish, 1999), frustration at work (e.g., Chen & Spector, 1992; Fortunato et al., 1999; Fox & Spector, 1999), job dissatisfaction (e.g., Cavanaugh, Boswell, Roehling, & Bourdreau, 2000; Dollard & Winefield, 1998; Schaubroeck, Judge, & Taylor, 1998) and intent to leave one's job (Van Katwyk, Fox, Spector, & Kelloway 2000). Further, Parkes (1999) found significant relationships between NA and physical symptoms associated with night shifts, such as sleep problems and gastric distress.

NA also has been associated with behavioral strains of counterproductive work behavior, such as abusive or aggressive behavior toward coworkers, sabotage, stealing, and wasting time (Douglas & Martinko, 2001; Fox & Spector, 1999; Fox, Spector, & Miles, 2001; Tepper, Duffy, & Shaw, 2001). Work injuries/accidents have been linked to high NA (Frone, 1998; Iverson & Erwin, 1997), although these are the result of both exposure and unsafe behavior. In sum, high NA has been associated with a multitude of dysfunctional outcomes for individuals as well as organizations. Finding possible antidotes for the dysfunctional consequences of NA may prove to be important for individual well being as well as organizational effectiveness.

Political Skill

Mintzberg (1983) coined the term "political skill" to refer to a necessary personal characteristic of individuals in effectively navigating interpersonal work arenas. Characterized as an intuitive sense regarding the effective use of power, political skill is an ability to "... to exercise formal power with a sensitivity to the feelings of others, to know where to concentrate one's energies, to sense what is possible, to organize the necessary alliances" (Mintzberg, 1983, p. 26). Although Mintzberg associated political skill with formal power, current use of the construct fits better with influence independent of formal authority (Kotter, 1985).

Ferris and his colleagues (e.g., Ferris, Berkson, Kaplan, Gilmore, Buckley, Hochwarter, & Witt, 1999) initiated research on delineating the construct domain space of political skill, provided initial evidence for its convergent and discriminant validity, and developed a concise unidimensional measure of this construct. In their conceptualization, and following Mintzberg's (1983) work, political skill refers to "the ability to effectively understand others at work, and to use such knowledge to influence others to act in ways that enhance one's personal and/or organizational objectives" (Perrewé et al., 2004, p. 142).

We see political skill as allowing individuals to create synergy among discrete behaviors that establish an interpersonal dynamic that contributes to personal and career success. Political skill implies a competence in working with and through others, a "how to" construct that combines knowing *what* to do in a particular work situation with *how* to execute the behaviors in a convincing manner (Ferris, 1999). This "how to" approach is in contrast to most of the work done on interpersonal influence tactics, which has focused on demonstrating specific behaviors (e.g., ingratiating and self-promotion). Unfortunately, this earlier research ignored the personal style component that largely explains the extent to which a specific tactic or behavior is successful (Jones, 1990).

Individuals high in political skill have a greater understanding of their environments, and therefore, evaluate and interpret environmental stimuli differently than those low in political skill (Perrewé et al., 2000). As they successfully influence others at work, individuals with political skill experience feelings of enhanced control as uncertainty is reduced, leading to less anxiety and tension (Ferris et al., 1999; Perrewé et al., 2000). As noted, Perrewé et al. (3004) provided empirical support for political skill's ability to neutralize the effects of role conflict on strain reactions. Because NA has been associated with perceived stressors and strains, the potential buffering effect of political skill may prove to be an important antidote for individuals high in NA.

Hypotheses

Following Lazarus' (1991) stress model, with its strong emphasis on individuals' appraisal of potential stressors, we apply findings of researchers (Moyle, 1995; Spector, Chen, & O'Connell, 2000) that suggest the fundamental importance of vulnerability and hyper-responsivity to stressors. Specifically, we examine how political skill affects the relationship between NA and psychological and physiological strains. Theorists have suggested that personality can be best understood if more attention is given to the influence of traits on what individuals are *trying* to do (Cantor & Zirkel, 1990). We suggest that political skill may provide individuals the necessary tools to navigate purposive social behaviors. According to Perrewé et al. (2000), the negative effects arising from a stressor should be reduced for individuals high in political skill because of their increased confidence and sense of control.

There is limited research on the interaction of individual differences in reacting to workplace conditions. Instead, much of the personality research has examined the moderating influence of situational variables such as autonomy (e.g., Barrick & Mount, 1993). Nevertheless, a "constellation approach" in examining the influence of personality on work behaviors has been called for in the literature (Hogan, Hogan, & Roberts. 1996; Organ, 1996), and researchers have acknowledged the need for studies examining cross-dimensional effects of personality traits (Hogan et al., 1996; Wright, Kacmar, McMahan, & Deleeuw, 1995).

Recently, Witt, Burke, Barrick, and Mount (2002) offered evidence of the interactive effects of conscientiousness and agreeableness on job performance. We are unaware of any similar studies in the stress literature that examines interactive effects of individual differences. We are not suggesting political skill is a personality trait; however, we do argue it is an important individual difference (that is partially dispositional and partly learned) that may interact with personality traits to influence reactions to stressors (Perrewé et al., 2000). In this sense, our work is similar to others (Hollenbeck, Brief, Whitener, & Pauli, 1988; Wright, Kacmar, McMahan, & Deleeuw, 1995), who report significant moderating effects of cognitive ability on the relationship between personality and job performance.

Combining the conceptual work of Lazarus (1991), and the theoretical and empirical work of Perrewé and her colleagues (Perrewé et al., 2004; Perrewé et al., 2000), we argue that although individuals high in NA are more likely to approach and evaluate situations more negatively than low NA individuals, high NAs, who are also high in political skill, may be able to alter their environments such that less strain is experienced. Thus, political skill is a unique coping resource and, thus, an antidote to the dysfunctional consequences of NA. Therefore, we formulate the following hypotheses:

Hypothesis 1: *Political skill moderates the relationship between NA and job tension such that the positive relationship between NA and job tension is reduced when political skill is high.*

Hypothesis 2: *Political skill moderates the relationship between NA and job satisfaction such that the negative relationship between NA and job satisfaction is reduced when political skill is high.*

Hypothesis 3: *Political skill moderates the relationship between NA and muscle tension such that the positive relationship between NA and muscle tension is reduced for those high in political skill.*

METHOD

Sample

We collected data from 230 full-time employees (99 had supervisory responsibilities and 131 did not have supervisory responsibilities) from three large oil companies in Brazil over a fifteen-month period. Participation in the study was voluntary. The sample was predominantly male (72.6%) and married (69%). The average number of years of work experience exceeded 19 years, and 82% of the sample had ten or more years of work experience. The questionnaire was translated from English to Portuguese and back translated by two English teachers, fluent in both languages. The two translators worked independently. Only a few minor discrepancies in wording emerged and were resolved by the translators as they talked through the differences.

Data were collected from each participant at two points in time as part of a large stress-related program sponsored by the companies. Each respondent completed a questionnaire containing personality and stressor items at a professional biofeedback clinic. In an effort to reduce concerns about common method variance for our survey items, the respondents returned to the clinic approximately one week later. Readings were taken for electromyography (EMG) by a professionally educated clinical psychologist (an author) with more than twenty years of experience in conducting and supervising biofeedback studies. During the second week, respondents also completed questionnaires that measured job satisfaction and job tension.

Measures

Political Skill

In addition to the Ferris et al. (1999) study, several other studies have assessed the factor structure of the 6-item political skill scale and found strong support for unidimensionality (e.g., Ahearn et al., in press). Respondents' political skill was measured using six items developed by Ferris et al. (1999) that utilized a 5-point Likert-type scale, with item responses ranging from "strongly disagree" to "strongly agree." Responses to the six items were summed and averaged into a composite with higher scores indicating greater political skill. The political skill items used in this study were:

1. "I find it easy to envision myself in the position of others."
2. "I am able to make most people feel comfortable and at ease around me."
3. "It is easy for me to develop good rapport with most people."
4. "I understand people very well."
5. "I am good at getting others to respond positively to me."
6. "I usually try to find common ground with others."

Negative Affectivity

Based on prior research linking negative affect (NA) and psychological symptoms (e.g., Spector, Chen et al., 2000), we measured NA using the PANAS scale developed by Watson, Clark, and Tellegen (1988). Using a 5-point scale ranging from "very slightly" to "extremely," respondents indicated the degree to which they generally felt to items such as "distressed" and "nervous". Higher scores indicate higher levels of NA.

Job Satisfaction

Job satisfaction was measured using a three-item scale of the Michigan Organizational Assessment Questionnaire (Cammann, Fichman, Jenkins, & Klesch, 1979). A sample item is "All in all, I am satisfied with my job." The seven-point scale had a response format that ranged from (1) *strongly disagree* to (7) *strongly agree.*

Job Tension

We measured job tension with a seven-item measure developed by House and Rizzo (1972). Sample items include "I work under a great deal of tension" and "If I had a different job, my health would probably improve." Participants responded to each item using a seven-point scale that ranged from (1) *strongly disagree* to (7) *strongly agree.*

Muscle Tension

Muscle tension, which changes in response to psychological or psychosocial stressors (Lundberg et al., 2002; McLean & Urgquhart, 2002), was measured by using electromyography (EMG). EMG involves monitoring electromyographic activity associated with muscle movement, and facial EMG measures that have shown to be affected by stressors (Neumann, 1994). We measured the facial muscles (i.e., Frontalis EMG) with 0.5-cm diameter silver-silver chloride electrodes placed above the eyebrow, over the pupil of each eye, with the ground centered. The skin was abraded to reduce resistance and cleaned with alcohol. The employee was in a seated and relaxed position during the measurement.

Control Variables

In order to ensure that the hypothesis tests were appropriately conservative, several variables previously shown to covary with strain were controlled in the regression analyses: total years of work experience with current employer, age, and gender. Finally, in order to make clear that political skill represents an interpersonal style and skill that is something beyond mere self-efficacy, we statistically controlled for general self-efficacy, which captures an individual's judgment regarding his or her abilities to succeed at a task (Bandura, 1977; Riggs & Knight, 1994). Respondents' general self-efficacy was measured with ten items developed by Riggs, Warka, Babasa, Betancourt, and Hooker (1994). Using a 7-point scale ranging from *strongly disagree* (1) to *strongly disagree* (7), respondents indicated the degree to which they possess confidence in their skills and abilities. Six items were reverse-coded. Higher scores indicated greater general self-efficacy.

Data Analysis

Means, standard deviations, and intercorrelations of the variables in the current study are shown in Table 7.1. Coefficient alpha internal consistency reliability estimates are shown along the diagonal. We tested the hypotheses using moderated regression. For each strain outcome, we entered the control variables (age, gender, years of work experience, and self-efficacy) in step one. NA and political skill were entered in step 2, followed by the interaction term (NA × political skill) in step 3. The regression results are shown Table 7.2.

RESULTS

The interaction term (step 3) significantly predicted job tension ($p < .01$), job satisfaction ($p < .05$), and EMG ($p < .10$), beyond the variance accounted for by the main effects and control variables. Pedhazur (1982) has argued that due to the typically small proportion of variance explained by interactions, using $p < .10$ significance level is acceptable, thus, we plotted the interaction for all three of our dependent variables. In order to examine the nature and form of the interactions more closely, we used procedures by Cohen and Cohen (1983) when plotting the interactions, and they are illustrated in Figures 7.1–7.3.

TABLE 7.1 Correlations, Means, Standard Deviations, and Reliabilities

Variable	M	SD	1	2	3	4	5	6	7	8	9
1. Job Tension	3.64	1.30	(0.80)								
2. Job Satisfaction	5.66	1.22	-0.47***	(0.76)							
3. EMG	8.30	2.10	0.25***	-0.20**							
4. Negative Affectivity	2.74	0.65	0.57***	-0.32***	0.27***	(0.83)					
5. Political Skill	3.76	0.62	-0.14*	0.27***	-0.11*	-0.40***	(0.71)				
6. Age	38.60	9.00	0.06	0.09	0.07	-0.05	0.03	-0.07			
7. Gender	1.27	0.45	0.12*	-0.03	-0.03	0.17**	0.14*	0.58***	-0.03		
8. Work Experience	11.69	7.60	0.05	-0.04	0.02	-0.08	0.06	0.19**	-0.10	0.02	
9. General Self Efficacy	5.16	0.93	-0.36***	0.34***	-0.15*	-0.32***	0.29***				(0.71)

Note: Listwise *N* = 230

* *p* < .05
** *p* < .01
*** *p* < .001

TABLE 7.2 Hierarchical Moderated Regression Analysis of the Interaction between Negative Affectivity and Political Skill on Job Tension, Job Satisfaction, and EMG

Variable	Step	Predictors	β	Std. Error	Adjusted R^2	ΔR^2
					Standardized	
Job tension	1	Age	.15*	.08		
		Gender	.10	.06		
		Work Experience	−.03	.08		
		Self Efficacy	−.38***	.06		
		$F(4,225) = 10.31***$			.14	.16***
	2	Negative Affectivity (NA)	.57***	.06		
		Political Skill (PS)	.15*	.06		
		$F(6,223) = 24.43***$			.38	.24***
	3	NA × PS	.79**	.30		
		$F(7,222) = 22.49***$			.40	.02**
Job satisfaction	1	Age	.08	.08		
		Gender	.01	.06		
		Work Experience	−.09	.08		
		Self Efficacy	.33***	.06		
		$F(4,225) = 8.00***$			.11	.13***
	2	Negative Affectivity (NA)	−.21**	.07		
		Political Skill (PS)	.12†	.07		
		$F(6,223) = 8.72***$			.17	.07***
	3	NA × PS	−.77*	.35		
		$F(7,222) = 8.31***$			.18	.02*
EMG	1	Age	.13	.08		
		Gender	−.04	.07		
		Work Experience	−.05	.08		
		Self Efficacy	−.18**	.07		
		$F(4,225) = 2.20†$			.02	.04†
	2	Negative Affectivity (NA)	.27***	.07		
		Political Skill (PS)	.03	.07		
		$F(6,223) = 3.85**$			.07	.06**
	3	NA × PS	−.71†	.37		
		$F(7,222) = 3.86**$			.08	.02†

† $p < .10$
* $p < .05$
** $p < .01$
*** $p < .001$

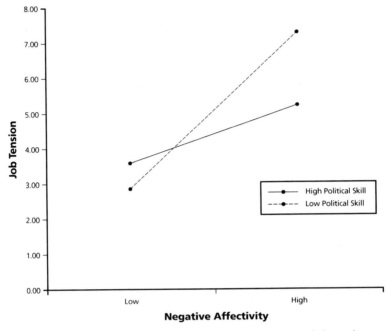

Figure 7.1   Negative affectivity and political skill interaction on job tension.

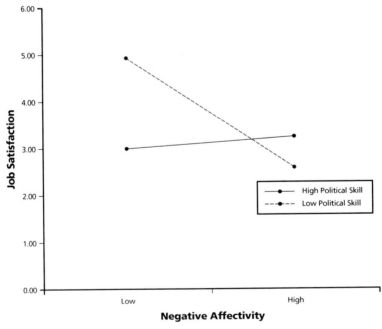

Figure 7.2   Negative affectivity and political skill interaction on job satisfaction.

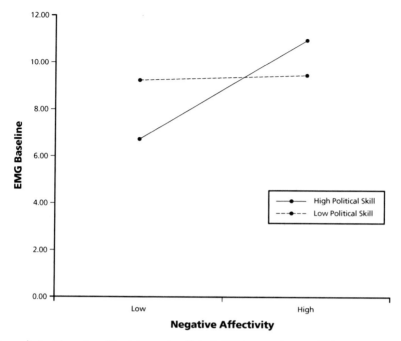

Figure 7.3   Negative affectivity and political skill interaction on EMG.

Evidence across two of the criterion variables supports the hypotheses that political skill attenuates the negative associations between NA and psychological strain. As shown, high NA is associated with more job tension and job dissatisfaction for individuals low in political skill as compared with those high in political skill, thus supporting Hypotheses 1 and 2. Whereas the interaction hypothesized for muscle tension, was significant, we found that, interestingly, EMG (i.e., muscle tension) was highest for individuals with high NA and high political skill. We discuss the possible reasons for this finding below.

DISCUSSION

Job stress continues to be a major problem, costing organizations billions of dollars in disability claims, absenteeism, and lost productivity (e.g., Xie & Schaubroeck, 2001). Because research has supported the dysfunctional personal and organizational effects of stressors (e.g., Spector, Chen et al., 2000), it is important to continue examining potential antidotes that can reduce strain and the related costs of strain to organizations.

Contributions of the Study

The results of this study contribute meaningfully to personality research and the job stress literature, as well as to the growing body of work on political skill. First, our study examines the interaction of two individual differences on strains, thus contributing to calls for filling the gap in the literature regarding studies examining cross-dimensional effects of individual differences. Extending the work of others (Hollenbeck et al., 1988; Wright et al., 1995) indicating interactive effects of cognitive skills and personality on performance, we found significant effects for political skill, an interpersonal ability, on three additional outcomes important to organizations and workers. Examining multiple individual differences simultaneously to examine their impact on strains may contribute to a greater understanding of the influence of individual differences on work outcomes than currently known.

Second, in the stress literature, the typical conclusion to positioning an inherent characteristic, like NA, as a stressor is that there is no known remedial intervention to change the state of affairs, as attempting to alter one's personality is difficult as well as problematic from an ethical standpoint. However, finding that another characteristic, like political skill (i.e., that is argued to be partially dispositional and partially learned), cannot just co-exist with NA, but can defuse or neutralize some of NA's dysfunctional consequences, is very important.

Perhaps high political skill increases the number of social contacts available to an individual, which has been shown to mitigate anxiety (Bolger & Eckenrode, 1991), an emotion frequently experienced by individuals high in NA. By viewing NA in conjunction with a skill that can be developed (at least to some extent), a more accurate picture of how NA influences strains can emerge. Finally, as we continue to study, and increase our understanding of political skill, we will be able to better comprehend the cognitive, behavioral, and emotional dynamics that underlie this complex construct.

The results for Hypothesis 3 deserve further investigation. One possibility for the finding that muscle tension was highest for individuals with high NA and high political skill is that political skill requires individuals to engage in self-monitoring behaviors to ensure personal success (Ferris et al., 1999). Perhaps because individuals high in NA approach situations expecting more negative outcomes, they are more likely to expend physical energy in order to behave in a politically skilled manner.

Thus, those high in political skill and high in NA will react more strongly physiologically because they are working harder to make their behavior socially appropriate. Indeed, possessing the savvy and astuteness (i.e., political skill) to know what behaviors particular situations call for, while simultaneously possessing an inherent tendency to be negative and ignore such conventional behavioral norms, can be expected to create the type of internal turmoil that could manifest itself as muscle tension (EMG). Clearly, however, conclusive assertions await further investigation.

Limitations and Directions for Future Research

Although NA has been well substantiated as an important personality construct for organizations, one of the limitations of this study is that only one personality dimension was examined. To some extent, we were constrained by the parameters of the data collection situation, and had to limit the amount of information that could be gathered. Another limitation is that political skill was measured only through self-report assessment. Although this might be acceptable as an initial test of these ideas, future efforts should include additional assessments of political skill (e.g., peer perspectives), in order to ensure the construct is being captured in a valid manner. Although recent research has demonstrated a significant relationship between employee self-reports of political skill and their supervisors' assessments of their political skill (Semadar, 2004).

Additionally, although several studies (e.g., Ahearn, Ferris, Hochwarter, Douglas, & Ammeter, 2004; Kolodinsky, Hochwarter, & Ferris, 2004; Treadway, Ferris, Douglas, Hochwarter, Kacmar, & Ammeter, 2004) have reported interesting results using the six-item, unidimensional measure of political skill developed by Ferris et al. (1999), Ferris and his colleagues recently have developed the more extensive, 18-item, multi-dimensional *Political Skill Inventory* (Ferris, Treadway et al., 2007; Ferris, Treadway et al., 2005; Ferris, Davidson, & Perrewé, 2005). Future research should employ this more extensive measure, and also examine how the different dimensions of political skill might demonstrate differential relationships with outcomes.

Also, although we can think of no reason that our results would not generalize to workers in large companies in the United States and elsewhere, additional research is needed across cultures to rule out cultural effects on political skill. Because our sample was predominantly male and experienced, it would also be informative to test our hypotheses in a more gender diverse sample.

We now have evidence that political skill can neutralize the potentially negative effects of personality characteristics (i.e., present study) and situational stressors (i.e., role conflict in Perrewé et al., 2004) on strain reactions. Future research should examine the moderating role of political skill on other stressor-strain relationships. For example, we cannot conclude that if political skill can neutralize role conflict's negative consequences, that it will do the same for role ambiguity and role overload. Similarly, we need more research examining the role of political skill in the relationship between other personality variables and job strain. It could be a general demands-strain paradigm is operating here, suggesting generally similar moderating effects for political skill. Or it could be that political skill is sensitive to, and perhaps more effective against the effects of personality based tendencies on psychological strains rather than physical strains. Clearly, additional research is still needed regarding these issues.

REFERENCES

Ahearn, K.K., Ferris, G.R., Hochwarter, W.A., Douglas, C., & Ammeter, A.P. (2004). Leader political skill and team performance. *Journal of Management, 30,* 309–327.

Bandura, A. 1977. Self-efficacy: Toward a unifying theory of behavioral change. *Psychological Review*, 84: 191–215.

Barrick, M.R., & Mount, M.K. (1993). Autonomy as a moderator of the relationship between the Big Five personality dimensions and job performance. *Journal of Applied Psychology,* 78, 111–118.

Bolger, N., & Eckenrode, J. (1991). Social relationships, personality, and anxiety during a major stressful event. *Journal of Personality and Social Psychology,* 61, 440–449.

Cammann, C., Fichman, M., Jenkins, D., & Klesh, J. (1979). *The Michigan Organizational Assessment Questionnaire.* Unpublished manuscript, University of Michigan, Ann Arbor.

Cantor, N., & Zirkel, S. (1990). Personality, cognition, and purposive behavior. In L.A. Pervin (Ed.), *Handbook of Personality* (pp.135–164). New York: The Guilford Press.

Cavanaugh, M. A., Boswell, W. R., Roehling, M. V., & Boudreau, J. W. (2000). An empirical examination of self-reported work stress among U.S. managers. *Journal of Applied Psychology,* 85, 65–74.

Chen, P. Y., & Spector, P. E. (1992). Relationships of work stressors with aggression, withdrawal, theft and substance use: An exploratory study. *Journal of Occupational and Organizational Psychology,* 65, 177–184.

Cohen, J., & Cohen, P. (1983). *Applied multiple regression/correlation analysis for the behavioral sciences.* Hillsdale, NJ: Erlbaum

Dollard, M. F., & Winefield, A. H. (1998). A test of the demand-control/support model of work stress in correctional officers. *Journal of Occupational Health Psychology,* 3, 243–264.

Douglas, S. C., & Martinko, M. J. (2001). Exploring the role of individual differences in the prediction of workplace aggression. *Journal of Applied Psychology,* 86, 547–559.

Ferris, G. R., Berkson, H. M., Kaplan, D. M., Gilmore, D. C., Buckley, M. R., Hochwarter, W. A., & Witt, L. A. (1999). *Development and initial validation of the political skill inventory.* Paper presented at the 59th Academy of Management Meetings, Chicago.

Ferris, G.R., Davidson, S.L., & Perrewé, P.L. (2005). *Political skill at work: Impact on work effectiveness.* Mountain View, CA: Davies-Black Publishing.

Ferris, G.R., Treadway, D.C., Perrewé, P.L., Brouer, R.L., Douglas, C., & Lux, S. (2007). Political skill in organizations. *Journal of Management, 33,* 290–320.

Ferris, G.R., Treadway, D.C., Kolodinsky, R.W., Hochwarter, W.A., Kacmar, C.J., Douglas, C., & Frink, D.D. (2005). Development and validation of the political skill inventory. *Journal of Management, 31,* 126–152.

Fortunato, V. J., Jex, S. M., & Heinish, D. A. (1999). An examination of the discriminant validity of the Strain-Free Negative Affectivity scale. *Journal of Occupational and Organizational Psychology, 72,* 503–522.

Fox, S., & Spector, P. E. (1999). A model of work frustration-aggression. *Journal of Organizational Behavior, 20,* 915–931.

Fox, S., Spector, P. E., & Miles, D. (2001). Counterproductive work behavior (CWB) in response to job stressors and organizational justice: Some mediator and moderator tests for autonomy and emotions. *Journal of Vocational Behavior, 59,* 1–19.

Frone, M. R. (1998). Predictors of work injuries among employed adolescents. *Journal of Applied Psychology, 83,* 565–576.

Hogan, R., Hogan, J., & Roberts, BW. (1996). Personality measurement and employment decisions: Questions and answers. *American Psychologist, 51,* 469–477.

Hollenbeck, J.R., Brief, A.P., Whitener, E.M., & Pauli, K.E. (1988). An empirical note on the interaction of personality and aptitude in personnel selection. *Journal of Management, 14:* 441–451.

House, R., & Rizzo, J. (1972). Toward the measurement of organizational practices: Scale development and validation. *Journal of Applied Psychology, 56,* 388–396.

Iverson, R. D., & Erwin, P. J. (1997). Predicting occupational injury: The role of affectivity. *Journal of Occupational and Organizational Psychology, 70,* 113–128.

Jones, E.E. (1990). *Interpersonal perception.* New York: W.H. Freeman.

Kolodinsky, R.W., Hochwarter, W.A., & Ferris, G.R. (2004). Nonlinearity in the relationship between political skill and work outcomes: Convergent evidence from three studies. *Journal of Vocational Behavior, 65,* 294–308.

Kotter, J.P. (1985). *Power and influence: Beyond formal authority.* New York: Free Press.

Lazarus, R.S. (1991). Progress on a cognitive-motivational-relational theory of emotions. *American Psychologist, 46,* 819–834.

Lundberg, U., Forsman, M., Zachau, G., Eklof, M., Palmerud, G., Melin, B., & Kadefors, R. (2002). Effects of experimentally induced mental and physical stress on motor unit recruitment in the trapezius muscle. *Work & Stress, 16,* 166–178.

McLean, L. & Urquhart, N. (2002). The influence of psychological stressors on myoelectrical signal activity in the shoulder region during a data entry task. *Work & Stress, 16,* 138–153.

Mintzberg, H. 1983. *Power in and around organizations.* Englewood cliffs, NJ: Prentice-Hall.

Moyle, P. (1995). The role of negative affectivity in the stress process: Tests of alternative models. *Journal of Organizational Behavior, 16,* 647–668.

Neumann, J.K. (1994). Influence of stress and blood type on toxicity-preventing activity and other cardiac risk factors. *Stress Medicine, 10,* 255–260.

Organ, D. (1996). Personality and organizational citizenship behavior. *Journal of Management*, 20, 465–479.

Parkes, K. R. (1999). Shiftwork, job type, and the work environment as joint predictors of health-related outcomes. *Journal of Occupational Health Psychology, 4*, 256–268.

Pedhazur, E. (1982). *Multiple regression in behavioral research: Explanation and prediction*. New York: Holt, Rinehart, and Winston.

Perrewé, P. L., Ferris, G. R., Frink, D. D., & Anthony, W. P. (2000). Political skill: An antidote for workplace stressors. *Academy of Management Executive, 14*, 115–123.

Perrewé, P.L. & Spector, P.E. (2002). Personality research in the organizational sciences. In G.R. Ferris (Ed.), *Research in personnel and human resources management* (Vol. 21, pp. 1–64). Oxford: JAI Press/Elsevier Science.

Perrewé, P. L., Zellars, K. L., Ferris, G. R., Rossi, A. M., Kacmar, C. J., & Ralston, D. (2004). Neutralizing job stressors: Political skill as an antidote to the dysfunctional consequences of role conflict stressors. *Academy of Management Journal, 47*, 141–152.

Riggs, M., & Knight, P. 1994. The impact of perceived group-success-failure on motivational beliefs and attitudes: A causal model. *Journal of Applied Psychology*, 75: 755–766.

Riggs, M.L.,Warka, J., Babasa, B., Betancourt, R., & Hooker, S. (1994). Development and validation of self-efficacy and outcome expectancy scales for job-related applications. *Educational and Psychological Measurement, 54*, 793–802.

Schaubroeck, J., Judge, T. A., & Taylor, L. A. (1998). Influences of trait negative affect and situational similarity on correlation and convergence of work attitudes and job stress perceptions across two jobs. *Journal of Management, 24*, 553–576.

Semadar, A. (2004). *Interpersonal competencies and managerial performance: The role of emotional intelligence, leadership self-efficacy, self-monitoring, and political skill.* Unpublished doctoral dissertation, Department of Psychology, University of Melbourne, Australia.

Spector, P. E., Chen, P. Y., & O'Connell, B. J. (2000). A longitudinal study of relations between job stressors and job strains while controlling for prior negative affectivity and strains. *Journal of Applied Psychology, 85*, 211–218.

Spector, P. E., & Jex, S. M. (1998). Development of four self-report measures of job stressors and strain: Interpersonal Conflict at Work Scale, Organizational Constraints Scale, Quantitative Workload Inventory, and Physical Symptoms Inventory. *Journal of Occupational Health Psychology, 3*, 356–367.

Spector, P. E., & O'Connell, B. J. (1994). The contribution of individual dispositions to the subsequent perceptions of job stressors and job strains. *Journal of Occupational and Organizational Psychology, 67*, 1–11.

Spector, P. E., Zapf, D., Chen, P. Y., & Frese, M. (2000). Why negative affectivity should not be controlled in job stress research: Don't throw out the baby with the bath water. *Journal of Organizational Behavior, 21*, 79–95.

Tepper, B. J., Duffy, M. K., & Shaw, J. D. (2001). Personality moderators of the relationship between abusive supervision and subordinates' resistance. *Journal of Applied Psychology, 86*, 974–983.

Treadway, D.C., Ferris, G.R., Douglas, C., Hochwarter, W.A., Kacmar, C.J., Ammeter, A.P., & Buckley, M.R. (2004). Leader political skill and employee reactions. *The Leadership Quarterly, 15,* 493–513.

Van Katwyk, P. T., Fox, S., Spector, P. E., & Kelloway, E. K. (2000). Using the Job-related Affective Well being Scale (JAWS) to investigate affective responses to work stressors. *Journal of Occupational Health Psychology, 5,* 219–230.

Watson, D., & Clark, L. A. (1984). Negative affectivity: The disposition to experience aversive emotional states. *Psychological Bulletin, 96,* 465–490.

Watson, D., Clark, L., and Tellegen, A. (1988). Development and validation of brief measures of positive and negative affect: The PANAS scale. *Journal of Personality and Social Psychology, 54,* 1063–1070.

Watson, D. & Pennebaker, J.W. (1989). Health complaints, stress, and distress: Exploring the central role of negative affectivity. *Psychological Review, 96,* 234–254.

Watson, D., Pennebaker, J. W., & Folger, R. (1987). Beyond negative affectivity: Measuring stress and satisfaction in the workplace. In J.M. Ivancevich & D.C. Ganster (Eds.), *Job stress: From theory to suggestion* (pp. 141–157). New York: Haworth Press.

Witt, L.A., Burke, L.A., Barrick, M.R., & Mount, M.K. (2002). The interactive effects of conscientiousness and agreeableness on job performance. *Journal of Applied Psychology,* 87, 164–169.

Wright, P.M., Kacmar, K.M., McMahan, G.C., & Deleeuw, K. (1995). P = f(M X A): Cognitive ability as a moderator of the relationship between personality and job performance. *Journal of Management,* 21, 1129–1140.

Xie, J. L. & Schaubroeck, J. (2001). Bridging approaches and findings across diverse disciplines to improve job stress research. In P. L. Perrewé & D. C. Ganster (Eds.), *Research in occupational stress and well being* (Vol. 1, pp. 1–53). Oxford, UK: JAI Press/Elsevier Science.

NOTE

1. Portions of the data collected for this chapter were published in an article in the *Journal of Organizational Behavior* in 2008. Correspondence should be addressed to: Kelly L. Zellars, Belk College of Business, University of North Carolina–Charlotte, Charlotte, NC 28223-0001, Ph: (704) 687-2087, Fax: (704) 687-3123, E-mail: kzellars@email.uncc.edu

CHAPTER 8

MEDITATION IN HEALTH

Definition, Operationalization, and Technique

Roberto Cardoso
Eduardo de Souza
Luiz Camano

In the last three decades, we have noted a growing change in the role of meditation in health. Previously understood as a procedure of an exclusively religious and/or philosophical nature, meditation has found, nowadays, an increasingly expressive position in the assistance and prevention of health problems.

In this chapter we will present the conceptual evolution that allows meditation to be understood as a well defined and gradually accepted technique in the medical-academic environment.

THE EVOLUTION OF THE CONCEPT OF MEDITATION

In order to speak about meditation, we must, first of all, understand exactly what meditation is all about, and this requires an adequate operational definition.

Stress and Quality of Working Life, pages 143–166
Copyright © 2009 by Information Age Publishing
All rights of reproduction in any form reserved.

Over the years, a few definitions have been proposed, in an attempt to describe this method. In their now already classical texts, Benson and collaborators (1974) used the term "relaxation response" to refer to meditation; however, this term describes the physiological characteristics obtained from meditation, rather than the operational method used by the technique. West (1979) defined meditation as "...an exercise that usually consists of training the individual to focus his or her conscious attention on one single object, sound, concept or experience"; however, this definition seems limited to the passive concentrating techniques (which use the so-called "positive anchors"–see below), and excludes the "perceptive" modalities, as well as does not mention the necessary "logic relaxation". Goleman (2004) defined the concept of meditation as "...a consistent attempt to achieve a specific position of attention..."; however, this concept does not emphasize either the fact that it is a self-induced method, or the "logic relaxation". Craven described meditation as something that involved "...relaxation, concentration, altered state of consciousness, 'logic relaxation', and attitude of self-observation..."; however, this definition does not include the "perceptive" techniques (that use the so-called "negative anchors"–see below), and does not stress the fact that it is a self-induced exercise, and neither does it emphasize the importance of a practice of self-focusing. Davis (1998) presents meditation as "...a group of attention practices, that lead to an altered state of consciousness characterized by the expansion of consciousness, and impression of a 'great presence' and a more integrating 'sensation of the I'..."; but his concept does not clearly indicate the existence of a stratagem of self-focusing, and does not address the need to avoid the sequences of thoughts in order the achieve the logic relaxation. Manocha (2000) considered that an authentic meditating technique would exist in face of "...a well-defined state of 'consciousness with rare thoughts', while focusing the attention onto the present moment and turning the attention away from the duel between the 'immutable past' and the 'undetermined future', thus reducing the unnecessary and unproductive basal 'mental noise'..."; but this definition sticks much more to the effects than to the technical aspects of the method. Cardoso & Leite (2000), in their first clinical testing, defined meditation as a procedure that would present "...a specific (clearly defined) technique and would involve an altered state of consciousness, with muscular relaxation at some point of the process, and "logic relaxation"; besides necessarily being a self-induced state, by using a "self-focusing" practice–called "anchor"–and by emphasizing non-sensorial self-perception..."; but this definition, at that time, was still considered somewhat extensive, besides incorporating psychophysical effects along with operational variables. Bishop and collaborators (2004) considered that meditation presented two basic components: the first, the so-called "...self-regulation of attention, involving sustained attention,

'connected' attention and the inhibition of the elaboration processes…";
the second, a "…quality to relate oneself with experience, with an orientation of curiosity, an openness to experience and acceptance…"; but this
definition is not sufficient to describe some types of "concentration" techniques.

In spite of so many efforts, it is our understanding that none of these
proposals has yet fully achieved the goal of adequately defining a meditating procedure.

CONCEPT AND OPERATIONALIZATION

In the almost totality of definitions that have been proposed up to now,
either the concepts presented are incomplete or technique and effect are
confounded. By the way, we have always said that this confusion (technique
vs effect) is the greatest misunderstanding in the history of meditation. The
technique consists of the steps to be followed with the goal of obtaining the
effect. The effect consists of psychophysical alterations resulting from the
technique. When we say that meditating is "Finding peace within oneself";
or "Getting in harmony with the Universe"; or "Being in the Peace of the
Eternal Now", we will be talking of the psychophysical effects and we will
not be teaching the apprentice how to meditate. Furthermore, this description only reflects the impression of the person reporting on the effect, i.e.,
this was the impression that that individual had while meditating; but it will
not necessarily be the same impression of the apprentice, who can meditate
and describe his or her impressions in entirely different words. And besides,
during the exercise, the beginner may be avidly seeking these sensations,
such as they were described to him or her, and this will eventually increase
logic even more, and abort the meditating process.

In an attempt to dissolving these conceptual difficulties, our group proposed (Cardoso, 2004) an operational definition that involves basically five
parameters: a necessarily (1) self-induced state, obtained by means of a (2)
specific (clearly defined) technique, by using a (3) practice of self-focusing
(called anchor), aiming at a (4) "logic relaxation" and presenting (5) muscular (psychophysical) relaxation at some point of the process, (Table 8.1).

In other words, meditating consists of self-applying a technique (previously
clearly defined), by using some "anchor" (practice of self-focusing) in order
to avoid getting involved in the sequence of thoughts, while aiming at and
obtaining the "logic relaxation", and finally reaching a state of psychophysical relaxation (conceptually, we speak only of muscular relaxation, as this is
the alteration that is the easiest to check in the clinical protocols).

TABLE 8.1   The Five Elements that Compose the Operational Definition of Meditation for Application in Health

Self-induced state	The method is self-applicable. Dependence on the instructor is not encouraged.
Specific technique	A specific technique is used, which is clearly specified before the process.
Self-focusing device	Some type of focus ("anchor") is used to avoid involvement with thought sequences.
"Logic relaxation"	Designed not to analyze, judge, or create expectations. Not getting involved in thought sequences.
Muscle relaxation	At some point in the process, a psychophysical relaxation takes place, with a measurable muscle relaxation.

Below, we will go a little further into the two items that are most difficult to understand, but are very important from the operational point of view: the "anchor" and the "logic relaxation".

THE "ANCHOR"

When learning a technique, the meditator needs to be introduced to the anchor of that technique, because that is where he or she will try to focus all their attention, in order to be able to "relax logic", i.e., not to get involved in the sequences of thoughts that will be emerging. When the NCCAM (National Center for Complementary and Alternative Medicine) presented its conceptual precepts on meditation to the health community in the USA, it clearly indicated, among the operational aspects, toward the so-called "focus of attention", which is nothing other than that which we have called anchor. This article can be found on the Internet (http://nccam.nih.gov/health/meditation/overview.htm).

The anchor, this fundamental aspect in any meditating technique, can be represented by several types of resources. There are very simple, very "tangible" anchors, such as a fixed point on the wall, or a specific sound pronounced repeatedly, or the attention to the movement of one's own abdomen, during respiration, the focus on the passage of air through the nostrils during respiration, or else, several counts during inspiration and/or expiration. Other anchors are more dynamic, as it occurs in the so-called "active techniques". In these, the focus can be the contact of the feet with the soil while we walk, or the attention on the feet and the lower womb while we turn the body around repeatedly. There are also more subtle anchors that we use to call "negative anchors". Here we use the term "negative", no in the depreciative sense, but rather, to represent the inversion of the original idea, as it occurs with the negative of a photographic film. These subtle anchors are used in the so-called "perceptive techniques". Hence, we can have as an anchor the attention (without judgment) on all of the noises and sensations of the moment, or only the "focus on now", or the so-called "focus on the vacuum", or, still, the mere act of witnessing (our own thoughts).

When a yogi, during his or her practice, focuses all his or her attention on his or her own respiration, this can be used as an anchor. When a meditator focuses all his or her attention on the repeated pronunciation of a sound, he or she will be using an anchor. When a Vietnamese monk focuses his attention on the contact of the feet with the soil, while walking, he will also be using an anchor. *Every meditation technique has an anchor.* It can be more or less evident, more or less subtle or wrongly taught, but there will always be an anchor. There is no way of relaxing logic without using a technical practice. Like the hindu Ramana Maharshi used to say, we cannot "ask the thief for help in order to catch the thief himself" (Maharshi R. Ensinamentos Espirituais (Spiritual Teachings). São Paulo, Cultrix, 1991). In fact, there is no way of using one's own thoughts in order to "reduce" the thoughts themselves. It is not possible to relax logic by using logic itself. Therefore, we need an operational resource, which is nothing other than the anchor.

THE "LOGIC RELAXATION"

Logic relaxation is, without any doubt, the most subtle among all aspects of the meditating practice. During the practice, it would consist of "intending not to analyze" thoughts or effects, "intending not to judge" thoughts or effects, and "intending not to create expectations" as to the practice or its effects. Therefore, the meditator will "*refrain from getting involved in the sequences of thoughts.*" Does it seem difficult? Maybe. But we will explain it here, step by step.

During the day, sequences of thoughts flood our mind. In general, an initial though is produced, and then a whole sequence is started. For example, the following though comes to our mind "... the noise on the car engine,..." and then the sequence starts getting formed immediately: "... I have to check this strange noise to see what it is,..." "... will I have time to do this today?..." "... maybe during the lunch hour,..." "... I have to decide where to take the car,..." "... I will talk to Joseph about it...." And then, all of a sudden, another though "invades" our mind and another sequence is formed: "... Mary has never called me again,..." "... could it be that she is angry at me?..." "... I guess I am going to call her,..." "... I don't know if I should,..." "... Yes, I guess I am going to call her,..." "... maybe I will call her tomorrow. . . ." And then, another thought "invades" our mind and another sequence is started, and so forth, many, many, and many times during the day. We use to say that if we were able to write with sufficient speed in order to make notes of all our thoughts, during a whole day, a whole notebook (of the large ones) might not be sufficient. At the end of the day, we would have written down in this notebook an enormous amount of thoughts, in vertiginously numerous and varied sequences, the major portion of which without any apparent productivity. Hence, we are, day after day, at the mercy of this stream of thoughts, and often at the mercy of this vertiginous zig-zag, just like a loose piece of paper in the wind.

Relaxing logic is exactly about refraining from getting involved in this sequence of thoughts. But how? After all, in order to "refrain from getting involved", we would have to use logic. We would have to "confirm" the existence of the sequence of thoughts, to "analyze" the possibility to avoid it, to "judge" whether we are being successful or not, and so forth. But, all these actions, such as confirming, analyzing, judging, are actions that require the use of logic and, therefore, could not help us to relax logic. By acting this way, we end up in a "deadlock". In order to meditate, we need to relax logic, but we will have to do this without using logic, or by using the smallest possible proportion of logic. So, then, how do we do it?

In order to solve this enigma, it was necessary to create some practice, an operational instrument that would allow us to relax logic without increasing logic itself, a technical trick that would allow us to "dribble" this problem: and this trick is what we described above as a practice of self-focusing, or "anchor". In the anchor, we "focus" our attention during the technique, and we return to the anchor when we find ourselves involved in some sequence of thoughts. While meditating, the apprentice remains focused on the anchor, and—at the same time—subtly attentive to the possible involvement in some sequence of thoughts. As soon as he or she finds himself or herself being taken by the stream of thoughts, he or she will gently turn all his or her attention to the anchor. Later on, he or she will find himself or herself involved in another sequence of thoughts, and will again return to the anchor. The interesting aspect of this is that when we find ourselves involved in the stream of thoughts, we generally notice that we are no longer focused toward the anchor and that, when we return to the anchor, we put aside the stream of thoughts; when we involve ourselves again in some stream of thoughts, we lose the focus on the anchor again, and so forth (Figure 8.1).

This way, we could say that technically meditation is operationalized through a basic duet, consisting of the anchor + logic relaxation. We focus on the anchor and relax logic; we lose the anchor and perceive ourselves involved in the stream of thoughts; we get back to focusing on the anchor and to relaxing logic; we realize a new loss of the anchor and a new involve-

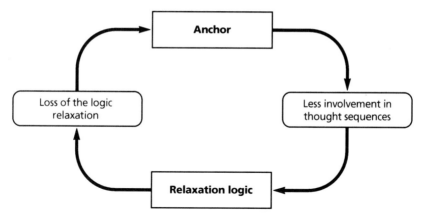

Figure 8.1 Basic components for the operationalization of the meditation exercise in health.

ment in the stream of thoughts; we return to the anchor and once again relax logic; and again, again, and again, until we reach the modified state of consciousness that is peculiar to the meditating practice, within which a subtle anchor exercise still persists, only now more stable and achieved with less effort.

Anchor and logic relaxation set up the primordial duet of meditation. They are the most important aspects to be highlighted by an instructor. While teaching a technique, it is vital to highlight this sequence of focusing on the anchor–relaxing logic; losing the anchor—getting involved in the stream of thoughts; focusing again on the anchor–relaxing logic again; in repetitive cycles, as this is the basis of the meditating exercise. The altered state of consciousness will only be the natural consequence of this repetitive exercise. Of course, in the beginning it is a little more difficult, as the beginner has the impression that he or she will get crazy with so many thoughts coming to the mind and taking the anchor away. But, with time, the apprentice will become trained in the anchor exercise, will increasingly master the technique, and will be able to achieve the modified state of consciousness with increasing ease. It is a question of exercise. It is a "neuronal workout". It is a continued and patient initiative, but with promising results.

MEDITATION OR CONCENTRATION?

Is spite of all efforts toward a clear operational definition of meditation, incorrect interpretations still exist (Cardoso, 2006). When they hear all these arguments that we have presented until now, some people ask: would this, that is described here, not be concentration instead of meditation? Like the yogis would say, wouldn't it be D*harana* (concentration), and not D*hyana* (meditation)? Not, not at all. There is a clear difference between concentration and meditation. Below we will clarify this classical misunderstanding.

First: in this statement, the technique and the effect are once again misunderstood. "Meditation technique" is confused with "meditating state". By the way, whenever someone asks us about what is the greatest misunderstanding regarding meditation, we promptly answer: confusing the effects with the technique. Meditation, in an operational point of view, consists of a practice, rather than of an effect. If the practice is privileged, the effect will emerge as a simple consequence.

Second: concentration uses a focus, while meditation uses an "anchor". While indicating a specific focus to the apprentice, we assume that he or she must try to maintain all his or her possible attention on this focus. Indicating the apprentice an "anchor" means to suggest a focus and, at the same time, to suggest the so-called "logic relaxation", i.e., orienting the apprentice so that whenever the individual finds him or herself in a sequence of thoughts, he or she returns his or her attention toward the "anchor". In concentration, the goal is solely to maintain the focus, and all effort is concentrated on this goal. In meditation, the focus, here called "anchor", is a way of not getting involved in the sequence of thoughts; it is a point to which we return when we find ourselves in the stream of our own thoughts. We soon realize that one single focus can serve as a focus of concentration or as an "anchor" for meditation. The main difference would be in the fact that, in meditation, the apprentice is oriented to observe the thoughts, to realize his or her occasional involvement and to return to the "anchor", whenever this occurs. In concentration, it is possible to maintain the focus and, at the same time, use logic, for example, focus the attention on a sound and think of the possible benefits of this practice; it is even possible to use logic during concentration, in order to better concentrate, by thinking, for example: "I need to concentrate on this sound; I really need to concentrate on this sound; it is important that I concentrate on this sound; concentrating on this sound is my major goal".

Actually, *Dharana* and *Dhyana* (concentration and meditation) are not only stages of one and the same path, as the yogis know so well; they would also be successive stages among themselves. We must realize that, as we progress in "subtilizing" the "anchor", we will gradually be passing from *Dharana* to *Dhyana*. For example, we can start with a concentration exercise for a few weeks, simply in order to train the focus. Later, we start a meditation technique with the focus on a sound, or on a mandala, i.e., with exercises that would still be very close to the *Dharana*. Little by little, we make this focus become more and more subtle, until we have the focus simply on the sensations of the exact moment. What happens is that, in order to use a focus such as this last one, so subtle, without wandering, dreaming or (most importantly) judging (bad; boring; good; sublime; spiritual), we will first need to have what we call "anchor training", i.e., we have to be **very well trained** in perceiving the loss of the anchor and providing our return to focus. The fact is that many apprentices want to go straight into very subtle anchors, and we have often seen that these individuals end up performing creative imagination, dreams, subtle self-hypnotic trances, etc., rather than the altered state of consciousness that characterizes meditation.

THE ALTERED STATE OF CONSCIOUSNESS

When it is adequately practiced, then the meditating technique finally leads to the altered state of consciousness that characterizes this method.

When meditating and following the appropriate operational precepts, a picture of bodily changes, already well described by medical literature, installs itself. Cardiac frequency decreases; respiratory frequency reduces; musculature relaxes; the corporeal metabolism decreases (the expenditure of energy of our body drops); cerebral waves alter; the functioning of some regions of the brain are altered; and so on.

Concomitantly to the changes described above, the so-called "altered state of consciousness", typical of meditation, installs itself. This is a state that is difficult to describe, because, since it would be "beyond logic", it would be very difficult to describe by using the logic of words. This is why we said that it is of no use telling the apprentice, for example, that meditating is "Finding peace within oneself"; or "Entering harmony with the Universe"; or "Being in the Peace of the Eternal Now". It is of no use to speak only of meditation. Rather, what we need to do is to teach the technique very well and then let the state "happen" to everyone.

In order to try to understand this state, we need to know that, as time goes by, and with the continued practice, the apprentice reaches the ultimate state of meditation, which we usually call "*non-sensorial self-perception, without the participation of logic.*" At first sight, it seems difficult to understand how there could exist a non-sensorial self-perception. After all, it seems that everything we perceive is perceived via the senses. We use to perceive something when we see it, or touch it, or hear it, and so forth. However, let us imagine that we are walking in the street, and all of a sudden we realize we are thinking of something (of a fact, of a person, etc). At this moment, we are exactly having an experience of non-sensorial self-perception. But, is this the type of self-perception that the experienced meditators know? Of course, not. This exercise resorts much to logic and the practice of meditation leads to the "logic relaxation", as we have said previously. The meditator perceives him or herself without the participation of the senses and, furthermore, without the participation of logic. It is neither a matter of feeling oneself nor perceiving oneself analytically. Rather, it is a matter of perceiving oneself, and only perceiving oneself; this and only this. This is why we talk about a "state of non-sensorial self-perception without the participation of logic". A state of pure existence. However, to explain this in words, through logic, becomes more and more difficult.

Here it can be seen that describing the ultimate result of meditation is an abstract, very subtle, idiosyncratic, and therefore impossible mission! . . . The mind would not be able to describe a "beyond-the-mind" state. Moreover, as it is idiosyncratic, the description may correspond to the perception (or description) by one person, which will not necessarily be equal to the perception (or description) of another person. As we have already said, this is even anti-didactical, as it will lead the apprentice to "look for" or "wait for" the described state, which will lead him or her to an exercise of logic and aborts the technical process of meditation.

Therefore, it should never be said that "*meditating is not to think of anything.*" This is a classical didactical mistake in the history of meditation. it is something very difficult to conceive, that will confuse the apprentice. Furthermore, by only trying to imagine this "not thinking of anything", we will start avidly thinking of how this would be possible and of how we could achieve it, and we will end up by reinforcing the exercise of logic.

The mind never stops producing thoughts. An evidence of this does not yet exist. What the meditator obtains is the non-involvement with the thoughts or, like others use to say, the involvement with the "Universal Thought". The complete involvement would then lead to the (almost impossible to describe) state of "two minds" within one and the same individual. One mind, physical, *strictu sensu*, that produces thoughts. Another mind, supra-physical, *latu sensu*, that is pure existence. The latter, does no longer get involved in the activity of the first, but the first does not stop existing, due to the fact that it continues perceiving.

The so-called "transcendence" then becomes possible, but only after overcoming the participation of logic, of judgment. And here all types of judgments are included, from value judgments; *even positive judgments*; up to even the so-called "spiritual" judgments. Subjectively, at this moment, we can say that the mind would "silence", and one would experience what is beyond it.

Our operational precepts have echoed within the health community. In 2005, the NCCAM (National Center for Complementary and Alternative Medicine), an organism linked to the American National Institute of Health (NIH) presented an official publication on the subject "Meditation for health purposes", which, as a basis and reference, indicated thirteen selected articles in world literature. Among these articles, ours was mentioned too, as the only one referring to the operational definition of the method (http://nccam.nih.gov/health/meditation/overview.htm).

In 2007, in a review for the AHRQ (Agency for Healthcare Research and Quality), an organism linked to the USDHHS (U.S. Department of Health and Human Services), Ospina presented an extensive review (Evidence Report) on the present status of the research in meditation. The lack of appropriate operational definitions for the application in study protocols was highlighted as one of the main limitations to international studies. Our proposal for a definition, as presented above, was then appointed as the only description now available, with sufficient detailing to be understood as an operational definition of meditation (http://www.ahrq.gov/downloads/pub/evidence/pdf/meditation/medit.pdf).

Well defined, well understood and well taught, we can present meditation as a promising method of behavioral intervention, which is efficient, of low cost and with an ample space in several health conditions. However, at first, we must remain watchful regarding its conceptual, didactical and operational aspects.

MEDITAÇÃO AND THE SUBSTANCES OF STRESS

Some works have proposed meditation as a method of approaching anxiety, through its action on the so-called "neuro-endocrinal axis" of stress. The main alterations would be in the alteration of the brain function, the decrease of the levels of catecholamines and cortisol. Let us see some examples below.

In 1991, Sudsuang, Chentanez & Veluvan, noticed a reduction in cortisol among Buddhist meditators. Moreover, they described a "reaction time" (time between a conventionalized stimulus and the response) 22% higher among meditators, when compared to that of other individuals studied. Such findings suggest a reduction in the state of alertness (of stress).

Glazer and collaborators, in 1992, carried out a study with a large number of individuals, and compared the dosage of dehydroepiandrosterone of 453 experienced meditators to 1252 control individuals. The apprentices showed higher levels of this hormone, regardless of the type of diet, body mass index or physical activity. In general terms, meditators showed blood dosages corresponding to members of the control group who were 5 to 10 years younger.

In 1995, Walton and collaborators compared 22 meditators (with an average practice of 8.5 years) to 33 healthy non-meditator students. Urinary samples were collected for suprarenal hormone dosages, besides sodium, potassium, magnesium, calcium and zinc. Among the meditators, lower levels of cortisol and aldosterone were noted, with higher levels of dehydroepiandrosterone and serotonine, besides a lower excretion of sodium, calcium, zinc and norepinefrine. In general terms, the biochemical alterations found in the meditators were the reverse of those found among the chronically stressed individuals, almost a "mirror image" of stress.

While applying a specific meditation technique ("*Body and mind Le Jing-fa*") for 20 minutes on young university students (19 to 21 years old), Fan and collaborators (2006) verified that there was a significant reduction in the release of salivary cortisol, which was attributed to the inhibition in the neuro-endocrinal axis of stress.

In 2007, Tang and collaborators evaluated the action of a very short training in meditation (5 days) on 40 Chinese students, and compared them to a control group without training. At the end of 5 days, the freshly trained individuals showed significantly lower levels of cortisol.

Infante and collaborators (1998) evaluated the stress axis of 18 meditators, with a practice of one year or more, and compared them to 9 healthy adults, via dosages of the adrenocorticotropic hormone (ACTH), cortisol and beta-endorfine (EP), in the morning and at dusk. Among the meditators, significant changes in the release of ACTH and EP were noted. According to the authors, the findings showed a different neuro-endocrinal state among regular long-term meditators.

In 2001, Infante and collaborators published another study, where they had researched catecholamine dosages, by comparing 19 experienced meditators to 16 healthy adult controls. Noradrenaline (in the morning and at dusk) and adrenanline (in the morning) were dosed. All dosages showed significant differences between the two groups, especially the morning dosage of noradrenaline, which would mean a reduction in these products of stress among long-term meditators.

In 2004, Goleman, presented a book that summarizes the conclusions of five days of international debates among scientists, philosophers and Tibetan monks, which draws the attention to the findings of Infante (2001), highlighting the lowest hormonal response shown by meditators, and considers it an indication that meditation seems to contribute toward the balance of cortisol in the corporeal economy, especially in stressful experiences.

While studying the neural basis of meditation, Newberg & Iversen (2003), stated that there are selective alteration of the neurotransmitters (substances that help in the transmission of impulses in the brain) during the meditating practice, with an increase in the production of excitatory substances (e.g., glutamate) in the areas with higher activation during the meditating practice (e.g., prefrontal cortex), and an increased production of inhibitory neurotransmitters, such as the γ-aminobutyric acid (GABA) in ordinarily inhibited regions, during meditation (e.g., specific talamic sectors). These alterations would be simultaneous with the higher production of dopamine (another neurotransmitter), that would function as a great regulator of production, selective action and functional balance of several brain areas. A drop in noradrenaline in some other selected regions (e.g., locus ceruleus) was also noted.

THE "BRAIN MAP" OF MEDITATORS

The electroencephalogram (EEG) also provided several studies on meditation. In 1996, Jacobs, Benson & Friedman followed 20 healthy volunteers without experience with meditating techniques, via the EEG. The sample was divided into two groups: the first one (the study group) was submitted to meditation through a tape with specific instructions; the second one (the control group) would only listen to tapes with recorded comments on the advantages of meditation, instead of meditating. Among the beginners that meditated, a higher reduction of the beta waves in the front lobe was found. No other significant difference was found, neither in intensity nor in the location of electroencephalographical alterations. According to the authors, even though limited by the use of inexperienced meditators, the work indicates that the effect of emotional regulation in meditating techniques may/can be drawn out from the self-regulation of the activity of the front cortex.

While studying the EEG during the altered state of consciousness of the meditators, Travis (2001) found the installation of high-amplitude alpha waves. Moreover, a coherence of alpha waves, i.e., a higher degree of spatial order of this type of waves was noted, suggesting a peculiar style of brain functioning during the practice, which was called "state of deep rest in alert."

In 2003, Davidson and collaborators, while applying an 8-week training program on healthy workers, found a significant increase of the electrical activity in the brain, in a front left location, which—according to the authors—suggested a possible increase of positive affective experiences during the technique.

While revising the literature on the aspect of the EEG in meditation in countless studies, Cahn & Polich (2006) mainly indicate an increase in the amplitude and the power of the alpha waves, with a moderate increase of the theta activity (pulses in theta waves) in experienced meditators.

In, 2004, Lutz and collaborators studied the so-called "neural synchronism" on meditators, in the frequency of gamma waves (20–70 Hz) of the EEG. The authors report that these "synchronisms" of neural discharges seem to be peculiar to moments when transitory neural circuits function, which characterize cognition and affection activities that are so high that they would even be capable of inducing synaptic changes (i.e., altering the connections between the neurons). In their study, Buddhist meditators were capable of self-inducing high-amplitude gamma synchronicity standards, suggesting that these neural integrating mechanisms, induced by meditation, could be capable of inducing neural changes at short and long term. According to the authors, these findings allowed to consider meditation as a possible instrument of induction of neuronal plasticity (formation of new neuronal connections), which might correlate to the outstanding cognitive-behavioral changes classically attributed to this method.

Cahn & Polich (2006) revised 20 articles that studied the reaction (evoked potential) induced by hearing, visual and other stimuli. They verified a general trend to a better control of attention and to a more selective perception by meditators. However, the authors criticized the methodological poverty of the major portion of these works.

More recent brain mapping techniques also found their space in the study on meditation.

In 1999, Lou and collaborators evaluated the distribution of the brain flow in meditators, through the PET Scan technique, with $150H_2O$. A change in the perfusion (blood circulation) in several brain regions was recorded, which allowed to identify the areas with higher circulation during the meditating practice.

Other articles with the use of the PET Scan highlighted the probable increase in activity in the frontal region of the brain, during meditation. In 1990, Herzog and collaborators were already reporting a higher frontal circulation, when compared to the parietal or occipital region. In 2001, Aazari and collaborators reported a special circulatory increase in the so-called dorsolateral region of the prefrontal cortex.

Newberg and collaborators (2001), followed Buddhist meditators through the mapping technique known as *Spect scan* (7 mCi HMPAO), and compared the results of the basal state with the meditating exercise. In this study, an increase of the blood flow to some regions of the brain, such as the prefrontal cortex and the thalamus, was noted, which suggests an important activity of maintenance of attention. The circulation in the prefrontal cortex showed inversely proportional to the circulation in the area known as the posterosuperior parietal region, suggesting that the higher the activity of maintenance of attention ("anchor") the lower the activity in the region responsible for physical limits and location, which would explain the altered perception of spatial location, commonly reported during meditation.

In 2001, Lehmann and collaborators published a tomographic analysis of an experienced meditator, obtained via a specific EEG system. During the self-induction stage, an increase of activity in the right rear region (related to viewing) and the left central region (related to verbalization) was verified. Meanwhile, during the altered state of consciousness, that the authors call the "dissolution and reconstitution" stage, a higher activity in the right front-temporal region (related to subjective experiences) was noted.

The brain mapping via functional magnetic resonance was presented by Sara Lazar and collaborators, in 2000. In this study, the meditators presented, during the meditating technique, an increase in activity in specific brain regions (and among them, the prefrontal cortex). Moreover, the findings varied with the time of practice of each meditator which, according to the authors, demonstrates the dynamic aspect of the neuronal activity during meditation, which would undergo slow and gradual alterations during the practices, coinciding with the subtle subjective changes commonly associated with the continued exercise of the method.

Other studies (Khushu and collaborators, 2000; Baerentsen and collaborators, 2001), also carried out with the use of the functional magnetic resonance resource, draw attention to the clear increase of the brain activity in the prefrontal region.

In 2005, Lazar presented a new study with magnetic resonance, involving 20 Western meditators, with a long experience (9.1 years of average practice) of daily practice, who were compared to 20 healthy volunteers, who were not meditators. Among the meditators, a greater cortical thickness in specific regions, such as the prefrontal cortex (involved with attention) and insula (involved with sensorial and perceptory phenomena) was noted. These findings suggest that meditation could have the capacity to promote more than neurochemical changes (alteration of the brain chemistry) or neurofunctional changes (alteration of the connection between the neurons). Apart from that, the regular meditating practice could also promote structural changes in the human brain. Moreover, the thickness was more pronounced in older meditators, which suggests a possible relationship of the anatomical alterations with the time of meditating practice.

In 2007, Hölzel and collaborators followed fifteen apprentices of a specific technique (*Vipassana*), and compared them to "control individuals" (who only performed arithmetic exercises when at rest). The idea was to stimulate the "attention cortex" (prefrontal cortex) with arithmetic operations, in order to study the differences between this type of cognitive activity and meditation, on this brain region, among others. In this study, the increased activity, in meditators, in the regions known as the cingular cortex and the prefrontal region was emphasized. However, while comparing the groups, there was even more significance in the difference of activity of the ventral portion of the prefrontal cortex, in favor of meditators, which suggests a possible emotional involvement, simultaneous to attention, in the meditating practice.

While revising all the neurophysiological findings of meditation available up to then, in 2003, Newberg & Iversen presented an extensive and admirable hypothetical model, which associated the advancements in the studies of neurotransmitters with the discoveries of the techniques of neuroimaging, present in scientific literature, concerning the exercise of meditation. If we were to describe here the sequence of alterations to the professionals in the area of health, we would say: in short, this model postulates that meditation starts with the activation of the prefrontal cortex and the cingular spin; followed by a talamic activation in chain; the sequence leads to the reduction of the activity of the posterosuperior portion of the parietal cortex; and at the same time, the activity in regions of the hippocampus and the tonsil are reinforced, this hippocampal alteration, in a positive *feedback* type axis, promotes a reinforcement of the activity in the prefrontal lobe, via *nucleus acunbens;* this set of alterations closes a reentry *loop*, which maintains the meditating process. Meanwhile, the hypotalamic alterations and the alteration of the autonomous nervous system begin.

While discussing its own previous articles, (Cardoso et al, 2007), our group presented an article on the apparent paradox of the clear activation of the prefrontal lobe during meditation. At first, this fact does not coincide with the classical precept that meditating involves "logic relaxation", "reduction of thoughts", among other descriptions regarding qualitative changes of the standard of mental functioning. The finding seemed paradoxical, since the brain region (prefrontal cortex) is classically associated with attention, logical planning and performance of tasks. However, we postulate that the prefrontal lobe is activated in this manner only because it reflects the installation of the so-called "anchor exercise", in which the meditator tries to maintain his or her focus of attention, which is a basic element of the meditating techniques. After all, it is only from the maintenance of the focus that it seems to be possible for the remaining brain effects, described in the literature, to install themselves. This sequence corroborates the impressions of Newberg & Iversen (2003), that highlight the prefrontal activation as the first event in the meditating practice, followed by several other neurophysiological changes.

The two publications above have a relationship to one another. In 2005, von Thomsen presented a monograph to the Loyola College (Maryland–USA), as a partial requirement for the degree of PhD in Psychology. In this writing, the author revised the knowledge related to the effects of meditation on the brain, and put special emphasis on the functional model proposed by Newberg & Iversen. In this model, von Thomsen identified the effect of positive feedback (through a region known and hippocampus), reinforcing the activity in the prefrontal cortex (the region responsible for the maintenance of the "anchor"). In other words, with a certain degree of training, meditation, from a certain point of the brain process, reinforces the meditating activity itself. The author states that, at this point, "... the handle of the positive neurological feedback, that was described by Newberg & Iversen, finds its cognitive correspondent at the handle of the positive feedback, which consists of 'anchor' and 'logic relaxation', as proposed by Cardoso and collaborators. . . ."

Today, by associating our clinical experience with the findings of the studies on brain mapping, we might say that the typical sequence of a meditating exercise would be as follows (Cardoso et al., 2007):

a) Presentation of a specific technique (with the instructor presenting the technique, explaining it clearly, including the anchor that will be used).
b) Application of the "anchor exercise" (see the topic "The anchor").
c) Logic relaxation (se the topic "Logic relaxation").
d) Moments of loss of logic relaxation.
e) "Return" to the anchor, by obtaining a new logic relaxation.
f) Several repeated cycles of the previous events (items "b", "c", "d" and "e"), in increasingly extensive periods.
g) Psychophysical relaxation gradually installed (concurrent with the process)

MEDITATION IN ANXIETY

In 1976, Williams, Francis, and Durham applied the inventory of Eysenck on apprentices of transcendental meditation, and studied the triad psychotism, extraversion and neuroticism. The authors intended to establish a personality profile, among the individuals that seek meditation, and to verify what changes would occur with the repeated practice. They noticed higher neuroticity and lower extroversion among the men and lower psychotism among the women. After 6 months of the practice had elapsed, a lower psychotism and a lower neuroticism was noticed among the men that meditated regularly during this period.

In 1979, West revised the literature existing at that time, and signaled, that, in general, the works referred to a lower neuroticity, a lower tendency to depression and less anxiety/irritability among the meditators. The decrease in alertness was also frequent in all studies. Moreover, there was an increase in self-control, in self-esteem and in the sensation of happiness. Higher indices of satisfaction regarding sleep were noticed. On that occasion, West drew the attention on the significant correlation between psychic changes and the regularity of the practice.

In 1982, Benson revised his findings regarding meditation, and referred to it as "relaxation response", noting that the individuals studied reported a sensation of mental peace, an impression that they were in harmony with the world and a sensation of well-being.

While following 40 Chinese students, and comparing them to the control group, Tang and collaborators (2007) noticed a significant improvement in the scores of attention, anxiety, depression, anger and fatigue tests, directly linked to the decrease of the levels of cortisol, as a result of the practice.

The approach of anxiety was studied by Miller, Fletcher and Kabat-zinn (1995), on 22 patients with anxiety defined by the DSM III. An evaluation was made through the scores of Hamilton and Beck, before and after the eight weeks of the recommended home meditation technique ("mindfulness meditation"). The punctuation of the scores resulted significantly reduced in 20 of the 22 cases, both in Hamilton's and Beck's score.

The reduction of stress among students of Medicine was researched by Shapiro, Schwartz & Bonner, in 1998, through "mindfulness meditation". The results indicated a lower level of stress and anxiety, besides a growth in empathy. The authors considered the technique recommendable for use among students of the medical area.

In, 2007, Coppola studied a specific meditating technique (*Natural Stress Relief*) for two times a day, on 25 volunteers, and compared the group to itself, at the beginning of the training program, after one week and after two weeks. A significant reduction was found in the anxiety-trace score, both in the first and in the second week, which allowed to infer the possible action of meditation, not only on the anxious state, but also on the anxious trace in the personality of the apprentice.

In 2005, In Brazil, Kozasa et al studied the effects of a meditation technique (*Siddha Samadhi Yoga*) on the scores of anxiety and depression. A significant reduction was noticed in anxiety-trace, anxiety-state and depression, among the meditators.

In 2006, Krisanaprakornkit and collaborators presented a revision on the Cochrane data base, by contemplating the role of meditation in anxiety trouble. According to the revision, two studies seemed to fully meet the criteria established for inclusion in the study, and posit the apparent advantage of meditation on relaxation techniques and on *biofeedback*, in the treatment of anxiety. However, the revision indicated that the methodological poorness and the heterogeneous aspect of the majority of articles available in literature, which jeopardizes a better assessment of the role of meditation in the situations of anxiety, which does not yet offer sufficient evidence that allows to attest the unequivocal effectiveness of this method among anxious patients. Moreover, they draw our attention to the high level of quitting, during the training, among volunteers of the selected works, which varies between 33 and 44%. No important side effects were reported. Finally, of course, more studies are suggested, in order to establish a clear and undisputed effect of meditation on anxiety.

BREATHING TO MEDITATE

Although a respiratory technique is not a synonym of meditation technique, we have noticed (data still unpublished) that the progress of the meditator that uses this resource (technique of breathing simultaneous to meditation), is almost four times quicker than when the instructor only teaches the meditation technique, with no concern for the respiration of the apprentice.

The respiratory model that we recommend consists of a variation of the one yogis call "abdominal respiration" or the behavioral therapists call "diaphragmatic respiration". This respiration has basically five aspects: it must be (1) abdominal, (2) nasal, (3) silent, (4) harmonic, and (5) as slow as possible. We will understand better below, item per item.

Abdominal. When inhaling, gently distend the abdomen, making the navel move forward. When exhaling, gently contract the abdomen, bringing the navel inward. Do this smoothly, without forcing the wall of the abdomen, so that it does not annoy you. If you prefer, you may hold the palm of one hand on the navel, in order to feel its movements. In case of great difficulty, start the technique by exhaling and, at the same time, pushing the navel inward with the hand that is on the abdomen.

Nasal. Both inhaling and exhaling must take place through the nose. In case of important difficulties (e.g., nasal obtrusion by rhinitis), you may leave the mouth discreetly open, with just a small slot, in order to help nasal respiration (as if you were holding a lollypop pick between the teeth).

Silent. The act of breathing must not be noisy. I use to say that, if there is another apprentice who is also breathing at a distance of 2 meters, he or she should not be disturbed by the noise of your respiration.

Harmonic. This harmony must exist, both from the temporal point of view and the emotional aspect. The inhaling time ant the exhaling time must be exactly equal. Moreover, establish a harmonious relationship with the air you breathe, refrain from fighting against it. Accept the air that enters your body, as if it entered your body while caressing you. Accept the air that exits your body, as if it were departing freely, without resistance.

Slow (as much as possible). Bit by bit, try to breathe slower, every time, until you achieve the slowest rhythm possible, but *without causing discomfort.* If you get the sensation of "lack of air", or any other type of discomfort, discreetly accelerate the respiratory rhythm, just enough to avoid discomfort.

Practice once or twice a day for 10 minutes. I suggest this to be your preparatory exercise for meditation, during the first 2 weeks, *before trying to meditate.* Soon, you will notice how this exercise does already reduce the activity of the nervous system (the one responsible for alarm reactions) and how it brings you a pleasant sensation of relaxation. However, this is not yet about meditation.

In our opinion, learning to breathe is the best first step for those who want to learn how to meditate. At our workshops, before teaching actual meditation techniques, we often train respiration with the people present, and recommend a daily home training of 10 minutes. Therefore, we suggest you to train this breathing method for a few days, as our meditation technique will be using this breathing standard.

A MEDITATION TECHNIQUE

Here we present a meditation technique. Before practicing it, make sure you *have very well understood* the concepts of "anchor" and of "logic relaxation". Without these concepts very clear in your mind, chances are you will fall asleep, or reach any other modified state of your consciousness, different from the so-called "meditating state". These concepts were well explained earlier in this chapter (see "The Anchor" and "Logic Relaxation"). If necessary, read them again, as often as necessary.

This is a basic meditation technique, modified from our book "Medicina e Meditação" ("Medicine and Meditation") (Roberto Cardoso), published by MG Editores (http://www.gruposummus.com.br/detalhes_livro.php?produto_id=939). This is an ideal technique for the first month (or for the first 30 practices, if you cannot meditate every day). It provides an "anchor" training for beginners, without excessive effort. Take my advice: start with it and do not change the technique, at least during the first 30 practices.

Even if you do already have some experience with meditation and/or yoga, read this technique carefully, as it provides very good examples of operationalization of a meditating exercise.

Anchors (what should be the focus of your attention)
 => Correct abdominal breathing
 => All attention on the vibration movement of the abdomen
 => Breathing count in three times (explained below)

Technique
Prepare yourself to stop for 15 to 20 minutes. If you prefer, play a very calm instrumental music (or several), with a total duration of 15 to 20 minutes.

Get seated the way you think is best, with the spinal cord erect (or close to erect), but *without discomfort*. Remember you have to stay quiet, without making any movement during the whole exercise.

Inhale, while you mentally count from one to three (ascending count). When inhaling, gently distend the abdomen, making the navel move forward.

Suspend breathing, and hold the air for a few moments. Only a short stop, just long enough to say mentally "one little stop"...

Exhale while counting from three to one (descending count). When exhaling, gently contract the abdomen, and bring the navel inward.

Remember that the inhaling and exhaling time must be exactly the same.

As you progress, try to count slower and slower, until you reach the lowest possible rhythm, but without causing discomfort.

Establish a harmonious relationship with the air you breathe. Refrain from fighting the air.

During the whole technique, keep the focus of attention out of your mind, and keep all your attention (observation without judgment) on the abdomen (2 to 3 fingers above the navel) and on the respiratory rhythm.

Avoid moving, scratching, balancing or making any movement.

Whenever a thought emerges and distracts you, as soon as you notice it, turn your focus of attention (anchor) toward the abdomen, very calmly, without anger and without force.

When the time is up (and when you feel like it), take 3 deep breaths and slowly open your eyes. Remain silent for 2 to 3 minutes.

Practice as regularly as possible. Refrain from speculating and do not try to interpret any effects you may notice.

Have a good practice!

REFERENCES AND SUPPLEMENTARY READING

Azari, N.P., Nickel, J., Wunderlich, G., Niedeggen, M., Hhefter, H., Tellmann, L., Herzog, H., Stoerig, P., Birnbacher, D., Seitz, R.J. (2001). Neural correlates of religious experience. *European Journal of Neuroscience*, 13, 1649–52.

Baerentsen, K.B. (2001). Onset of meditation explored with fMRI. *Neuroimage*, 13, S297.

Benson, H. (1982). The Relaxation Response: History, Physiological Basis and Clinical Usefulness. *Acta Med Scand* (Suppl), 660, 231–7.

Benson, H., Beary, J.F., Carol, M.P. (1974). The Relaxation Response. *Psychiatry*, 37, 37–46.

Bishop, S.R., Lau, M., Shapiro, S., Carlson, L., Anderson, N.D. (2004). Carmody, J., Segal, Z.V., Abbey, S., Speca, M., Velting, D., Devins, G. *Mindfulness: a proposed operational definition. Clinical Psychology: Science and Practice*, 11, 230–41.

Cahn, B.R., Polich, J. (2006). Meditation States and Traits: EEG, ERP, and Neuroimaging Studies. *Psychological Bulletin*, 132, 180–211.

Cardoso, R. (2004). *Medicina e Meditação: um médico ensina a meditar* (1st ed.). São Paulo, MG Editores.

Cardoso, R, Leite, J.R. (2000). *Noções Básicas sobre Meditação–Apostila explanatória destinada aos aprendizes de técnicas de meditação em saúde*. Universidade Federal de São Paulo–Departamento de Obstetrícia/Departamento de Psicobiologia. São Paulo.

Cardoso, R., Leite, J.R. (2007). Técnicas de meditação e sua aplicação no ciclo gravídico puerperal. In: Bortoletti F.F., Moron A.F., Bortoletti-Filho J., Nakamura M.U., Santana R.M., Mattar R. R. *Psicologia na prática obstétrica.* São Paulo, Manole, 344–51.

Cardoso, R., Souza, E., Camano, L., Leite, J.R. (2004). Meditation in health: an operational definition. *Brain Research Protocols,* 14, 58–60.

Cardoso, R., Souza, E., Camano, L., Leite, J.R. (2006). Meditação em saúde: aspectos operacionais e didáticos. *Anais do VI Congresso Internacional de Stress da ISMA-Brasil* (International Stress Management Association). Porto Alegre, Brasil.

Cardoso, R., Souza, E., Camano, L., Leite, J.R. (2007). Prefrontal Cortex in Meditation. When the Concrete Leads to the Abstract. A schematical hypothesis, concerning the participation of the logic for "logic relaxation". *NeuroQuantology,* 5, 233–40.

Cardoso, R., Souza, E., Camano, L., Leite, J.R. (in press). Meditation for Health Purposes: conceptual and operational aspects. In: De-Luca B.N. *Mind-Body and Relaxation Research Focus.* New York, Nova Publishers.

Coppola, F. (2007). Effects of natural stress relief meditation on trait anxiety: a pilot study. *Psychol Rep.* 101, 130–4.

Davidson, R.J., Kabat-Zinn, J., Schumacher, J., Rosenkranz, M., Muller, D., Santorelli, S.F., Urbanowski, F., Harrington, A., Bônus, K., Sheridan, J.F. (2003). Alterations in Brain and Immune Function Produced by MindfulnessMeditation. *Psychosom Méd.,* 65, 564–570.

Davis, J. Notes on psychology of meditation. Part 1: definition. (1998). Disponível em: http://www.naropa.edu/faculty/johndavis/tp/medit2.html. Acessed em February 03, 2008.

Fan, Y., Tang, Y., Feng, S., Yu, Q., Wang, J., Lu, Q., Sui, D., Zhao, Q., Ma, Y., Jin, J., Wang, W., Gu, L., Cai, X. (2006). Effect of Hi-method for body regulation on heart rate and salivary cortisol level after stress reaction. *Chinese Journal of Clinical Rehabilitation,*10, 31–3.

Glaser, J.L., Brind, J.L., Vogelman, J.H., Eisner, M.J., Dillbeck, M.C., Wallace, R.K., Chopra, D., Orentreich, N. (1992). Elevated serum dehydroepiandrosterone sulfate levels in practitioners of the Transcendental Meditation (TM) and TM-Sidhi programs. *J. Behav. Med.,* 15, 327–41.

Goleman, D. (Ed.). (2004). *Destructive Emotions: a scientific dialogue with The Dalai Lama.* New York, Random House, p. 179.

Herzog, H., Lele, V.R., Kuwert, T., Langen, K.J., Kops, E.R., Feinendegenm L.E. (1990). Changed pattern of regional glucose metabolism during yoga meditative relaxation. *Neuropsychobiology,* 23, 182–7.

Hölzel, B.K., Ott, U., Hempel, H., Hackl, A., Wolf, C., Stark, R., Vaitl, D. (2007). Differential engagement of anterior cingulate and adjacent medial frontal cortex in adept meditators and non-meditators. *Neuroscience Letters,* 421, 16–21.

Infante, J.R., Peran, F., Martinez, M., Roldan, A., Poyatos, R., Ruiz, C., Samaniego, F., Garrido, F. (1998). Aacth and β-Endorphin in Transcendental Meditation. *Physiol. Behav.* 64, 311–5.

Infante, J.R, Torres-Avisbal, M., Pinel, P., Vallejo, J.A., Peran, F., Gonzalez, F., Contreras, P., Pacheco, C., Roldan, A., Latre, J.M. (2001). Catecholamine levels in practitioners if the transcendental meditation technique. *Physiol. Behav.*, 72, 141–6.

Jacobs, G.D., Benson, H., Friedman, R. (1996). Topographic EEG Mapping of the Relaxation Response. *Biofeedback Self Regulation*, 21, 121–9.

Khushu, S., Telles, S., Kumaran, S., Naveen, K.V., Tripathi, R.P. (2000). Frontal activation during meditation based on functional magnetic resonance imaging. *Indian Journal of Physiology and Pharmacology*, 44,34.

Kozasa, E.H., Krshnam, L.I,, Mohandas, S., DesideriI, A.V., Rueda, A.D., Silva, A.A.B., Martins, I., Leite, M.P., Mendes, L.; Leite, J.R. (2005). Cognitive effects and subjective feelings after Siddha Samadhi Yoga (SSY), training–a meditation procedure associated to respiratory exercises–in volunteers with anxiety complaints. In: *5th International Congress of Cognitive Psychotherapy*. Göteborg, Sweden, p. 164.

Krisanaprakornkit, T., Krisanaprakornkit, W., Piyavhatkul, N., Laopaiboon, M. (2006). Meditation therapy for anxiety disorders. *Cochrane Database Syst. Rev.* (1): CD004998.

Lazar, S.W., Bush, G., Gollub, R.L., Fricchione GL, Khalsa G, Benson H. (2000). Functional brain mapping of the relaxation response and meditation. *NeuroReport*, 11, 1581–5.

Lazar, S.W., Kerr, C., Wasserman, R., Gray, J., Greve, D., Treadway, M., Mcgarvey, M., Brian, T., Dusek, J., Benson, H., Rauch, S., Moore, C., Fischl, B. (2005). Meditation experience is associated with increased cortical thickness. *Neuroreport*, 16, 1893–7.

Lehmann, D., Faber, P.L., Achermann, P., Jeanmonod, D., Gianotti, L.R., Pizzagalli, D. (2001). Brain sources of EEG gamma frequency during volitionally meditation-induced, altered states of consciousness, and experience of the self. *Psychiatry Res.*, 30, 111–21.

Lou, H.C., Kjaer, T.W., Friberg, L., Wildschiodtz, G., Holm, S., Nowak, M. (1999). A 150-H2O PET study of meditation and the resting state of normal consciousnesss. *Hum Brain Mapp*, 7, 98–105.

Lutz, A., Greischar, L.L., Rawlings, N.B., Ricard, M., Davidson, R.J. (2004). Long-term meditators self-induce high-amplitude gamma synchrony during mental practice. *PNAS*, 101, 16369–73.

Manocha, R. (2000) Why meditation? *Australian Family Physician*, 29, 1135–38.

Miller, J.J., Fletcher, K., Kabat-Zinn, J. (1995). Three-year follow-up and clinical implications of a mindfulness meditation-based stress reduction intervention in the treatment of anxiety disorders. *Gen Hosp Psychiatry*, 17, 192–200.

National Center for Complementary and Alternative Medicine. (2005). *National Institutes of Health. NIH-Backgrounder. Meditation for Health Purposes*, Bethesda, EUA. Disponível em: <http://nccam.nih.gov/health/meditation/overview.htm>. Acessed February. 03, 2008.

Newberg, A., Alavi, A., Baime, M., Pourdehnad, M., Santana, J., D'aquili, E. (2001). The measurement of regional cerebral blood flow during the complex cognitive task of meditation: a preliminary SPECT study. *Psychiatry Res.*, 106, 113–22.

Newberg, A.B., Iversen, J. (2003). The neural basis of the complex mental task of meditation: neurotransmitter and neurochemical considerations. *Med Hypotheses*, 61, 282–91.

Ospina, M.B., Bond, T.K., Karkhanen, M., Tjosvold, L., Vandermeer, B., Liang, Y., Bialy, L., Hooton, N., Buscemi, N., Dryden, D.M,, Klassen, T.P.(2007). *Meditation Practices for Health: State of the Research. Evidence Report/Technology Assessment No. 155.* (Prepared by the University of Alberta Evidence-based Practice Center under Contract No. 290-02-0023.) AHRQ Publication No. 07-E010. Rockville, MD: Agency for Healthcare Research and Quality, June.

Shapiro, S.L, Schwartz, G.E., Bonner, G. (1998). Effects of mindfulness-based stress reduction on medical and premedical students. *J Behav Med,* 21, 581–99.

Tang, Y., May, Y., Wang, G.J., Fan, Y., Feng, S., Lu, Q., Yu, Q., Sui, D., Rothbart, M.K., Fan, M., Posner, M.I. (2007). Short-term meditation training improves attention and self-regulation. *PNAS,* 104, 17152–6.

Travis, F. (2001). Autonomic and EEG patterns distinguish transcending from other experiences during transcendental meditation practices. *International Journal of Psychophysiology,* 42, 1–9.

Von Thomsen, C. (2005). *Meditation and the Brain.* A monography presented to the Loyola College–Maryland in partial fulfillment of the requirements for the degree of PhD in Psychology. Loyola College in Maryland , p.2.

Walton, K.G., Pugh, N.D., Gelderloos, P., Macrae, P. (1995). Stress reduction and preventing hypertension: preliminary report for a psychoneuroendocrine mechanism. *J Altern Complement Med,* 1, 263–83.

West, M. Meditation. (1979). *Brit J Psychiatr,* 135, 457–67.

Williams, P., Francis, A., Durham, R. (1976). Personality and Meditation. *Percept Motor Skills ,* 43, 787–92.

SECTION 3

UNDERSTANDING AND EXAMINING WORK LIFE QUALITY

The bases of this appraisal process are not yet known, but research has indicated that two neuroendocrine systems are the principle drivers of integrated stress responses. Upon recognition of threat or demand, the sympathetic nervous system (SNS) and the hypothalamic-pituitary-adrenocortical (HPA) axis respond and accomplish a number of basic and excitatory functions. The SNS innervates most regions of the body, descending from the hypothalamus and extending to most organ systems and tissues throughout the body. Activation of the SNS results in increased heart rate, blood pressure, respiration, and other functions that distribute nutrients to the body. Changes in hemodynamic responses result in greater blood flow, delivering oxygen and glucose to the cells and organs of the body. Increased respiration increases oxygen available, and other changes liberate energy into early transportable form. This permits stronger, faster responses. At the same time, SNS activity modifies the distribution of blood to specific parts of the body: constriction of some blood vessels causes reduction of blood flow to the gut, skin and reproductive systems and selective dilation of other blood vessels, resulting in increased muscle tone, strength, and performance. SNS activation as a consequence of perceived threat or demand produces an aroused, alert and strengthened organism in preparation for coping (e.g., fight or flight).

The initial arousal of the SNS is a function of the nervous system, but neural stimulation of the SNS is relatively short-lived and may not be sufficiently intense to evoke strong enough responses. To some extent, prolonged and more intense responses are associated with endocrine system release of epinephrine from the adrenal medullae and norepinephrine from the adrenal and from sympathetic neurons. The release of these hormones into circulation have the same effects as SNS arousal accomplished by direct neural stimulation, but take longer to clear and may produce a more intense response. The release of epinephrine, for example, stimulates the same heart and respiratory changes that accompany neural stimulation of the SNS, but the different mechanisms that convey these effects (e.g., receptor binding vs. synaptic transmission) alter the strength and persistence of responding. Some effects of SNS arousal appear to be exclusive to endocrine responses but, for the most part, these neuroendocrine responses work together. The HPA axis is different and, although it is also an integrated neuroendocrine response originating in the hypothalamus, it unfolds in different ways and accomplishes different things. Activity in this system is initiated by release of corticotrophin-releasing hormone (CRH) in the brain, which stimulates the pituitary to produce adrenocorticotropic hormone (ACTH), which travels to the adrenals and stimulates release of corticosteroids from the adrenal cortex. In humans, these glucocorticoids are primarily cortisol, a hormone that has important anti-inflammatory and metabolic effects. Stress appraisals are believed to be associated with CRH release, and the arousal of the HPA has been considered another principal driver of the overall stress response.

The two systems work together and provide redundant coverage of some survival functions and complementary coverage of others. The SNS and HPA differ in how responsive they are; the SNS causes measurable changes in circulating sympathetic hormones and increased cardiac and respiratory function, almost immediately after stimulation, but the HPA axis is more sluggish, taking up to 20–30 minutes to show responses after stimulation (Dickerson & Kemeny, 2004). However, the effects of SNS activation can dissipate as rapidly as they appeared, while HPA responses are more long-lived. Both are catabolic in nature, breaking down energy stores, and increasing capture and transport of oxygen and distribution of glucose to areas of the body. Each has a number of important targets and functions, some of which overlap with stress. Together, they provide the regulatory basis for the energizing effects of stress.

These systems, and the effects that they have on biology and behavior, provide a context for understanding how and why stress has a number of consequences that affect health and well-being. This basic syndrome is present in many species and the elements of response fit together so well, they appear to be linked together for some reason. These responses were most likely to have been selected because of their benefits for adaptation to the environment. Response patterns like these evolve over very long periods of time, as elements are selected or not through natural processes and survival. Those that are present in survivors (presumably some or all of them are responsible for or associated with survival) and remain in the human genome. This process began before humans had appeared and unfolded through thousands of years of human development. It is possible, and some have suggested, that because the world that was the basis for evolution of stress responses was the world of thousands of years ago, the nature of the selected responses may not be useful or adaptive in our modern world. The stressors were different and "successful" responses different as well. At the time these integrated responses evolved, the earth was likely filled with immediate threats such as those posed by predators, geological or meteorological events, famine, and the like. If the primary stressors in one's life include avoiding predators and providing food, the fight or flight responses described by Cannon (e.g., 1939) would clearly confer an advantage and facilitate survival. In modern settings, where stressors may include overload, alienation, crowding, and financial and occupational woes that ultimately may threaten one's ability to provide, the value of some of these energizing effects may be less. Although these basic responses are still useful for some stressors (e.g., sudden life threat, accidents, challenges), they may not be effective in resolving others and may give rise to persistent and/or unusually intense responses, which may damage the body and cause distress, disease and disability.

STRESS RESPONSES AND CONSEQUENCES

The activity of the stress "drivers" described above can be expected to have broad effects on the body, mood, and behavior. Generally, those may be considered to be *stress responses* or *consequences*. The distinction between them is generally derived from the relevance of the change for adaptation. Stress responses are changes, mostly mediated directly by SNS or HPA activation, that are either part of the emergency response or that are directly related to coping or adaptation to stressful circumstances. The arousal of the SNS causes, among other things, increases in blood flow, respiration, muscle tone, alertness, focused attention, and changes in patterns of blood flow. As we have noted, these changes are related to meeting the metabolic demands of strong and/or rapid responding, or to strengthening physical response, early identification of stressors, and coping. However, this arousal ordinarily causes feelings of discomfort and may affect bodily systems that are not directly related to adaptation, or may cause wear and tear on systems used too often. These latter aspects of stress are more readily considered to be consequences and form a basis for the pathophysiology of disease and mental health problems. Although the discomfort associated with stress arousal clearly motivates people to address the sources of stress, it does not directly increase ability to overcome them and may engender anxiety, depression, fear, anger, or irritability. In the workplace, this may contribute to absenteeism, poorer performance, conflict with co-workers, and the like.

Stress responses, ordinarily thought of as facilitating adaptation, may do so if the stressors in question are addressable with the kinds of physical responses selected. If the stressors are unusually strong or persistent, adaptation may not be achieved and stress responses may increase. Under these conditions, unusually intense or prolonged SNS and HPA arousal, as well as arousal of the systems of the body affected by these neuroendocrine systems, may cause stress consequences. Excessive use of these systems, often at high levels of activity, can cause aging of the cells and systems of the body. In most cases, the major sources of stress are more readily avoided, accommodated, or eliminated and responses do not engender severe consequences.

Stress and Health

It should be noted that the more widely embraced recognition of the influence of stress on health is a relatively recent advance in our conceptualization of health and illness (Baum, Gatchel, & Krantz, 1997). The forerunner of recent research on stress was Hans Selye's general adaptation syndrome (Selye, 1946), which initially highlighted the importance of environmental factors on disease. Subsequently, Lazarus and Folkman (1984) provided a more general conceptualization of stress as the physiological, psychological or mental influences that exert pressure on the organism, taxing or exceeding its capacity to respond. The emerging field of psychoneuroimmunology has also increased our understanding of the complex connections between stress and illness. This area of research has demonstrated that, during times of stress, immune functioning is changed (e.g., Ader, Felton & Cohen1990), leaving one more susceptible to minor illnesses such as the cold or flu. Psychosocial stressors that tax the immune system include major life events (such as marital discord and bereavement), as well as occupational work stressors.

Stress and Occupational Health

In terms of the cumulative "wear and tear" on physiological systems prompted by long-term overactivation of the stress response, McEwen (1998) coined the term "allostatic load." This construct refers to the costs or demands associated with adaptation. It is a cumulative load, but consists of the demands and costs of coping with discrete stressors. As a consequence it allows consideration of unique instances of stress in the context of the organism's load history. McEwen reviewed studies that showed serious negative health consequences of such allostatic load on the rest of the body. Such studies are growing in number and demonstrating health problems such as heart disease, intestinal problems, depression, PTSD, and even cancer(Wargo, 2007). For heart disease, the data are quite striking. For example, a recent study by Aboa-Éboulé, Brisson, Maunsell et al. (2007) demonstrated that chronic job strain increases the risk of a first coronary heart disease and chronic job strain after a first myocardial infarction was associated with an increased risk of recurrent coronary heart disease events. Indeed, it had been shown in numerous earlier studies that occupational job strain (consisting of a combination of high psychosocial demands and low decision-making latitude) increased the risk for a first coronary heart disease event (e.g., Alfredsson, Spetz, & Theorell, 1985; Haan, 1988; Kornitzer et al., 2006; Kuper & Marmot, 2003). In fact, one of the leading causes of the epidemic of cardiovascular disease in industrialized countries has long been shown to be due to occupational work stress (Olsen & Kristensen, 1991; Ragland et al., 1987; Schnall et al., 1990).

Relatedly, research on metabolic syndrome has also shown links between occupational stress and illness. Metabolic syndrome is a cluster of symptoms or risk factors for diabetes and heart disease, a group of predisposing factors that heighten one's risk for several illnesses. It is primarily characterized by obesity (abdominal), high levels of circulating triglycerides and cholesterol, hypertension, inflammation, and insulin resistance. Metabolic syndrome, then, is a useful and heuristic construct, and studies have reported evidence that work stress is associated with aspects of the syndrome (Brunner et al., 1997; Raikkonen, Matthews, & Kuller, 2007). Recent study of more than 10,000 men and women over a more than 10-year period found a positive relationship between chronic work stress and metabolic syndrome, defined as the cluster of symptoms noted above (Chandola, Brunner, & Marmot, 2006). These and other findings underscore the importance of work stress as a risk factor for serious chronic illness.

OCCUPATIONAL STRESS

Stress is ubiquitous in the workplace. Many jobs involve pressures to complete increasing amounts of work, and these pressures can contribute to social overload and stress (e.g., Baum et al., 1997; Cohen, 1978; Frankenhaeuser & Gardell, 1976). Resulting job pressures and social problems can cause stress directly that may also be associated with role ambiguity, role conflict and resulting conditions of absenteeism, low productivity, turnover, burnout, and, ultimately, mental and physical health problems (e.g., Kahn et al., 1964; Spielberger et al., 2003). Pressures that derive from the nature of the work being done, the worker's role in the organization, the social context or support that characterizes the worker's relationships at work, and the organizational climate or structure are all related to the propensity of an occupational setting to be stressful (e.g., Cooper & Marshall, 1976). Schultz, Feuerstein, Gatchel, and Stowell (2006)have recently provided a comprehensive review of the various models developed to account for the better understanding of the multidimensional aspects of many health problems in the work place.

Increasingly sophisticated and inclusive models of occupational stress have been developed over the last 25 years of the 20th century. Most of these generally consider four types of stressors, including: physical demands of a job; job role demands; job task demands; and social/interpersonal issues (Quick & Quick, 1984). There is overlap among these models and across these sources of demand, but brief consideration of them and integrating them with stress theory is informative.

Demand-control models represent an attempt to combine the stressful conditions associated with level of demand (work to be done), and the moderating or exacerbating influences of a worker's ability to control the rate of work or the timing of work demands (e.g., Karasek, 1979). High demand jobs are more likely to be stressful; as demand approaches excessive or unattainable levels, workers' responses are likely to become increasingly negative. However, among these workers, those who have considerable decision latitude and can control the pace or timing of work can moderate this stress. The combination of high demand and low levels of perceived control can produce stress and health-related problems (e.g., Theorell & Karasek, 1996).

This model has been adapted so that other conditions and moderating variables can be added. For example, social support has been described as a moderating factor like perceived control (Karasek et al., 1998). These modified models, together with the original formulation, has been heuristic despite difficulties in measuring decision latitude and perceived control and in validating them given the many other sources of variance in the work setting. However, it remains an intuitive, appealing characterization of work stress and provides testable hypotheses about how characteristics of work may cause disease and reduce quality of life.

A different perspective emphasizes the extent to which workers can derive reward or satisfaction from the work that they do. Siegrist (1996) suggested that when the level of reward is too low, particularly when demand is high, workers may perceive an imbalance between reward and effort, leading to stress. Finally, a number of theories suggest that interpersonal conflict, leadership mismatches, and other social conditions or characteristics of an occupational setting can cause stress and, potentially, consequences of that stress. Occupational settings are recurrent and episodic in people's lives, and persistent stress in such settings represents large, long-lasting, repetitive exposure to stressors.

Figure 9.1 depicts the general prevailing perspective on occupational stress with the important role of these mechanisms superimposed on it. Stressful conditions are appraised by individual workers and, to the extent that this appraisal suggests that they are experiencing stress, will spark a cascade of biological and psychological changes that can lead directly to stress-relate consequences. Specification of these processes and mechanisms are important in prevention of stress on the job and of interventions designed to minimize the consequences of experienced stress.

Considering this situation in the context of our discussion above, suggests ways in which job stress many cause problems for workers. The level of demand described by Karasek can be characterized from too high to too low. A worker encountering very high demand on the job many benefit from the energizing effects of stress arousal; increased alertness and mental acuity should be associated with better performance, particularly for very well-learned tasks or tasks that demand physical exertion. Whether or not these demands are so persistent as to cause unhealthy changes in mood, outlook, or physical health can be debated but, in general, for some jobs,

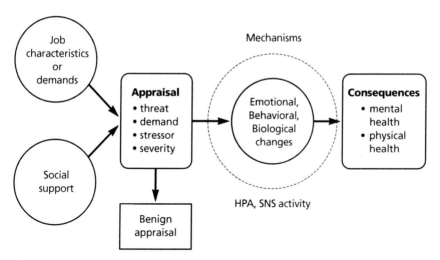

Figure 9.1 A model of work stress consequences.

the physical arousal characteristic of stress is useful in coping with demand. The "closer" one's job is to the likely conditions facing organisms as the stress response evolved, the stronger this benefit is likely to be.

The impact and control over work or work pace on the stressful nature of demand suggests that high demand and low control would produce workers who are experiencing energizing effects of stress but are in a situation in which there are few options available for coping and adaptation. It is possible in some instances that workers may find themselves pressed for decisive action in a situation where there are few or no options for action. This could result in responses "with nowhere to go", leading to chronic and sometimes excessive levels of distress and arousal.

There are stressors for which these responses also seem less appropriate or effective. Interpersonal stressors related to numbers of workers or underemployment, boredom, and stressors associated with environmental characteristics (e.g., lighting, architectural layout) seem less intense relative to the responses associated with the general stress response. Increasing strength, for example, may be irrelevant for these stressors and these effects of the stress response may contribute to excessive or prolonged physical arousal. The stress-reducing effects of exercise may in part be due to its value in releasing this pooled, unused, energy. However, coping responses that may be useful in reducing the effects of such mismatches may provide ample opportunity for adaptation.

Regardless of whether the general stress response is relevant to effective coping with a stressor, there are consequences whenever these responses are aroused. Quick adaptation will neutralize these changes, often before they can exert any effects, but to the extent that stress is experience in occupational settings, some changes will occur.

INTERVENTION IMPLICATIONS

In addition to the fact that occupational stress can lead to increased illness rates in workers, there is also another potentially significant cost to employers—higher rates of absenteeism, job turnover, job dissatisfaction and poor job performance(e.g., Kivimaki et al., 2002), as well as higher rates of substance abuse (e.g., Greenberg & Grunberg, 1995). In response to this, there have been attempts to reduce occupational stressors and improve health. One such early attempt was a program developed by the Johnson & Johnson Corporation. In 1979, they initiated a *Live for Life* (LFL) program for more than 28,000 employees in 50 different plant sites (Bly, Jones, & Richardson, 1986). The LFL program was free for the employees at company sites, and included the basic elements of a wellness program: a lifestyle assessment and general health screening; a lifestyle seminar that provided employees with an overview of the essential components of wellness and the LFL program; various classes for smoking cessation, weight loss, nutrition, stress management, yoga, alcohol education, and physical fitness; alteration of the work environment (e.g., more nutritious food in the cafeteria; exercise facilities; flexible scheduling of work time; car pools; programs to improve employee-supervisory relationships); and systematic feedback and follow-up.

A number of studies were conducted to assess the efficacy of the above program. For example, Bly et al. (1986) compared a large group of employees at LFL plants who participated in the program for two years versus employees at non-LFL plants. Results revealed significant improvements in LFL-plant employees in exercise, fitness, work satisfaction, smoking cessation, as well as decreases in coronary heart disease risk and stress. Subsequent to this study, several other large companies began introducing similar programs for their employees (e.g., New York AT&T; Blue Cross/Blue Shield), with comparable positive benefits. It should be noted, though, that such programs are "at the mercy" of economics. When the economy goes down, and companies try to reduce costs, then the first things that are cut are programs such as these that do not add anything to the "bottom line of quarterly profit earnings reports."

The significance of the above programs was the clear demonstration of how occupational stress, if adequately addressed, can be reduced, with resultant positive health outcomes. Such results again show a link, albeit indirect, between occupational stress and health consequences. Subsequently, several occupational stress researchers have delineated methods to sub-

---

TABLE 9.1   Methods to Reduce Workplace Stress

- Reduce as much as possible physical work stressors such as noise, harsh lighting, crowding, temperature extremes, etc.
- Minimize unpredictability and ambiguity in expected performance tasks and levels.
- Involve workers as much as possible in important decisions that may affect workplace stress (e.g., control over certain job characteristics such as the order and rate at which certain tasks are performed).
- Make jobs-tasks as interesting and rewarding as possible.
- Provide workers with social and recreational facilities, in order to development and promote meaningful social support, during break times, lunch time and after-hours free time.
- Provide tangible rewards to workers for good work (such monetary rewards as bonuses, time off, etc.)
- Train supervisors to monitor potential signs of stress (e.g., apathy, anger, absenteeism, boredom, carelessness), and then intervene before the stress becomes problematic.

---

stantially reduce workplace stressors. Taylor (2006) has summarized these methods (Table 9.1).

SUMMARY AND CONCLUSIONS

In this Chapter, we have reviewed the extant scientific literature on the important biobehavioral mechanisms involved in occupational stress, health and quality of life. The significant role played by stress in the workplace was discussed, especially as it affects physiological functioning, such as CNS activity, SNS arousal, HPA axis reactivity, and the potential for excessive allostatic load on the body. Such excessive allostatic loads can result in serious negative health consequences, such as cardiovascular disease, intestinal problems, depression, and even cancer. Research demonstrating this toxic occupational stress-illness relationship was reviewed.

A number of models of occupational stress have been developed over the years that have emphasized four major types of stressors: physical demands of the job; job role demands; job task demands; and social/interpersonal issues at the workplace. These often overlap, but they all have been found to individually contribute to the degree of occupational stress that can be experienced by a worker. A general perspective of how these major types of stressors impact biobehavioral mechanisms was presented. Finally, the potential intervention implications of this accumulated scientific knowledge base was discussed. Successful interventions introduced into the workplace, as well as research summarizing methods to reduce workplace stress, have provided additional empirical support (albeit indirect) for the strong link between occupational stress and negative health consequences.

REFERENCES

Aboa-Eboule, C., Brisson, C., Maunsell, E., Masse, E., Bourbonnais, R., Vezina, M., et al. (2007). Job strain and risk of acute recurrent coronary heart disease events. *JAMA, 298*(14), 1652–1660.

Ader, R., Felton, D., & Cohen, N. (Eds.). (1990). *Psychoneuroimmunology.* San Diego: Academic Press.

Alfredsson, L., Spetz, C. L., & Theorell, T. (1985). Type of occupation and near-future hospitalization for myocardial infarction and some other diagnoses. *International Journal of Epidemiology, 14*(3), 378–388.

Baum, A., Gatchel, R. J., & Krantz, D. S. (Eds.). (1997). *An Introduction to Health Psychology* (3rd ed.). New York: McGraw-Hill.

Bly, J., Jones, R., & Richardson, J. (1986). Impact of worksite health promotion on health care costs and utilization. *JAMA, 256*, 3235–3240.

Brunner, E. J., Marmot, M. G., Nanchahal, K., Shipley, M. J., Stansfield, S. A., Juneja, M., et al. (1997). Social inequality in coronary risk: Central obesity and the metabolic syndrome. *Diabetologia, 40*(11), 1341–1349.

Cannon, W. B. (1939). *The Wisdom of the Body.* New York: Norton.

Caplan, R. D., Cobb, S., & French, J. R. J. (1975). Relationships of cessation of smoking with job stress, personality and social support. *Journal of Applied Psychology, 60*(2), 211–219.

Chandola, T., Brunner, E. J., & Marmot, M. (2006). Chronic stress at work and the metabolic syndrome: A prospective study. *British Medical Journal, 332*, 521–525.

Cohen, S. (1978). Environmental load and the allocation of attention. In A. Baum, J. E. Singer & S. Valins (Eds.), *Advances in Environmental Psychology* (pp. 1–30). Hillsdale, NJ: Fullbaum.

Cooper, C. L., & Marshall, J. (1976). Occupational source of stress: A review of the literature relating to coronary heart disease and mental ill health. *Journal of Occupational Psychology, 49*(1), 11–28.

Dickerson, S. S., & Kemeny, M. E. (2004). Adult stressors and cortisol responses: A theoretical integration and synthesis of laboratory research. *Psychological Bulletin, 130*, 355–391.

Frankenhaeuser, M., & Gardell, B. (1976). Underload and overload in working life: Outline of a multidisciplinary approach. *Journal of Human Stress, 2*(3), 35–46.

Frankenhaeuser, M., Lundgerg, U., & Forsman, L. (1980). Note on arousing Type A persons by depriving them of work. *Journal of Psychosomatic Research, 24*(1), 45–47.

Greenberg, E. S., & Grunberg, I. (1995). Work alienation and problem alcohol behavior. *Journal of Health and Social Behavior, 36*, 83–102.

Haan, M. N. (1988). Job strain and ischaemic heart disease. *Annals of Clinical Research, 20*(1–2), 143–145.

Kahn, R. L., Wolfe, D. M., Quinn, R. P., Snock, J. D., & Rosenthal, R. A. (1964). *Organizational Stress: Studies in Role Conflict and Ambiguity.* New York: John Wiley & Sons.

Karasek, R. A. (1979). Job demands, job decision latitude and mental strain. *Administrative Science Quarterly, 24*, 285–307.

Karasek, R. A., Brisson, C., Kawakami, N., Houtman, I., Bongers, P., & Amick, B. (1998). The job content questionnaire (JCQ): An instrument for internationally comparative assessments of psychosocial job characteristics. *Journal of Occupational Health Psychology, 3*(4), 322–355.

Kivimaki, M., Leino-Arjas, P., Luukkonen, R., Riihimaki, H., Vahtera, J., & Kirjonen, J. (2002). Work stress and risk of cardiovascular mortality: Prospective cohort study of industrial employees. *British Medical Journal, 325*(7369), 857.

Kornitzer, M., deSmet, P., Sans, S., Dramaix, M., C., B., DeBacker, G., et al. (2006). Job stress and major coronary events: Results from the Job Stress, Absenteeism and Coronary Heart Disease in Europe study. *European Journal of Cardiovascular Prevention and Rehabilitation 13*(5), 695–704.

Kuper, H., & Marmot, M. (2003). Job strain, job demands, decision latitude, and risk of coronary heart disease within the Whitehall II study. *Journal of Epidemiology and Community Health, 57*(2), 147–153.

Lazarus, R. S., & Folkman, S. (1984). *Stress, Appraisal and Coping.* New York: Springer.

McEwen, B. S. (1998). Protective and damaging effects of stress mediators. *New England Journal of Medicine, 338,* 171–179.

Nelson, D. L., & Simmons, B. L. (2003). Health psychology and work stress: A more positive approach. In J. C. Quick & L. E. Tetrick (Eds.), *Handbook of Occupational Health Psychology* (pp. 97–119). Washington, DC: American Psychological Association.

Olsen, O., & Kristensen, T. S. (1991). Impact of work environment on cardiovascular diseases in Denmark. *Journal of Epidemiology and Community Health, 45,* 4–10.

Quick, J. C., & Quick, J. D. (1984). *Organizational Stress and Preventive Management.* New York: McGraw Hill.

Ragland, D. R., Winkleby, M. A., Schwalbe, J., Holman, B. L., Morse, L., Syme, S. L., et al. (1987). Prevalence of hypertension in bus drivers. *International Journal of Epidemiology, 16*(2), 208–214.

Raikkonen, K., Matthews, K. A., & Kuller, L. H. (2007). Depressive symptoms and stressful life events predict metabolic syndrome among middle-aged women. *Diabetes Care, 30,* 872–877.

Schnall, P. L., Pleper, C., Schwartz, J. E., Karasek, R. A., Schlussel, Y., Devereux, R. B., et al. (1990). The relationship between "job strain," workplace diastolic blood pressure, and left ventricular mass index. *JAMA, 263*(14), 1929–1935.

Schultz, I. Z., Feuerstein, M., Gatchel, R. J., & Stowell, A. W. (2006). *Models of Return to Work in Pain Disability.* Unpublished manuscript, Milan, Italy.

Selye, H. (1946). The general adaptation syndrome and the diseases of adaptation. *Journal of Clinical Endocrinology, 6,* 117.

Siegrist, J. (1996). Stressful work, self-experience, and cardiovascular disease prevention. In K. Orth-Gomer & N. Schneiderman (Eds.), *Behavioral Medicine Approaches to Cardiovascular Disease Prevention.* Hillsdale, NJ: Lawrence Erlbaum Associates.

Spielberger, C. D., Vagg, P. R., & Wasala, C. F. (2003). Occupational stress: Job pressures and lack of support. In J. C. Quick & L. E. Tetrick (Eds.), *Handbook of Occupational Health Psychology* (pp. 185–200). Washington, DC: American Psychological Association.

Taylor, S. E. (2006). *Health Psychology* (6th ed.). New York: McGraw-Hill.

Theorell, T., & Karasek, R. A. (1996). Current issues relating to psychological job strain and cardiovascular disease research. *Journal of Occupational Health Psychology, 1*(1), 9–26.

Wargo, E. (2007). Understanding the have-knots: The role of stress in just about everything. *Association for Psychological Sciences: Observer, 20*(11), 18–23.

CHAPTER 10

QUALITATIVE AND QUANTITATIVE METHODS IN OCCUPATIONAL-STRESS RESEARCH

Irvin Sam Schonfeld
City College and the Graduate Center of the City University of New York

Edwin Farrell
City College of the City University of New York

ABSTRACT

The chapter examines the ways in which qualitative and quantitative methods support each other in research on occupational stress. Qualitative methods include (a) eliciting from unconstrained descriptions of workers' experiences, (b) careful first-hand observations at the workplace, and (c) participant-observers describing "from the inside" a particular work experience. The paper shows how qualitative research stimulates theory development, hypothesis generation, and the identification of job stressors and coping responses. The limitations of qualitative research, particularly in the area of verification, are also described.

Stress and Quality of Working Life, pages 183–204
Copyright © 2009 by Information Age Publishing
183

The purpose of this chapter is to advance the idea that qualitative methods and more highly controlled quantitative methods applied to occupational-stress research, together, can provide a clearer picture of the stress process. Plewis and Mason (2005) wrote that quantitative and qualitative methods represent "mutually informing" strands of research. Hugentobler, Israel, and Schurman (1992) underlined the view that every method has weaknesses, and that by applying manifold methods to the study of occupational stress, weaknesses in one method will be compensated for by strengths in other methods. They go on to show how qualitative and quantitative methods converge in identifying the sources of stress in workers in a manufacturing firm. Qualitative research, moreover, can be useful to quantitative researchers in instrument development (Blase, 1986; Schonfeld, 2006b).

Qualitative methods, particularly methods associated with grounded theory (Glaser & Strauss, 1967), emphasize the emergence from data of theoretically important categories as well as hypotheses bearing on the relations among those categories. There is no dearth of literature on using multiple methods (Cresswell, 2003; Tashakkori & Teddlie, 2003). Smith (2006), justifying the application of multiple methodologies in educational research, points out that "any methodology has inherent deficiencies and fails to capture the chaos, complexity, and contextuality of applied fields such as education" (p. 458). We would add the field of occupational-stress research. Methods must fit the research questions. It is appropriate to use survey methods, for instance, when one wants to quantify variables in the occupational-stress context. To characterize descriptively the intensity of work-related stressors experienced by individual workers, however, qualitative methods may be profitably used (Jex, Adams, Elacqua, & Lux, 1997).

There are at least three types of qualitative methods that have been employed in occupational-stress research. The first, and most commonly used, method involves having members of occupational groups describe, in their own words—in writing or orally—their everyday work experiences. This type of method has been applied to a variety of occupation roles (Browner, Ellis, Ford, Silsby, Tampoya, & Yee, 1987; Büssing & Glaser, 1999; Carradice, Shankland, & Beail, 2002; Dewe, 1989; Dick, 2000; Gomme & Hall, 1995; Goodwin, Mayo, & Hill, 1997; Hugentobler et al., 1992; Hutchinson, 1987; Isaksen, 2000; Jex et al., 1997; Kahn, 1993; Keenan & Newton, 1985; Khowaja, Merchant, & Hirani, 2005; Kidd, Scharf, & Veazie, 1996; Lee, 1998; MacDonald & Korabik, 1991; Maki, Moore, Grunberg, & Greenberg, 2005; Mears & Finlay, 2005; Molapo, 2001; Noonan, Gallor, Hensler-McGinnis, Fassinger, Wang, & Goodman, 2004; Polanyi & Tompa, 2004; Reid et al., 1999; Tewksbury, 1993; Tracy, Myers, & Scott, 2006; Weyman, Clarke, & Cox, 2003) including that of teachers (e.g., Blase, 1986; Blase & Pajak, 1986; Engelbrecht, Oswald, Swart, & Eloff, 2003; Farber, 1991; Farber, 2000; Ginsberg, Schwartz, Olson, & Bennett, 1987; Griffith & Brem, 2004; Mykletun, 1985; Schonfeld & Ruan, 1991; Schonfeld & Santiago, 1994; Smith & Smith, 2006; Steggerda, 2003; Younghusband, 2008). In this type of qualitative research, workers' descriptions of their working conditions would not be constrained to fit the response alternatives found in structured interviews and questionnaires, the stock-in-trade of quantitatively oriented occupational-stress investigators.

The second method involves investigators who situate themselves in a workplace (without obtaining a position in the workplace), and observe, first-hand, workers on the job (e.g., Ginsberg et al., 1987; Gomme & Hall, 1995; Kahn, 1993; Kaiman, 1994; Molapo, 2001; Tracy et al., 2006). The third method involves participant observation. Here the researcher obtains the kind of job (Browner et al., 1987; Hutchinson, 1987; Mears & Finlay, 2005; Palmer, 1983; Tewksbury, 1993; see particularly Sachar, 1991) that he or she intends to study, and describes elements of the occupational stress process from the inside. Sometimes the participant observer obtains a partial work role that includes some but not all job tasks (Browner et al., 1987; C. H. Browner, personal communication, September 20, 2007). Although this first-hand experience on the job provides an insider's perspective, participant observers, like the investigators in the second category, also closely observe other workers first hand. Although some investigators label as participant observation, scrutiny at close quarters without necessarily occupying the same occupational role as the workers under study (e.g., Gomme & Hall, 1995; Tracy et al., 2006), we do not.

Teaching is a particularly stressful occupation because the profession is built on a fundamental conflict, namely, the tension between the socializing agent and those being socialized (Mykletun, 1985). The examples to follow will show how qualitative research helps to add theoretical depth to findings obtained from a longitudinal study of new teachers. The qualitative research includes teachers' descriptions of their jobs and a participant observer's description of her year as a junior high school math teacher.

A QUANTITATIVELY ORIENTED APPROACH TO MEASURING STRESSFUL SCHOOL CONDITIONS

To describe how qualitative research is utilized in a research program devoted to teachers, we first briefly describe the series of quantitatively oriented studies and measurement concerns related to those studies. Within the framework of two cross-sectional studies of veteran teachers (Schonfeld, 1990, 1994) and one longitudinal study of newly appointed female teachers (Schonfeld, 1992a, 2001), one of us developed self-report instruments that were designed to assess teachers' exposures to adverse working conditions.

The occupational-stress scales have solid measurement characteristics. The alpha coefficients of scales measuring episodically occurring work events and ongoing job conditions were satisfactory. In the veteran- and new-teacher samples, the occupational-stress scales were more highly related to each other than they were to a measure of non-work stressors. In the longitudinal study of new teachers, workplace scales administered during the fall term demonstrated convergent and discriminant validity: the fall-term workplace measures were more highly related to spring-term depressive symptoms and job satisfaction four and a half months later than to summer, pre-employment depressive symptoms and anticipatory levels of job satisfaction, measured four and a half months earlier (Schonfeld, 2000). Compared to other measures found in the occupational stress literature, the teacher stressor measures were relatively uncontaminated by negative affectivity or prior psychological distress (Schonfeld, 1992b, 1996).

Like qualitatively oriented researchers, quantitatively oriented investigators are concerned with the richness and informativeness of the data they collect. Quantitatively oriented investigators have shown great concern about the value and accuracy of both "objective" and self-report data, and have thought carefully about the best ways to ensure the validity of quantitative data (Frese & Zapf, 1994; Kasl, 1987). In view of these considerations, one of us secured official, objective data bearing on the quality of the workplaces of the new teachers who were employed in New York City public schools. The data included the school-by-school rates of assaults, robberies, and sex offenses against teachers. One of the project's aims was to link the official data, which were independent of the responses of the New York City participants in the longitudinal study, to various outcome measures, including depressive symptoms and job satisfaction. Interestingly, the objective data proved to be of little merit. An audit of the official data revealed widespread underreporting by administrators who were charged with officially recording and aggregating crimes occurring in the City's schools (Dillon, 1994); the problem of underreporting violent incidents continues to occur in New York City schools (Gootman, 2007) and across the country (Schonfeld, 2006a). Information (Sachar, 1991; Schonfeld, 1992b) obtained independently of audits was consistent with the view that there is serious underreporting of violent incidents. This situation amounted to an instance in which self-report data that became part of the abovementioned episodic and ongoing stressor scales were of superior quality than so-called objective data.

The longitudinal research on new teachers identified sizable mean differences in depressive symptoms and job satisfaction among new women teachers confronting different levels of adversity in working conditions (Schonfeld, 2001). Teachers who frequently faced highly aggressive and defiant youngsters were considerably more likely to show higher depressive symptom levels and diminished job satisfaction compared to their colleagues who worked in more pacific circumstances. Importantly, these differences were largely independent of the women's (a) pre-employment symptom profiles, (b) anticipatory levels of job satisfaction measured prior to their entry into the teaching profession, and (c) stressors occurring outside of work.

QUALITATIVE DATA THAT ENRICH
THE QUANTITATIVE DATA

As a supplement to the longitudinal study, the new teachers were given an opportunity to write, with no constraints, about their work experiences. As the longitudinal study progressed, hundreds of pages of the teachers' written descriptions of their work lives accumulated.

Given the labor required by the quantitative side of the research, a quantitatively oriented investigator may initially view qualitative research as an interested spectator; it is something best done by ethnographers who seek to describe diverse subcultures. By contrast, the research activities of a quantitative investigator are best devoted to scale construction, power analyses, the writing of computer programs to identify response sets, etc., in adherence to the methodological canons of quantitative research. How does one assess the reliability of workers' characterizations of their phenomenal worlds? Despite the difficulties involved in "processing" the qualitative data, a reading of the teachers' descriptions proved to be highly compelling and demanded a closer look.

The qualitative data collected to supplement the quantitative research on new teachers provided a detailed examination of the transactions occurring in schools (Schonfeld & Santiago, 1994). These data vividly depict the working conditions that give rise to psychological distress in teachers. For example, a former elementary school teacher, a participant in the longitudinal study, wrote:

> I loved the teaching profession but because of my experience at P.S. xxx I doubt I'll ever teach again. If I do, it will not be for the New York City Board of Education. My present job requires me to work many more hours and much harder but I am a much happier person. The stress caused by teaching a rough class is incredible. I used to come home crying every night.

Crying can be construed as a symptom of depression; it is captured in items on the Center for Epidemiologic Studies Depression Scale (Radloff, 1977) and the Depression subscale of the SCL-90 (Derogatis, Lipman, & Covi, 1973). This teacher's words and the words of many other teachers richly describe the human context to which the quantitative findings pertain. Consider the words of the following elementary school teacher:

> The students in my school are physically violent. It seems that fighting is the only solution to their problems. I was previously working in this school as a substitute teacher. It is discouraging and depressing to me to see that even first graders are fighting. There seems to be no love, friendship, or caring going on among the students.

Notice that she used the terms "discouraging" and "depressing" to describe how she feels about the student-to-student transactions she observed as part of her job. The longitudinal study found that teachers in the most dangerous, worst-run schools manifested high levels of depressive symptoms (Schonfeld, 2000).

Also consider the fear in the next teacher and its impact on her health and life decisions:

> One of the worst classes I have is a fourth grade Gates class[1] in which the children are around age 13. They are very rough children and I have to break up fights regularly. Last week as I was getting the children ready to be dismissed, an object which looked like a gun fell out of a child's pocket. I was in a panic until the boy picked it up turned it over and it was red and purple. In this class I would not have been surprised if it were a real gun. Weapons are constantly being taken away from children in this class. Also lately there has been a big security problem in the building. Several times intruders have entered the building. Last week children reported being threatened by a man with a knife and a gun. Since I have been teaching my health has declined. I am constantly sick with whatever the kids have and I have developed an ulcer-like condition. Last year I was perfectly healthy. I have decided that since I have the grades, in two years I will start law school.

Participant-observer research, another form of qualitative research, also sheds light on teachers' working conditions. Emily Sachar (1991), who had been a journalist, left her job at a newspaper to obtain a teaching position in one of New York City's more chaotic schools, Walt Whitman Junior High School in Brooklyn. As a participant observer, she wrote what amounts to an ethnographic account of one year in the life of a mathematics teacher. She described a high level of day-to-day disrespect and insult:

> My problems with Jimmy promptly worsened. By the third week, he had a ritual prank—raising his hand constantly to pose questions that had nothing to do with class work. I fell for the bait every time. His questions were tame enough at first. "Mrs. Sachar, could I get a drink? I'm gagging in my throat," or "Mrs. Sachar, how about a night of no homework?" Their innocent tone did not last long. One day after waving his hand frantically, Jimmy asked,

"Mrs. Sachar, where do babies come from?" Calmly I told him to ask his health instructor. Another day he tried, "Mrs. Sachar, do you like sex?....Do you have orgasms, Mrs. Sachar?...Do you masturbate Mrs. Sachar?" (pp. 76-77)[2]

This student was not a rarity.

Later Sachar (1991) wrote:

We were not officially informed of the gun incident until the monthly faculty conference on January 23rd [about three weeks after the incident occurred]. Then we learned that one student had been inches away from death in the accident. Winfield [the principal] told us that a twelve-year-old boy had brought a loaded gun to school, and that it had accidentally fired in class. The bullet tore a large hole through the coat of a girl standing next to him, then ricocheted off a desk. "If the girl had larger breasts, they would have been eliminated," Winfield said, "and if she'd been turned in another direction, she'd probably be dead." (p. 146)[2]

Despite the seriousness of the situation, the principal's flippancy is evident. Sachar (1991) went on to write:

This was only the first of a series of weapons incidents. In February, one dean told me, a sixth-grade girl hit another student over the head with a hammer and was suspended for five days. A few days later, another sixth-grader brought a custom-made .410-gauge shotgun to school, and was arrested. The boy had borrowed the weapon from his fourteen-year-old brother, a drug dealer, to scare another kid at school who was "giving him trouble." A detective from the local precinct said that the boy showed no remorse: "He was quite callous, in fact." (p. 146)[2]

To compound problems like these, Sachar (1991) noted that many administrators were not forthcoming in helping the teachers tackle classroom management problems. On the other hand, Sachar (1991) observed that the administrators tended to squelch reports of school violence.

Qualitative material from Barry Farber (1991) in his book on teacher burnout depicts a young idealistic teacher working in an inner city school. Farber described her incessant problems controlling her class, the lack of help from an otherwise "caring" principal, and how "beat" she felt at the end of the day.

Sachar (1991) also described the physical toll of the job including exhaustion and other bodily complaints. She wrote, "I phoned this teacher on a Sunday to chat about the coming year and to gossip a bit about the school administration.

"'I'm in the midst of a diarrhea spell,' he said.

"'What's wrong? Did you eat something bad?'

"'You know what's wrong,' my friend said. 'I've got to go back there in two days.'

"This was a veteran teacher with a good reputation at Whitman, a man whose company I cherished during the year." Later the man reports "I feel helpless. You have a principal who says the school is great when the school stinks. He tells you about all these great programs that exist" (p. 215).[2]

Other teachers spoke of chronic depression.

MAKING SENSE OF QUALITATIVE DATA

Given the wealth of descriptive material gathered from the new teachers in the longitudinal study, the project needed a method for categorizing the teachers' writings. Brenner (2006) suggested an analytic framework for interview data consisting of five phases: transcription, description, analysis, interpretation, and display. Although she presented them as a linear progression, she emphasized that working with data is often a cyclical process. In this case, the transcription was relatively easy since the data were already written.

For the qualitative data collected in the longitudinal study, a provisional set of themes emerged "naturally" from the new teachers' writings according a method described by Farrell (1990). The readers' goal was to adhere to the principle that no preconceived theory guide this stage of the qualitative research, the readers following the groundbreaking dictum of Glaser and Strauss (1967) who advanced the view that theory arise from the data. Of course, the idea that important categories emerge from data is idealized. Popper (1963) underlined the fact that "observation is always selective," and that so much of what one observes is presupposed by a host of factors. Nonetheless, qualitative methods have a role to play in occupational-stress research.

It should, of course, be noted that qualitative researchers dispute positivist social scientists on the role of methodology. Kirk and Miller (1986) maintain that quantitative definitions of reliability and validity are rarely appropriate to the way qualitative researchers work. They argue for a theoretical rather than an apparent validity. They are less charitable when discussing reliability, calling a single method of observation continually yielding an unvarying measurement a quixotic reliability. They support linking the two concepts while realizing that there are tradeoffs between them when conducting qualitative research. Qualitative researchers lean toward validity as the more important concept with experimental controls and triangulation to increase objectivity (cf. Goodwin et al., 1997; Hugentobler et al., 1992; Kidd et al., 1996).

Notwithstanding Kirk and Miller's (1986) admonitions about reliability, Schonfeld and Santiago (1994) needed a way to make sense of hundreds of pages of teachers' descriptions of their working conditions that were collected in the context of the longitudinal study. After the initial content analysis, the two readers independently read through a series of about 75 writings, categorizing the writings by the provisional set of themes. After the readers examined their disagreements, they slightly altered the categorical scheme. The readers then proceeded to classify another series of about 75 descriptions using the revised scheme, checked how reliably they classified the writings, and made additional adjustments in the categorical scheme based on the location of disagreements. They blindly and incrementally refined the initial set of categories. With the final set of categories, the pair of readers obtained coefficient *kappas* (Cohen, 1960) of .79 or greater for every category, indicating a satisfactory level of inter-rater agreement. *All* the teachers' writings were reread and sorted on the basis of the final categorical scheme.

With rare exceptions (Isaksen, 2000; Keenan & Newton, 1985; Kidd et al., 1996; MacDonald & Korabik, 1991, Schonfeld & Santiago, 1994), among the 40 qualitatively organized studies of occupational stress that the authors reviewed, most investigators neglected to apply *kappa* to assess the reliability of their results. Kidd et al. (1996) reported on a validity check that involved the successful application of their agricultural stressor coding scheme, which they developed for one sample of farmers, to another farm sample. Goodwin et al. (1997) developed a validity check by having (1) salespersons scrutinize the transcripts of their responses to a semi-structured interview and (2) outside experts review transcripts and codes in this research on salespersons' responses to a major job stressor. Although most qualitative research is, by definition, interpretative (Erickson, 1986; Farrell, Pegero, Lindsey, & White, 1988; Rabinow & Sullivan, 1987), we suggest that some of the tools (e.g., *kappa*) employed by quantitative researchers can be used to strengthen qualitative research.

FOUR THEMES EMERGE FROM THE TEACHER DATA

Four major categories emerged from the new teachers' descriptions: (a) interpersonal tensions and lack of support among colleagues/supervisors, (b) happiness with one's job, (c) violence and other security problems, and (d) classroom management problems. Teachers' descriptions sometimes reflected more than one theme. The themes illuminate problems with which quantitatively oriented occupational-stress researchers have grappled. The first two themes to emerge from the teachers' writings accord with quantitative research literature on social support. Many new teachers described their distress when supervisors absented themselves from the supervisory role or when they obtained jobs in schools characterized by interpersonal tensions among the faculty or between faculty and administrators. By contrast, when new teachers reported being happy with their jobs, they often described the importance to their well-being and success in managing a classroom, of good relationships with colleagues and supervisors. For example, a fourth-grade Catholic school teacher wrote:

> Where I work the teachers are very close. They help each other when help is needed. There is only one [other] teacher who is also teaching for the first time and we are close. We usually talk about school and our own personal life but we don't do any recreation together.

Although some parochial schools offer important clues for improving public schools (Bryk, Lee, & Holland, 1993), the above teacher went on to complain about the difficulties she experienced in making ends meet because she earned a considerably lower salary than her public school colleagues. In general, when teachers expressed satisfaction with their jobs, they tended to mention reliable colleagues and administrators who were available to help them (Schonfeld & Santiago, 1994).

The theme of violence in the schools is particularly troubling. Violent and overly aggressive behavior is often evidenced in qualitative research on teachers (Engelbrecht et al., 2003; Ginsberg et al., 1987; Schonfeld & Santiago, 1994; Smith & Smith, 2006; Steggerda, 2003; Younghusband, 2008). Teachers reported on the personal consequences of having been victimized by violent students. Teachers also reported being affected by the *prospect* of violence even on occasions in which student violence was not in evidence. For many teachers, violence often seemed to be lurking. The picture is troubling enough to warrant public health concern.

Apart from the violence, teachers described having students who were verbally, if not physically, assaultive (recall Sachar's Jimmy). The disruption caused by the behavior of some children sabotaged lessons, causing teaching to proceed haltingly, in a stop-and-go manner, if at all. Thus even if teachers did not become victims of violence, they had to be concerned about being targets of endemically disrespectful behavior that makes managing classrooms difficult.

The qualitative findings just described suggest that if the qualitative and quantitative research traditions can be linked, a truer, more rounded picture can emerge of what it is like to work in a variety of school environments and the consequences those environments hold for teachers. The qualitative findings provide a context for the discovery (Reichenbach, 1951) of insights that contribute to a theory of job stress. Sachar's (1991) participant-observer investigation and Schonfeld and Santiago's (1994) study of teachers' descriptions of their jobs provide insights into why working in some schools may be normatively stressful. Although there are a number of different models of the stress process (Dohrenwend & Dohrenwend, 1981), a model of the stress process to emerge from the qualitative findings from both the longitudinal study and from the work of Sachar (1991) dovetails with Dohrenwend's (1979) pathogenic-triad theory of stress.

Dohrenwend (1979), in reviewing research on extreme situations, found that stressful life events can engender psychopathology in individuals in whom evidence of psychopathology had previously been absent. This is not to argue that teachers are in a position similar to that of combat infantry. Research, however, suggests that combinations of undesirable life events are particularly toxic when such events (a) are unanticipated, unscheduled, and outside the individual's control; (b) lead to physical exhaustion; and (c) reduce social support. The elements of Dohrenwend's (1979) theory of stress are well illustrated by the above examples. Clearly many teachers are affected by a dangerous level of violence in the schools that is a cause for anxiety.

It is, moreover, unlikely that academically trained individuals seeking entrance into a profession would foresee violence and endemically discourteous and disrespectful behaviors as everyday working conditions. Louis (1980) highlighted the demoralizing effect of the unrealistic expectations many new workers bring to their jobs. By contrast, among individuals entering the teaching profession only to work in the most chaotic and threatening schools, commonplace expectations regarding workplace safety and respect are not met (also see Steggerda, 2003).

Qualitative findings of the longitudinal study, more than the quantitative results, underscore the *shock* and uncontrollability of teachers' encounters with aggressive students (Schonfeld & Santiago, 1994; Smith & Smith, 2006), showing the applicability of Dohrenwend's (1979) theory of stress to teaching. Sachar's (1991) participant-observer findings also highlight this sense of shock in encountering so much violence and disrespect as a normal and, too often, uncontrollable part of one's work role. The sense of violence and shock is illustrated by an incident, this time occurring in the neighborhood of Sachar's (1991) school, in which one Walt Whitman student, who began by bullying another Whitman student, set the other student on fire, severely burning, and almost killing, the victim. The appalling event brought to mind the words of the school's namesake, "I mourn'd, and yet shall mourn with ever-returning spring."

Some of the above described qualitative findings highlight another element of the pathogenic triad. Although examples cited earlier suggest that exhaustion can accompany the job, such exhaustion does not betray ill conditioning on the part of the teacher incumbent. One new male teacher, who had contributed qualitative data to a pilot study, had been an intercollegiate trackman and cross-country runner. He obtained a job in a New

York City junior high school in which only a small proportion of students read on grade level. He reported going to sleep just after he got home from work at about four o'clock in the afternoon. He attributed his fatigue to two sources: the energy he expended trying to maintain order within his classes and the piercing noise, as manifest in students' loud talking and yelling, that permeated the school building throughout the day. One of the school's deans, a former starter on a major college football team, evolved into a three-pack-a-day chain smoker.

As mentioned earlier, teachers in the longitudinal study who reported satisfaction with work often indicated that collegial relations with coworkers and, sometimes, administrators contributed to that sense of satisfaction. By contrast, other beginning teachers who participated in the longitudinal study complained about being cut off from their more senior colleagues. They described administrators who rarely helped them develop the skills required to manage classrooms. Sachar (1991) described a principal who rarely helped new teachers adjust to the classroom, frequently isolating himself in his office, and a dean who seldom helped teachers with the violent students who were his responsibility to discipline; the principal's lack of involvement continued for years after Sachar left the school, ending only when he was relieved of his job owing to his inaction over a case of sexual molestation (Steinberg, 1997). Events and conditions that deny the individual support are part of the pathogenic triad.

Sachar's (1991) insider's description of an urban public school and qualitative data from the longitudinal study pointedly indicate that many of the difficulties teachers encounter come as a package, if not as a triad. One observes in the same school many troubled and violent students who block effective instruction for all students as well as imperil everyone's safety, administrators who do not extend themselves to help teachers gain skill and competence, and a generally poorly managed, isolating, dirty, and noisy environment, a workplace from which teachers return home drained. Qualitative research thus paints a picture that suggests that some school environments are quite toxic to any teaching candidate with ordinary expectations about starting out in an honorable profession.

THE STRENGTHS AND LIMITATIONS OF QUALITATIVE AND QUANTITATIVE RESEARCH

Qualitative research will not help investigators test hypotheses derived from theory, nor of course is it meant to. The history of science, however, indicates that the strength of qualitative observation—we include uncontrolled, practical observation—is in theory development and hypothesis generation. We highlight four examples from diverse areas of medicine to underline this point. We chose medicine because of the value the research has had for the well-being of large numbers of people. First, *en route* to mankind's conquest of smallpox, what might termed qualitative observations, often made by ordinary people long before Jenner's discovery of a vaccine, suggested the proto-hypothesis that inoculating susceptible individuals with small amounts of secretion from the pustules of affected individuals affords the inoculees immunity from the disease (Hopkins, 1983; Razzell, 1977). This experience contributed to the development of a theory of contagion, and helped undermine rival humoral theories of smallpox (Miller, 1957).

Similarly, the experience of sailors dating back to the time of Francis Drake suggested that fresh fruit, particularly citrus fruit, prevents and cures scurvy (Carpenter, 1986). Carpenter (1986) showed that from the beginning of the seventeenth century, the men of the Hudson's Bay Company kept scurvy to a minimum by sending small amounts of lime juice with its crews. We can call this an action hypothesis based on qualitative observational data. When fresh vegetables were unavailable, fresh game supplied by Hudson's Bay hunters throughout the year, kept scurvy at bay. In the eighteenth and nineteenth centuries there were a number of ill conceived theories of the disease (e.g., cold moist climates, potassium deficiencies) that led to ineffective treatments and preventive measures. Later, highly controlled research, built upon the clues provided by earlier uncontrolled observation, linked vitamin C to the prevention of scurvy.

The discovery of fluorides' protective effects began with uncontrolled observations by dental practitioners who first described brown mottled tooth enamel in children living in a region of the Rocky Mountains (Black & McKay, 1916). Black and McKay (1916) believed they identified a new kind of dental pathology, noting the "general evil effect of the countenance of the individual" (p. 142). They observed that the amount of mottling was directly related to the age at which each child entered the region and that "as to caries, the teeth of these children compare favorably with those of other communities where endemic mottled enamel is unknown" (p. 145). More than ten years later the mottling was linked to the presence of fluorides in the drinking water as well as to a lower incidence of dental caries (Ainsworth, 1932). These early observations paved the way for controlled hypothesis-based research on the protection from dental caries fluorides afford (Ward & Miller, 1978).

In psychiatry, uncontrolled, clinical observation first identified infantile autism (Kanner, 1943), a syndrome reflecting "the presence of markedly abnormal development in social interaction and communication and a markedly restricted repertoire of activity and interests" (American Psychiatric Association, 1994, p. 66). The syndrome is distinct from other debilitating mental disorders including schizophrenia. Kanner's case study description of the syndrome has been well supported in the research literature (Rimland, 1964; Rutter & Schopler, 1979). Kanner's description of the very-early developing and highly unusual behavior associated with the disorder has suggested an organic cause (Rimland, 1964).

These examples from the history of science emphasize, albeit in different contexts, an idea underlined by Kidd et al. (1996), namely, that "qualitative methods are preferred to quantitative methods when there is little information known about a phenomenon, the applicability of what is known has not been examined, or when there is reason to doubt the accepted knowledge about a given phenomenon" (p. 225; cf. Goodwin et al., 1997). By contrast, when qualitative methods are employed in a field that has been well explored, it is likely that the theoretical insights that emerge from the data will make contact with existing theories.

Popper (1963) was right about the selective nature of observation. It is too unrealistic to hold to the view that theory will emerge from qualitative data untainted by the investigator's prior exposure to existing theory and research findings. For example, in research on stressors affecting farmers, a coding scheme for stressors was developed based on a coding dictionary developed from the extant literature on agricultural stressors (Kidd et al, 1996). Blase (1986; Blase & Pajak, 1986) in his qualitative research on teachers found that work overload is a prominent stressor although the quantitatively oriented literature has viewed overload this way in research antedating his. Despite adhering to the Glaser and Strauss's (1967) canon of letting theoretically important categories emerge from the data, Goodwin et al. (1997), in one of the methodologically soundest qualitative studies we reviewed, found problem- and emotion-focused coping strategies in salespeople's responses to major account loss, coping strategies long known to the quantitatively oriented investigators. Schonfeld and Santiago (1994) anticipated stress-related themes as best they could but "took care to avoid imposing [existing theory]" on the data. Schonfeld and Santiago were aware that they should enter the qualitative phase of the research with an open mind and let themes and theory emerge from the data *á la* Glaser and Strauss (1967); they were nonetheless aware of the existence of Dohrenwend's (1979) pathogenic triad as well as other models of the stress process. There is thus an unavoidable tension in qualitative research.

There are two other limitations to qualitative research that need to be mentioned. One is the problem of reactivity. People who are observed sometimes change in response to the presence of an observer (Shai, 2002). The second is the concern that the researcher may overidentify with the workers being observed. The first author was once a mathematics teacher, and was concerned about the potential for his overidentifying with teachers, which in turn would affect his interpretation of the qualitative findings. One way to at least partly overcome these limitations is through the deployment of multiple observers and multiple interpreters, and the subjecting of hypotheses generated by qualitative research to rigorous testing using quantitative methods.

Qualitative research nonetheless is valuable, even in fields where much is already known. Insights from qualitative research can call attention to new ways of categorizing data when the data are relatively unstructured (Blase & Pajak, 1986). Even in well trodden avenues of research, qualitative methods can provide surprising new ideas. Qualitative methods can identify important occupational stressors that research has overlooked. For example, incidents involving time wasting among engineers (Keenan & Newton, 1985) and difficulties women managers have in motivating subordinates (MacDonald & Korabik, 1991) are stressors that previous research had missed. Qualitative research has helped to identify coping responses such as self-care activities in nurses (Hutchinson, 1987) that previous research has missed. Whether in well-studied areas or new areas of research, qualitative methods can help investigators understand the meaning and intensity stressful incidents hold for workers (Dewe, 1989; Dick, 2000; Isaksen, 2000; Jex et al., 1997; Polanyi & Tompa, 2004; Steggerda, 2003), helping to lay a foundation for hypothesis testing and scale construction in quantitative research.

It should be noted that both quantitative and qualitative data have been misinterpreted. Gould (1981) gives myriad examples of the former happening in his survey of the early research on human intelligence and race. An example of the latter error comes from Kanner (1943, 1949) who described the parents of autistic children as extremely cold and undemonstrative; in the popular press he went as far as to describe them as "just happening to defrost enough to produce a child" (The child is father, 1960, p. 78). Even if Kanner's observations were accurate, quantitative research shows that the observations would only apply to Kanner's clinical sample, and would be unrepresentative of the population of parents of autistic children.[3] A good deal of theorizing followed Kanner's papers suggesting that parental personality and behavior contributed to the etiology of the disorder (Cantwell, Baker, & Rutter, 1979; McAdoo & DeMeyer, 1979). Although the preponderance of evidence from rigorously designed, quantitatively organized studies is much more compatible with biological than psychological causal theories of autism (Dawson & Castelloe, 1992; Dawson & Osterling, 1997; Rutter & Schopler, 1979), an unfortunate effect of psychogenic theories that precipitated out of qualitative observational research is that of adding to the distress of parents of mentally disabled children, by falsely suggesting to the parents that their defective caregiving gave rise to their children's disability (Rimland, 1964).

This paper advances the view that qualitative observation and quantitative methods in research on occupational stress help investigators push toward a common goal, namely, understanding, and doing something about, the stressors affecting workers. The history of scientific research teaches that uncontrolled, observational inquiry has contributed significantly to theories of the etiology of physical and mental disorder. Teachers' and participant-observers' descriptions of day-to-day work activities have contributed to theories of teacher stress (Jackson, 1968; Kohl, 1976).

It is, however, important to emphasize the limits of both qualitative observational and quantitative research. Qualitative research should not substitute for appropriate quantitative methods of verification; qualitative research is ill suited for hypothesis testing. Consider the damage done by qualitative researchers (e.g., Bettelheim, 1967) who, on the basis of uncontrolled, clinical-observational evidence, wrongly attributed autism to deviant parental behavior (see Pollak, 1997) or mistakenly attributed schizophrenia to "the severe warp and early rejection" of important figures such as the so-called "schizophrenogenic mother" (Fromm-Reichmann, 1948). Qualitative research can be helpful in contexts of discovery; quantitative research is more applicable to understanding measurable differences in discreet phenomena than to "thick descriptions" (Geertz, 1973) of workers in stress-producing settings. At the same time, we stress that it would be unfortunate to write off quantitative methods as a source of theoretical insight. Quantitative methods also play an important role in the context of discovery. For example, Trow (1957) pointed out that Durkheim's (1897/1951) crude quantitative data, data that were far removed from the experiential context, added "much to our understanding of some of the most subtle and complex aspects of social life" (p. 35).

The four themes that emerged from the examination of the qualitative data which the teacher studies produced were incorporated into research questions relevant to the analyses of the quantitative data generated by the longitudinal study (Schonfeld, 2001). Both the contexts of discovery and verification are essential to the research process (Reichenbach, 1951). We advance the view that in occupational-stress research qualitative methods can be helpful in the context of discovery because such methods can contribute to (a) theory development, (b) hypothesis generation, (c) the identification of heretofore unidentified stressors and coping responses, and (d) a rich description of stressful transactions that humanize what quantitatively oriented researchers endeavor to study.

ACKNOWLEDGMENT

Preparation of the paper was supported by NIOSH/CDC grants no. 1 01 OH02571-01 to -06 and PSC-CUNY Award Program grants nos. 667401, 668419, 669416, 661251, and 63593. We extend special notes of thanks to Phillip Morgan, Sigmund Tobias, and George Schonfeld. All correspondence concerning the paper should be sent to Irvin Schonfeld, Dept. of Psychology, City College of the City University of New York, New York, NY 10031 or to the email address ischonfeld@ccny.cuny.edu.

REFERENCES

Ainsworth, N. J. (1932). Mottled teeth. *British Dental Journal, 55,* 233–250.

American Psychiatric Association. (1994). *Diagnostic and statistical manual of mental and disorders* (4th ed.). Washington, DC: Author.

Bettelheim, B. (1967). *The empty fortress: Infantile autism and the birth of the self.* New York: Free Press.

Black, G. V., & McKay, F. S. (1916). Mottled teeth; endoic developmental imperfection of the enamel. *Dental Cosmos, 58,* 129–156.

Blase, J. J. (1986). A qualitative analysis of sources of teacher stress: Consequences for performance. *American Educational Research Journal, 23,* 13–40.

Blase, J. J., & Pajak, E. F. (1986). The impact of teachers' work life on personal life: A qualitative analysis. *Alberta Journal of Educational Research, 32,* 307–322.

Brenner, M. E. (2006). Interviewing in educational research. In J.L. Green, G. Camilli, & P. B. Elmore (Eds.), *Handbook of complementary methods in education research* (pp. 357–370). Mahwah, NJ: Erlbaum.

Browner, C. H., Ellis, K. A., Ford, T., Silsby, J., Tampoya, J., & Yee, C. (1987). Stress, social support, and health of psychiatric technicians in a state facility. *Mental Retardation, 25,* 31–38

Bryk, A. S., Lee, V. E., & Holland, P. B. (1993). *Catholic schools and the common good.* Cambridge, MA: Harvard University Press.

Büssing, A., & Glaser, J. (1999). Work stressors in nursing in the course of redesign: Implications for burnout and interactional stress. *European Journal of Work and Organizational Psychology, 8,* 401–426.

Cantwell, D. P., Baker, L., & Rutter, M. (1979). Family factors. In M. Rutter & E. Schopler (Eds.), *Autism: A reappraisal of concepts and treatment* (pp. 269–296). New York: Plenum.

Carpenter, K. J. (1986). *The history of scurvy and vitamin C.* Cambridge, UK: Cambridge University Press.

Carradice, A., Shankland, M. C., & Beail, N. (2002). A qualitative study of the theoretical models used by UK mental health nurses to guide their assessments with family caregivers of people with dementia. *International Journal of Nursing Studies, 39,* 17–26.

Cohen, J. (1960). A coefficient of agreement for nominal scales. *Educational and Psychological Measurement, 20,* 37–46.

Cresswell, J. W. (2003). *Research design: Qualitative, quantitative, and mixed methods approaches* (2nd ed.). Thousand Oaks, CA: Sage.

Dawson, G., & Castelloe, P. (1992). Autism. In C. E. Walker & M. C. Roberts (Eds.) *Handbook of clinical child psychology* (pp. 375–397). Wiley: New York.

Dawson, G., & Osterling, J. (1997). Early intervention in autism. In M. J. Guralnick (Ed.). *The effectiveness of early intervention.* Baltimore: Brookes.

Derogatis, L. R., Lipman, R. S., & Covi, L. (1973). SCL-90: An outpatient psychiatric rating scale. *Psychopharmacology Bulletin, 9,* 13–28.

Dewe, P. J. (1989). Examining the nature of work stress: Individual evaluations of stressful experiences and coping. *Human Relations, 42,* 993–1013.

Dick, P. (2000). The social construction of the meaning of acute stressors: A qualitative study of the personal accounts of police officers using a stress counselling service. *Work and Stress, 14,* 226–244.

Dillon, S. (1994, July 7). Report finds more violence in the schools: board says principals covered up incidents. *The New York Times,* pp. B1, B7.

Dohrenwend, B. P. (1979). Stressful life events and psychopathology: Some issues of theory and method. In J. E. Barrett, E. M. Rose, & G. L. Klerman (Eds.), *Stress and mental disorder* (pp. 1–15). New York: Raven.

Dohrenwend, B. S., & Dohrenwend, B. P. (1981). Life stress and illness: Formulation of the issues. In B. S. Dohrenwend & B. P. Dohrenwend (Eds.), *Stressful life events and their contexts.* New York: Prodist.

Durkheim, E. (1951). *Suicide, a study in sociology.* (J. A. Spaulding & G. Simpson, Trans.). Glencoe, IL: Free Press. (Original work published 1897)

Engelbrecht, P., Oswald, M., Swart, E. & Eloff, I. (2003). Including learners with intellectual disabilities: Stressful for teachers? *International Journal of Disability, Development and Education, 50,* 293–308.

Erickson, F. (1986). Qualitative methods in research on teaching. In M. C. Whitrock (Ed.), *Handbook on research in teaching* (3rd ed., pp. 119–161). New York: Macmillan.

Farber, B. A. (1991). *Crisis in education: Stress and burnout in the American teacher.* San Francisco: Jossey-Bass.

Farber, B. (2000). Treatment strategies for different types of teacher burnout. *Journal of Clinical Psychology, 56,* 675–689.

Farrell, E., Pegero, G., Lindsey, R., & White, R. (1988). Giving voice to high school students: Pressure and boredom, ya know what I'm sayin'? *American Educational Research Journal, 25,* 489–502.

Farrell, E. (1990). *Hanging in and dropping Out: Voices of at risk high school students.* New York: Teachers College Press.

Fleiss, J. L. (1981). *Statistical methods for rates and proportions* (2nd ed.). New York: Wiley.

Frese, M., & Zapf, D. (1994). Methodological issues in the study of work stress: Objective vs subjective measurement of work stress and the question of longitudinal studies. In C. L. Cooper & R. Payne (Eds.), *Causes, coping and consequences of stress at work* (pp. 375–411). Chichester: Wiley.

Fromm-Reichmann, F. (1948). Notes on the development of treatment of schizophrenia by psychoanalytic psychotherapy. *Psychiatry: Journal for the Study of Interpersonal Processes, 11,* 263–273.

Geertz, C. (1973). *The interpretation of cultures: Selected essays.* New York: Basic Books.

Ginsberg, R., Schwartz, J., Olson, G., & Bennett, A. (1987). Working conditions in urban schools. *The Urban Review, 19,* 3–23.

Glaser, B., & Strauss, A. (1967). *The discovery of grounded theory: Strategies for qualitative research.* Chicago: Aldine.

Gomme, I. M., & Hall, M. P. (1995). Prosecutors at work: Role overload and strain. *Journal of Criminal Justice, 23*, 191–200.

Gootman, E. (2007, September 20). Undercount of violence in schools: Defective reporting is found at 10 sites. *The New York Times*, pp. B1, B4.

Goodwin, C., Mayo, M., & Hill, R. P. (1997). Salesperson response to loss of a major account: A qualitative analysis. *Journal of Business Research, 40*, 167–180.

Gould, S. J. (1981). *The mismeasure of man.* New York: Norton.

Griffith, J. A., & Brem, S. K. (2004). Teaching evolutionary biology: Pressures, stress, and coping. *Journal of Research in Science Teaching, 41*, 791–809.

Hopkins, D. R. (1983). *Princes and peasants: Smallpox in history.* Chicago: University of Chicago Press.

Hugentobler, M. K., Israel, B. A., & Schurman, S. J. (1992). An action research approach to workplace health: Integrating methods. *Health Education Quarterly, 19*, 55–76.

Hutchinson, S. (1987). Self-care and job stress. *Image: Journal of Nursing Scholarship, 19*, 192–196.

Isaksen, J. (2000). Constructing meaning depsite the drudgery of repetitive work. *Journal of Humanistic Psychology, 40*, 84–107.

Jackson, P. W. (1968). *Life in classrooms.* New York: Holt, Rinehart, & Winston.

Jex, S. M., Adams, G. A., Elacqua, T. C., & Lux, D. J. (1997). A comparison of incident-based and scale measures of work stressors. *Work and Stress, 11*, 229–238.

Kahn, W. A. (1993). Caring for the caregivers: Patterns of organizational caregiving. *Administrative Science Quarterly, 38*, 539–563.

Kainan, A. (1994). Staffroom grumblings as expressed teachers' vocation. *Teaching and Teachers Educaiton, 10*, 281–290.

Kanner, L. (1943). Autistic disturbances of affective contact. *Nervous Children, 2*, 217–250.

Kanner, L. (1949). Problems of nosology and psychodynamics in early infantile autism. *American Journal of Orthopsychiatry, 19*, 416–426.

Kasl, S. V. (1987). Methodologies in stress and health: Past difficulties, present dilemmas, future directions. In S. V. Kasl & C. L. Cooper (Eds.), *Stress and health: Issues in research methodology* (pp. 307–318). New York: Wiley.

Keenan, A., & Newton, T. J. (1985). Stressful events, stressors and psychological strains in young professional engineers. *Journal of Occupational Behaviour, 6*, 151–156.

Khowaja, K., Merchant, R. J., & Hirani, D. (2005). Registered nurses [*sic*] perception of work satisfaction at a Tertiary Care University Hospital. *Journal of Nursing Management, 13*, 32–39.

Kidd, P., Scharf, T., & Veazie, M. (1996). Linking stress and injury in the farming environment: A secondary analysis. *Health Education Quarterly, 23*, 224–237.

Kirk, J., & Miller, M. (1986). *Reliability and validity in qualitative research.* Beverly Hills, CA: Sage.

Kohl, H. (1976). *On teaching.* New York: Schocken.

Lee., D. (1998). An analysis of workplace bullying in the UK. *Personnel Review, 29*, 593–608.

Louis, M. R. (1980). Surprise and sense making: What newcomers experience in entering unfamiliar organizational settings. *Administrative Science Quarterly, 25,* 226–251.

MacDonald, L. M., & Korabik, K. (1991). Sources of stress and ways of coping among male and female managers. *Journal of Social Behavior and Personality* (Special Issue on Occupational Stress, P. Perrewé, Ed.), *6,* 185–198.

Maki, N., Moore, S., Grunberg, L., & Greenberg, E. (2005). The responses of male and female managers to workplace stress and downsizing. *North American Journal of Psychology, 7,* 295–312.

McAdoo, W. G., & DeMeyer, M. K. (1979). Personality characteristics of parents. In M. Rutter & E. Schopler (Eds.), *Autism: A reappraisal of concepts and treatment* (pp. 251–267). New York: Plenum.

Mears, A., & Finlay, W. (2005). Not just a paper doll. *Journal of Contemporary Ethnography, 34,* 317–343.

Miller, G. (1957). *The adoption of inoculation for smallpox in England and France.* Philadelphia: University of Pennsylvania Press.

Molapo, M. P. (2001). *A biosocial study of high blood pressure among underground mineworkers in a South African gold mine.* Unpublished doctoral dissertation. Emory University, Atlanta, Georgia.

Mykletun, R. J. (1985). Work stress and satisfaction of comprehensive school teachers: An interview study. *Scandinavian Journal of Educational Research, 29,* 57–71.

Noonan, B. M., Gallor, S. M., Hensler-McGinnis, N. F., Fassinger, R. E., Wang, S., & Goodman, J. (2004). Challenge and success: A qualitative study of the career development of highly achieving women with physical and sensory disabilities. *Journal of Counseling Psychology, 51,* 68–80.

Palmer, C. E. (1983). A note about paramedics' strategies for dealing with death and dying. ; *Journal of Occupational Psychology, 56,* 83–86.

Plewis, I., & Mason, P. (2005). What works and why: Combining quantitative and qualitative approaches in large-scale evaluations. *International Journal of Social Research Methodology, 8,* 185–194.

Polanyi, M., & Tompa, E. (2004). Rethinking work-health models for the new global economy: A qualitative analysis of emerging dimensions of work. *Work: Journal of Prevention, Assessment and Rehabilitation, 23,* 3–18.

Pollak, R. (1997). *The creation of Dr. B: A biography of Bruno Bettelheim.* New York: Simon and Schuster.

Popper, K. (1963). *Conjectures and refutations: The growth of scientific knowledge.* New York: Basic Books.

Rabinow, P., & Sullivan, W. H. (1987). *The interpretive turn: A second look.* Berkeley: University of California Press.

Razzell, P. (1977). *The conquest of smallpox: The impact on smallpox mortality in eighteenth century Britain.* Firle, Sussex, UK: Caliban Books.

Reichenbach, H. (1951). *The rise of the scientific philosophy.* Berkeley: University of California Press.

Reid, Y., Johnson, S., Morant, N., Kuipers, E., Szmukler, G., Thornicroft, G., et al. (1999). Explanations for stress and satisfaction in mental health professionals: A qualitative study. *Social Psychiatry and Psychiatric Epidemiology, 34,* 301–308.

Rimland, B. (1964). *Infantile autism.* New York: Appleton-Century-Crofts.

Rutter, M., & Schopler, E. (Eds.). (1979). *Autism: A reappraisal of concepts and treatment.* New York: Plenum.

Sachar, E. (1991). *Shut up and let the lady teach: A teacher's year in a public school.* New York: Poseidon Press.

Schonfeld, I. S. (1990). Distress in a sample of teachers. *Journal of Psychology, 123,* 321–338.

Schonfeld, I. S. (1992a). A longitudinal study of occupational stressors and depressive symptoms in first-year teachers. *Teaching and Teacher Education, 8,* 151–158.

Schonfeld, I. S. (1992b). Assessing stress in teachers: Depressive symptoms scales and neutral self-reports on the work environment. In J. Quick, L. Murphy, and J. Hurrell, Jr. (Eds.), *Work and well-being: Assessments and instruments for occupational mental health* (pp.270–285). Washington, DC: American Psychological Association.

Schonfeld, I. S. (1994, May).The impact of working conditions on depressive symptoms: The case of newly appointed woman teachers. International Conference on Social Stress Research, Honolulu.

Schonfeld, I. S. (1996). Relation of negative affectivity to self-reports of job stressors and psychological outcomes. *Journal of Occupational Health Psychology, 1,* 397–412.

Schonfeld, I. S. (2000). An updated look at depressive symptoms and job satisfaction in first-year women teachers. *Journal of Occupational and Organizational Psychology, 73,* 363–371.

Schonfeld, I. S. (2001). One-year longitudinal study of the effects of working conditions social support, coping, and locus of control on depressive symptoms and job satisfaction in women. *Genetic Psychology Monographs, 127,* 133–168.

Schonfeld, I. S. (2006a). School violence. In E.K. Kelloway, J. Barling, & J.J. Hurrell (Eds.). *Handbook of workplace violence* (pp. 169–229). Thousand Oaks, CA: Sage.

Schonfeld, I. S. (2006b). The daily show: Teachers at work. American Psychological Association-NIOSH Conference on Work, Stress, and Health. Miami.

Schonfeld, I. S., & Ruan, D. (1991). Occupational stress and preemployment measures: The case of teachers. *Journal of Social Behavior and Personality* (Special Issue on Occupational Stress, P. Perrewé, Ed.), *6,* 95–114.

Schonfeld, I. S., & Santiago, E. A. (1994). Working conditions and psychological distress in first-year women teachers: Qualitative findings. In L. C. Blackman (Ed.), *What works? Synthesizing effective biomedical and psychosocial strategies for healthy families in the 21st century.* Indianapolis: School of Social Work, University of Indiana.

Shai, D. (2002). Working women/cloistered men: A family development approach to marriage arrangements among ultra-Orthodox Jews. *Journal of Comparative Family Studies, 33,* 97–115.

Smith, D. L., & Smith, B. J. (2006). Perceptions of violence: The views of teaches who left urban schools. *The High School Journal, 89,*34–42.

Smith, M. L. (2006). Multiple methodology in education research. In J. L. Green, G. Camilli, & P.B. lmore (Eds.), *Handbook of complementary methods in education research* (pp. 457–476). Mahwah, NJ: Erlbaum.

Steggerda, D. M. (2003). *If I tell them, will they listen? Voices of former teachers.* Unpublished doctoral dissertation. Drake University, Des Moines, Iowa.

Steinberg, J. (1997, July 24). "Strong disciplinary action' is recommended for principal. *The New York Times*, p. B3.

Tashakkori, A., & Teddlie, C. (Eds.). (2003). *Handbook of mixed methods in social and behavioral research*. Thousand Oaks, CA: Sage.

Tewksbury, R. (1993). On the margins of two professions: Job satisfaction and stress among post-secondary correctional educators. *American Journal of Criminal Justice, 187,* 61–77.

The child is father. (1960). *Time, 76,* 78.

Tracy, S. J., Myers, K. K., & Scott, C. W. (2006). Cracking jokes and crafting selves: Sensemaking and identity management among human service workers. *Communication Monographs, 73,* 283–308.

Trow, M. (1957). Comment on "participant observation and interviewing: A comparison." *Human Organization,* 16, 33–35.

Ward, H. L., & Miller, H. (1978). *A preventive point of view*. Springfield, IL: Thomas.

Weyman, A., Clarke, D. D., & Cox, T. (2003). Developing a factor model of coal miners' attributions on risk-taking at work. *Work and Stress, 17,* 306–320.

Wing, L. *Autistic children: A guide for parents and professionals* (2nd ed.). New York: Brunner/Mazel.

Younghusband, L. J. (2008, March). Violence in the classroom: The reality of a teacher's workplace. Paper presented at the Work, Stress, and Health 2008 Conference, Washington, D.C.

NOTES

1. A Gates class comprises students who were held back because of poor achievement.

2. The excerpts from Emily Sachar's book *Shut up and let the lady teach: A teacher's year in a public school* were quoted by permission of the publisher.

3. Berkson's fallacy, a principle from the highly quantitative field of epidemiology, indicates that if all potential research subjects are *not* equally likely to be incepted into a study sample, investigators will have difficulty concluding that an association, found in the sample, between a factor and a disorder applies to the population (Fleiss, 1981). The fallacy explains why it is often difficult to draw firm conclusions when studying factors associated with a disorder in clinical samples. Factors that propel potential research subjects into a clinical setting, where they may be recruited for a study, often differ from factors that increase individuals' risk for a disorder. Studies of clinical samples may result in the investigator misidentifying factors that are associated with subjects' arrival at a clinical setting as factors that increase subjects' risk for a disorder. In the era of the Great Depression, it is likely that families that took their autistic children to see Kanner were mostly patrician in background. Their background wealth could explain why the families could afford to visit Kanner (1943) at his Baltimore practice—many families traveled considerable distances—and may partly account for the coolness he observed in the parents of the affected children (cf. Wing, 1985).

CHAPTER 11

MANAGEMENT OF QUALITY OF LIFE AT WORK IN HEALTHCARE ORGANIZATIONS

Káthia de Carvalho Cunha

The Human Resources Management at the Department of Health, which is in charge of coordinating the Humanization Policy and the establishment of the Promotion of Quality of Life at Work service designed to humanize all state, hospital and outpatient services, established the Center for the Improvement of Quality of Life and Work Environment through Decree 49.343 from 01/24/2005, which is designed mainly to propose and develop Programs to improve quality of life and safety (SES, 2008).

In Brazil, the Program for Improvement and Structuring of Work Management and Education at the National Healthcare System (ProgreSUS) was established through administrative act 2.261, from September 22, 2006, taking into account the weakness of Work Management and Education in Healthcare areas in the various State and City Departments of Health, as shown by surveys conducted in 2004 by the National Council of Health

Stress and Quality of Working Life, pages 205–234
Copyright © 2009 by Information Age Publishing
All rights of reproduction in any form reserved.

Secretaries (CONASS) and the Observatory Network of Human Resources in Healthcare (ROREHS-MS) (Brasil, 2007).

Although these are examples of important and more recent initiatives and investments in the management of work in healthcare and in the improvement of the quality of work processes, signs and symptoms continuously observed and voiced by workers in hospitals show that these professionals might be at the service of policies committed to quality, but that do not yet fully take into account the management of the quality of life at work.

According to Ruas and Antunes (1997, p. 169–70), the productive restructuring which started in the 1980s and was intensified after the 1990s required new forms of management, with total quality management being a widely disseminated strategy in organizations that should involve and get the commitment of workers, leading them to assume multiple roles and tasks and the responsibility, as internal customers, for the quality of their actions and for productivity. Organizational policies and practices were established based on the principles of Total Quality Management, focusing particularly on the commitment of workers to organizational purposes and goals. The management of the quality of live at work-MQLW emerged from concepts and practices related to total quality (Limongi-França, 1997).

Albuquerque and Limongi-França (1998) analyzed the "apparent paradox" of the coexistence of the search for productivity and the change to a better competitive position by companies in the market with academic and business discussion on the quality of life at work-QLW, which led to questions on the reasons behind the focus placed on QLW by organizations; if QLW would encompass people management strategies for competitiveness; if QLW programs would be related to ISO 9000 certification and to a company's business policy.

The dissemination of the QLW concept was triggered, in the past decade, by the revision of the links and the structure of the personal and professional lives, by socioeconomic factors, by business targets and organizational pressures. The QLW concept contains choices of well-being and a perception of what can be done to meet the expectations of managers and workers (Limongi-França, 2001; 2003).

QLW is a concept and a philosophy of work that aims at improving the life of workers in organizations. "It is a management style through which employees have a feeling of ownership, self-control, responsibility and self-love" (Dolan, 2006, p. 3–4). QLW can be understood as the result of intra- and extraorganizational macro and micro policies that outline organizational practices, in interaction and harmony with personal and professional characteristics and needs and with the nature of the work process and relationships.

QLW derives from the management of the quality of life at work-MQLW. In this regard, QLW is the result of a network of interdependent variables which affect the environment, the organization, workers, the work process and relationships. The complexity of this concept becomes evident when we analyze the multiple factors that affect each and every one of these variables which, as a consequence, change over time and in different scenarios.

The management of the quality of life at work- MQLW is seen by França (2007, p. 167) as "the ability to manage the set of actions, including diagnosis, implementation of management, technology and structural improvements and innovations at the work environment which are in line with and built into the organizational culture, with absolute priority given to people's well-being".

MQLW is influenced by the organizational strategy that can make it feasible or not, since it provides it with a direction and consistency, resulting from a decision-making process that involves the whole organization and its relationship with the environment, involving content and process issues at different levels. Thus, the strategy includes the "establishment of a mission and objectives for the organization, as well as policies and action plans to achieve them, considering the impacts of the forces of the environment and competition" (Albuquerque, 2002, p. 37–8). When this is the strategy focus, it can become an instrument to generate and maintain MQLW in the organization, thus having an impact on QLW.

If in every step of the process designed to integrate the HR strategy to the company's strategy managers consider QLW in their decisions, organizational practices will reflect these guidelines. The dynamism, temporality and subjectivity resulting from contingency are shown in the interrelational process between QLW and the MQLW. QLW can result from some organizational benefits, but not only from them. It can, to certain people, include meeting needs of individualization such as self-esteem and self-achievement. Understanding QLW is a multifaceted process directed by the diversity of benchmarks and world views that support individual and collective points of view. The awareness can either open or close the "visual field" of these points of view, making them clearer or turbid, more superficial or deeper, closer or farther from the reality lived and observed.

Commitment to QLW happens through a "committed act" which, according to Freire (1983, p. 16), can only happen when individuals are able to act and reflect with critical conscience. Therefore, commitment to QLW goes through individual and collective awareness, which points to the interface between quality demands and the educational level of any given society, organization, group and individual, which underlines the relevance of organizational learning and corporate education. The commitment to QLW requires people who, either individually or collectively, are against an anti-change attitude, neutrality, anti-historicity and naivety in organizations, which influence the values and premises that guide the organizational mission, vision, philosophy, structure, culture and practices. The MQLW is influenced by the convictions of managers about its relevance at the individual, collective, organizational or societal level.

Additionally, QLW and MQLW depend on what people think of corporations, and it may include the concept of citizen corporation, organizations as promoters of excellence, ethics and morality, of the flexible and innovative force responsible for the development and well-being of society, protecting those who are part of them and who through them give meaning to their lives (Freitas, 1997).

QLW and MQLW coexist in organizations in different degrees, from insufficiency to excellence, implicitly or explicitly, managed and experienced with varying degrees of commitment, reciprocity and awareness. Figure 11.1 shows the dynamism and complexity of the relationship between Quality of Life at Work (QLW) and the Management of the Quality of Life at Work

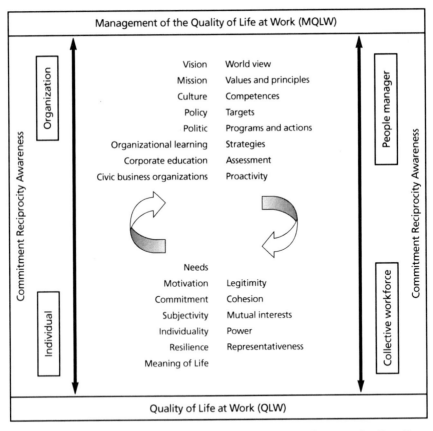

Figure 11.1 Dynamism and complexity of the relationship between Quality of Life at Work and the Management of the Quality of Life at Work. São Paulo, 2008. Adapted from Cunha, 2004.

(MQLW), i.e., the mutual influence of the variables at the individual, collective and organizational levels.

An important assumption is that QLW and MQLW should be supported by values that aim at generating individual, collective and organizational well-being, which is key to the vitality, survival and the functional and psychological health of organizations. "In order for an organization to achieve a high level of performance, their members should believe that what it is doing is ultimately the contribution to the community and to the society on which everyone depends" (Drucker, 2000, p. 8).

There can be conflicts between professional aspirations and projects and the interest the company may have that individuals do no develop (Dutra, 1997). "If the culture of an organization and the values of its community are in conflict, the community should have precedence—otherwise it will not give its social contribution" (Drucker, 2000, p. 8).

Healthy organizations working as a system get updated information from its subsystems; they are managed considering the vision of the future; they use several structures and team management; they respect internal and external customers, they share access to information; they decentralize decision-making and maintain communication channels open; they identify learning points; they accept innovation and creativity; they tolerate ambiguity and different ways of thinking; they respect tensions between professional and family demands; they encourage work at home, whenever appropriate; they keep an explicit social agenda; community citizenship; they are responsible for maternity leave and childcare; they protect the environment; they support the arts; they pay attention to quality and safety in their operations; they identify and manage change for a better future (Beckhard, 1997).

According to Platt (1997, p. 343), workers' attitudes and expectations are changing. 72% of the North-American workforce state that they need a job that does not interfere with their personal or family life and that provide them with a balanced life style. [...] Healthy organizations need to focus on the balance between work and personal life. "[...] they need to be committed to providing favorable conditions so that people can make choices in order to achieve an acceptable level of balance" (Dahlberg et al., 1997, p. 390).

However, the prevailing premise is that "Bosses do not want you to give up your family or fun. Their only purpose is to capture all your energy and use it in the company" (Welch, 2005, p. 292). "The organizations of the future will have to solve people's real concerns if they intend to lead their sectors and establish committed and talented workforces" (Platt, 1997, p. 340).

Although Stalk Jr et al. (2000, p. 28–9) afirm that the tested managerial skills are related to speed, consistency, acuity, agility and innovation, another managerial competence is associated to the condition of promoting the alignment of the mission, policy and goals with practices that include QLW. A new management model that highlights QLW as one of its values should necessarily go through a process in which, someday, somehow organizational learning will occur, because commitment to MQLW can happen through disseminated organizational knowledge applied by everyone. Organizational learning includes experiencing the transition between tacit and explicit knowledge, the former rooted in action, commitment and involvement in a specific context and the latter transmissible in formal, systematic language (Nonaka, 2000).

In the knowledge management process conducted by a company, there are three important steps: knowledge acquisition and development, knowledge dissemination and memory building. Knowledge management in organizations is related to learning processes (Fleury, 2001, p. 103).

Learning processes can also be favored by corporate education, understood as a strategy of investment in personal growth and development. Eboli (2001, p. 110–1) focuses on the new trends directed to people's education and development. "The new management style will demand the establishment of a true business culture of competence and results, which assumes deep changes not only in the structure, systems, policies and practices, but also, and mainly, in the organizational and individual mindset".

The professionals working in the people management area should be the agents of continuous change, designing processes and implementing a culture that increases the capacity an organization has to adapt and improve, including strategies that promote learning. This new style of management should be based on the commitment, reciprocity and awareness required to enable the inclusion of MQLW in the organizational strategic plan.

In Brazil, the maintenance of some organizational practices is reason for concern. Organizations must be aware of the importance of letting go of attitudes that do not favor the development and self-achievement of people. Strategies and indicators should be established to monitor QLW. The success of organizations will be measured having among the measurement criteria the assessment of their contribution to meeting the expectations and needs of citizens. Leaders should take actions that improve QLW and MQLW. This perspective has to be consolidated. MQLW requires the monitoring of processes and results through indicators (Limongi-França, 1996).

Dahlberg et al. (1997, p. 383) stated that "one of our challenges is to continue to develop our organizational health and vitality as we grow amidst massive changes". The concept of healthy corporation implies to determine the ideal way of giving attention both the performance parameters and employee satisfaction. Welch (2001, quoted by Quick et al., 2003, p. 21) stated that "My only job in life is to remain healthy".

Policies that enable MQLW are linked to the social responsibility of organizations. They can generate a qualitatively positive impact on the life of the community where they operate. Organizations should be responsible for their impact on employees, the environment, customers and everything else they deal with (Drucker, 2000). Historically, however, companies have been reactive vis-à-vis the demands connected to their legal responsibilities.

> All organizations now say routinely "People are our greatest asset". However, few practice what they preach, and even fewer truly believe in it. Most organizations still believe, maybe not consciously, in what 19th century employers believed: people need us more that we need them (Drucker, 2000, p. 11).

Many organizations look for employees with initiative that solve problems and work hard for customers. Some of them do not make an effort to invest in employees and in their future (Kanter, 1997, p. 156). Working in many organizations can be dangerous, because thousands of workers die in occupational accidents or due to work-related diseases and this is a systemic problem (Morgan, 1996, p. 280–301).

The study of MQLW is based on humanitarian values that can promote reciprocity, legitimacy, respect, autonomy, participation, emancipation, happiness, achievement, health, well-being, commitment and these are only some of the elements of the complex conceptual network that supports an organizational culture directed to MQLW. MQLW is one of the management models designed to promote QLW, the diagnosis of risks and susceptibilities resulting from the work organization process, the intervention to minimize or eliminate risks and vulnerabilities, the promotion and recovery of the individual, collective and organizational physical and psychological health.

Quick et al. (2003) analyzed the Achilles heel, the risks and the vulnerability, connecting them to prevention strategies and measures that promote health, balance, well-being and QLW. Mendes (1995, p.37) said that "as one of the expressions of the full exercise of citizenship rights we see, as an universal trend, individuals and societies becoming increasingly more demanding regarding the health risks and what they consider to be the 'adverse effects', 'damages' or 'losses'". Among them, there are those that are difficult to objectively characterize that have an economic impact and that show through symptoms that include early aging, fatigue, stress and burnout.

Suffering, adversities and the banalization of unfair conduct have already been analyzed, including in hospital organizations (Dejours, 2003). Resilience is associated with the ability of workers to live with and survive under such circumstances. "Resilience is not a set of qualities an individual has. It is a process that, from birth to death, continuously connects us with the environment around us" (Cyrulnik, 2001, p. 239).

Organizations with policies that exclude MQLW are to some degree neglecting elements that would guarantee their operational health and the health and well-being of their workers. Dejours (1992) has contributed to provide the foundations in favor of MQLW by stating that there is a feeling of mental sclerosis, imagination paralysis, intellectual regression and depersonalization by workers. This situation shows the importance of the management of quality of life at work based on a consistent, critical, contemporary and ethical-legal theoretical-methodological framework.

According to Chanlat (1996) a management method is a set of administrative practices implemented by the top management of an organization to achieve objectives. The management method includes the establishment of work conditions, work organization, the nature of hierarchical relationships, the type of organizational structures, the systems for results assessment and control, policies connected to management and objectives, the management values and philosophy that inspire them. Management modes incorporate the abstract, prescribed, formal and static component and the real, informal and dynamic component resulting from the relationship between what the organization formalizes and what the practices of groups and individuals incorporate or reinvent based on this formal apparatus. The formal components of a people management model are defined by principles, policies and processes that interfere in human relationships within organizations (Fischer, 2002, p. 17–20).

Human resources policies should focus on subjects valued by people that help them build their own futures and reap the rewards for their contributions (Kanter, 1997, p.162–64). Sethi (1997, p. 252–3) believes that motivation will occur when policies and practices speak to the hearts and minds of all involved in the production process. The role of the human resources area is to be the indispensable catalyst to make people enthusiastic and lead this process.

QUALITY OF LIVE AT WORK AND MANAGEMENT OF QUALITY OF LIFE AT WORK: THE PROBLEM IN THE HEALTHCARE AREA

Healthcare workers around the world are experiencing an increase in stress and unsafety (WHO, 2006). A study conducted by the National Institute for Occupational Safety and Health characterized the scenario of violence that involved people who work in hospitals and recommended that they should all develop a prevention program for the diagnosis of risk factors in each unit under the guidance of the workers (NIOSH, 2002). A program was established to provide healthcare professionals with the means to counter fear, aggression, humiliation and homicides at their workplaces (OMS/OIT/CIE/ISP, 2002).

The various forms of violence healthcare workers are subjected to are stressors and generate risks to the quality of care given by them, to productivity and to the development and may compromise the efficiency of healthcare systems (Di Martino, 2002). This organizational stress has become a contemporary concern. Workers in different organizational settings and dynamics experience levels of stress and there are frequently consequences affecting their performance, morale, turnover rates, absenteeism and violence at the workplace (Rossi, 2005).

The prolonged exposure to stressors leads to a chronic condition that may lead to burnout, which is characterized by exhaustion, skepticism and disconnection from work (Maslach, 2005, p. 41). Physical and emotional stress has been a concern of people working in professions that involve the care of human beings for over 20 years, but today it is taking epidemic proportions (Maslach & Leiter, 1999).

The diagnosis in the healthcare sector points to fragmented systems, inequalities, governability problems, inefficiencies in managing the system and services. Changes will take place with the permanent development of people, with the focus on equality, on the quality of healthcare actions and the satisfaction of the population and the workers (Motta, 2001).

In Brazil, there is still a lack of healthcare professionals, considering that for every 1,000 inhabitants there are 1.71 physicians, 1.16 dentists, 0.65 nurses; 0.21 dietitians; 0.42 physical therapists, 0.05 occupational therapists; 0.76 physical education professionals; 0.34 social workers; 0.20 biologists, 0.55 pharmacists, 0.82 psychologists, 1.34 nursing technicians and 1.99 nursing assistants (Brasil, 2007).

Fernandes and Gutierrez (1988) have already stated that "it might even sound paradoxical, at the challenging and competitive time experienced by companies, in which there is a constant lack of resources, to speak about improving the quality of life at work to increase the level of satisfaction of employees". The deficiency of human resources in the healthcare area is already a variable that impacts the organizational dynamics and the quality of life at work–QLW.

There is already a body of knowledge systematized by studies conducted over the past decade in Brazil focusing on the QLW dimensions with evidence of a situation that deserves attention and of new practices by managers of healthcare organizations and their services(Anabuck, 2001; Araujo, 2003; Bachion, 1998; Barros, 2003; Bianchi, 1990, 1999; 2000; Borges, 2002; Cordeiro et al., 2006; Costa, Almeida & Lima, 2003; Cunha et al., 2007; Cunha et al., 2007a; Faria, 2005; Gatti, 2005; Gaspar, 1997; Hoga, 2002; Lemos, Cruz & Botomé, 2002; Lima & Ésther, 2001; Martins, 2000; 2003; Mauro, 1996; MenzanI, 2006; Murofuse et al., 2005; Peniche & Nunes,

2001; Robayo-Tamayo, 1997; Santos & Soler, 2003; Santos & Trevizan, 2002; Stacciarini & Troccoli, 2001; Silva, 1996).

Case studies conducted by Cunha & França (2003); Cunha (2003) and Cunha & Souza (2004) on bullying, stress and violence provide new insights about the issue of QLW in healthcare organizations in the city of São Paulo.

The first case study was designed to identify situations considered as bullying by nursing workers in hospitals. The subjects were 40 students graduating from the Nursing School in a Higher Education Organization, aged 20 to 43 years, members of nursing staffs, who had been working for 2 to 17 years at 6 healthcare organizations of the public, private and third sector in São Paulo.

Data was collected through interviews with the following guiding questions: "please reflect on your experience as a nursing worker and talk about bullying, understanding it as a frequent abusive conduct shown through gestures, words and attitudes that affect your dignity, physical and/or psychological integrity and the work environment, putting your job at risk". After fully transcribing the answers, data content was analyzed. Results showed that 25% of subjects had experienced bullying. The remaining 75% reported having experienced, as spectators, routine situations that led to embarrassment and that physically and psychologically affect their coworkers who are subjected to this practice.

Bullying described by the respondents was characterized by the following key words: "pressure", "coercion" and "aggressiveness". The resulting feelings were associated with "embarrassment", "isolation" and "feeling demeaned". As a conclusion, bullying was characterized as repetitive and embarrassing situations where the victim was humiliated, their work demeaned and where they were reproached in front of the healthcare staff, with references to the risk of losing the job, of being dismissed for cause, of being suspended and to the fact that it interferes in the performance appraisal. This experience was associated with stress, headache, sleeplessness, irritability, insecurity, lack of motivation and gastrointestinal disorders. Bullies were characterized as being "stressed, mean and uninformed".

The second case study was designed to identify stressful situation for nursing assistants and technicians. The same previously mentioned 40 respondents were the subjects.

Data was collected through interviews with the following guiding question: "please talk about situations at work that trigger stress in the nursing staff". After fully transcribing the answers, data content was analyzed.

The stressors found were excessive workload, time pressure, violence resulting from the contact with specific customers, demands from the different roles taken in the family, school and work contexts, poor quality of relationships at work and in life in general, the feeling of loss arising from the possibility of a patient's death, inadequate conditions regarding physical, material and financial resources and the absence of positive links that could generate credibility, trust, respect, generosity, cooperation and support at the workplace. Impersonality was valued and encouraged among employees and supervisors, while total dedication to patients and the organization was demanded. There was no perception of concern by supervisors with their employees. The stress experience was associated with constant fatigue, sleeplessness, irritability, gastrointestinal disorders, tachycardia, hypertension, concentration difficulties and memory problems.

In sum, the nursing process and work relationships were generating stress among the investigated nursing workers; there was the perception of mismatch between the quality of life of internal customers (the nursing staff) and that of external customers (users) of the hospital organizations; stress was associated with poor quality of life inside and outside the work environment; no preventive measures against stress at the personal and professional level were mentioned; the perception was that supervisors emphasized the commitment to users and the organization, without the organization committing itself to the workers who "cared for customers and who did not feel cared for by the organization".

The third case study diagnosed violence to which the healthcare teams were subjected at four Basic Healthcare Units-BHUs where the Family Health Strategy was followed in São Paulo; this study identified the perception by customers and users of the violence in the BHU coverage area; it also characterized the type of violence and its impact on the work process and relationships.

"Violence against workers is now recognized as an important occupational health issue. [...] In spite of the considerable progress achieved in the past decade regarding the recognition, definition and prevention of violence against workers, a lot still needs to be done" (Loomis, 1998, p. 153–66). Approaching the issue of violence at the healthcare area requires interdisciplinary attitude and practices (Minayo, 1992). Marziale (2004) discusses violence in the healthcare sector.

Questionnaires were administered to the teams, users and local informants who made up the sample of 250 respondents, 14% male and 86% female. The following questions were asked: How do you see the existence of violence in the area? What type of violence exists in the area? Have you ever been a victim of violence? What type of violence did you suffer? What type of violence did your family members suffer? Do you feel afraid? What type of events in this area are you and your family afraid of? Does violence in the area affect your professional activity? How does violence affect your professional activity? Do you think violence in the area is affecting the service provided to the users of the BHU? Data was treated and transferred to

Excel spreadsheets showing that violence affects the healthcare teams, the elderly, women, children and the community at large, being characterized by events such as robberies, kidnapping, intimidation, homicide, domestic violence and drug dealing. Violence was found to have a significant impact on the work process and relationships in these BHUs.

57% of respondents had already been victims of violent events, predominantly robbery, intimidation and physical assault, in the area of the BHU where they worked and lived. 74% of respondents said they were afraid of the violence in the area. The events they feared most were robberies, physical assault, intimidation and kidnapping. 66% of respondents considered that violence in the BHU area affected the performance of professional activities. 51% of respondents said that violence partially prevented them from performing their professional activity. 12% said that violence totally prevented them from performing their professional activity and 37% said that it did not affect their professional activity. 29% said they considered that violence did not affect the service provided to users and 15% could not answer.

Figure 11.2 shows the relationship between violence perceived by the respondents in the areas of the Basic Health Units where they worked in São Paulo with the quality of life and quality of life at work.

Violence in Brazil was characterized, at the end of the last century, as one of the main public health problems (Minayo; Souza, 1993; 1999; Minayo,

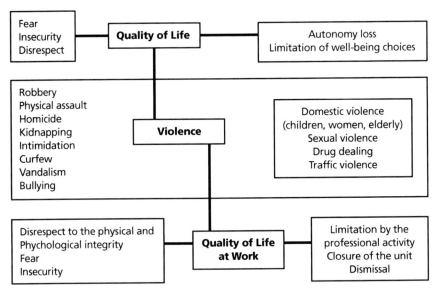

Figure 11.2 Perception of violence and its connection with quality of life and quality of life at work. São Paulo, 2008.

1994).This condition weakens people and generates insecurity. Regarding this issue, Souza and Minayo (1995, p.115) stated that:

> [...] the most significant challenges associated with the issue of violence are the establishment of agencies that guide and better define the actions to be taken in the sector regarding violence; intensification of analyses, planning and allocation of resources for prevention and damages, reorganization or reallocation of services to meet new needs, training and education of professionals or the introduction of this subject in the training and education of healthcare workers, both regarding awareness of the issue and care techniques; emphasis on intersectorial and multidisciplinary work together with the civil society.

According to Agudelo (1989; 1997), violence generates diseases and affects the physical and psychological integrity, leads to death, interfering with the life cycle. Violence immobilizes by terror and silences by force. Collective defense mechanisms are characterized by inversion and euphemization. In inversion, the danger is challenged, in euphemization, dangers are ridiculed.

Dejours (2003, p. 51) focuses on the defensive strategy of silence, blindness and deafness. "In order to resist, therefore, one should shut one's eyes and ears to the misery and injustice caused to others [...] everybody, from operators to managers, defend themselves the same way: by denying other people's suffering and silencing their own." In the healthcare area, professionals not always have institutionalized strategies to deal with the demands generated by the different types of violence they are subjected to during the performance of their work. This experience affects the quality of life at work, requiring the commitment and competence of all those involved with the management of quality of life at work.

SURVEY ABOUT THE MANAGEMENT OF QUALITY OF LIFE AT WORK IN HOSPITALS IN SÃO PAULO[1]

Some questions gave rise to this survey:

- "Are hospital organizations in the city of São Paulo that provide healthcare services and value the promotion of quality of life incorporating models of management of quality of life at work in their strategies?
- Are these organizations connecting the management of quality of life at work to an organizational commitment?
- Is the management of quality of life at work a priority for these healthcare organizations?
- Is the management of quality of life being connected to an organizational competence related to well-being?

- Is management of quality of life at work part of the mission and strategic vision of these organizations?
- What are the values that guide people managers and the management of quality of life at work programs at these organizations?

Purpose

The purpose of this survey was to understand the values that guide management of quality of life at work programs in Hospital Organizations in the city of São Paulo; identify the actions designed to manage the quality of life at work; characterize the vision people managers have of quality of life at work programs; and analyze the concept of management of quality of life at work used in these Hospital Organizations.

Methodology

An exploratory study was conducted using multiple case studies (Triviños, 1995). Case studies, as a research method, are used in exploratory endeavors to analyze one or few objects in order to enable a broad and detailed knowledge of it, without the concern of generalizing findings. The case study is adequate to explore typical, extreme or marginal cases. The case units in the present research were selected based on the typicity criteria (Gil, 1995; Chizzotti, 1991; Lüdke & André, 1986; Marconi & Lakatos, 1996).

The sample was composed of hospitals with one hundred or more beds included in the Registry of São Paulo State Hospitals that are part of the Hospitals of the State Department of Health -CSRMGSP-DIR-I-Capital. (Source: Establishment Registry –FCES).

Data was collected through a questionnaire containing closed and open questions and a Likert scale with statements based on the theoretical framework, in line with the specificity of the object and the objectives of the study. For each statement, respondents chose the most adequate answer in the scale. A pilot test designed to identify the need to improve the process and the instrument was performed in two hospitals in a capital city in Southern Brazil. After this pre-test, the instrument was analyzed by three instrument judges, university professors, with a background in statistics and experience with scales. The suggestions made by the three judges were considered to improve the quality of the instrument used to collect data, which was composed of 14 questions designed to characterize the organization; 4 questions on the organizational information of the respondent; 8 questions with respondent's personal information; 3 questions related to organizational guidelines; and 11 questions related to the quality of life at work program.

A Term of Information about the Research and the Term of Free and Informed Consent were attached to the Likert scale. Ethical issues related to the performance of research were respected. The sample was composed of 35 hospitals, with the hospitals who refused to participate claiming as the main reasons to do so the non-existence of a Policy for the Management of the Quality of Life at Work, prioritization of other intra- and extra organizational demands, the need to follow a lengthy internal flow to request the organizational authorization, which would not enable data collection within the scheduled timeframe.

Statistical techniques were used according to the purpose of the analyses and the nature of data. The same applied to the graphic representations used. In order to describe the sample, the mean, standard deviation, minimum, maximum and ratio calculation (percentages) were used. In terms of diagrams, histograms and bar graphs were used. Differences among groups were analyzed using the Mann-Whitney U test because this is the adequate test for this type of analysis of ordinal data and/or with non-Gaussian distribution (non-matched and non-parametric hypotheses test). As for the comparisons between two variables, they were made using the Wilcoxon's test Matched pairs which is applicable to this type of analysis of ordinal and/or non-Gaussian data (matched and non-parametric hypotheses test). The degree of relationship between variables was assessed using a correlation coefficient. The Spearman R test was used because it is applicable to ordinal and non-Gaussian data. In case of multiple variables, at once, or of one variable with multiple nominal alternatives, the Variance Analysis

TABLE 11.1 Profile of the Hospitals Surveyed in São Paulo, 2008

Characteristics of Hospitals				
Profile of the Hospitals				
Private	Public	Third Sector	Mixed	Other
49%	34%	9%	6%	2%
Profile of the Hospitals According to the Time of Operation				
0 a 20 years	21 a 40 years	41 a 60 years	61 a 80 years	more than 80 years
23%	20%	34%	11%	12%
Profile of the Hospitals According to Professional Categories				
MDs		Nursing staff		Other employees
28,60%		32,40%		39%
Profile of the Hospitals According to the Type of Employment Contract				
Hired under Brazilian labor law	Public examination	Contractors	Other	
61%	17,90%	12,10%	9%	
Profile of the Hospitals According to the Annual Average of Procedures				
Admissions	Emergency care	Laboratory tests	Image tests	Surgeries
16.434,80	97.756,70	669.830,40	136.348	9.298,00

TABLE 11.2   Profile of the Subjects, São Paulo, 2008

	Average Working Time	**Average Time at the Position**	**Gender**	
			Males	Females
	108,4 months	64,6 months	34%	66%
	Working Area			
	Hospital administration	HR	Other	**Average Age**
	23%	60%	17%	43,5 years
	Education			
	Technical training	Undergraduate	**Number of dependents**	
	3%	97%	1,1	
	Field of Undergraduate Degree			
	Human Sciences	Health	Other	
	57%	26%	17%	
	Graduate Degree			
	Lato sensu	Stricto sensu	No graduate degree	
	74%	9%	17%	
	Field of Graduate Degree			
	Human Sciences	Health	Applied Social Sciences	
	59%	34%	7%	

(Left margin label: **Profile of the Subjects**)

(ANOVA) was used. For the graphic illustration of differences or similarities between the statistical behavior of different variables, the Box & Whiskers diagram was used.

Regarding the profile of the hospitals according to the organizational mission, respondents not always chose one single focus area. A relevant predominance was found for "healthcare" (60%), "all areas" (20%), "social work" (9%) and "teaching and research" (6%).

Regarding the organizational priority, some respondents also chose more than one option, with "improvement of the healthcare services" representing 74% of the choices, "increase in revenues" 14%, "better management of the QLW" 6% and 12% said that they had other organizational priorities.

Regarding the organizational priority for people management, one option was chosen by the vast majority of respondents. However, some chose more than one alternative and a minority did not choose any. "Skill development" was chosen by 46% of respondents; "internal customer satisfaction" by 23%, "investment in QLW" was chosen by only 14% of respondents and "performance appraisal" by 6%. Other priorities were mentioned by 6%.

The main focus of the mission of these hospitals was to provide healthcare services to the population. Their priority was to improve the healthcare services they provided and, therefore, people management was mainly focused on the development of skills. These data are coherent, because in order to provide better healthcare services, one of the strategies can be to develop skills.

The "investment in Quality of Life at Work" as one of the organizational priorities for people management was mentioned by 14% of the respondents, with only 6% of them stating that "better management of QLW" is an organizational priority. These data show that although the issue of QLW and MQLW was present, it did not show as relevant enough to be considered a priority in organizational strategies.

Regarding the features of the organizational initiatives for QLW, around 23% of organizations declared they had a formal QLW policy; 29% affirmed they had a specific management for QLW, 69% of organizations answered that their QLW actions were directed at workers at the operational level.

The formalization of a policy becomes essential for the alignment, maintenance and development of institutionalized practices. The formalization of the organizational commitment to MQLW and to QLW in these organizations still has a lot of room for improvement, because at the time of the survey they had other priorities.

The attribute considered as very significant by these Organizations for a QLW program was the importance it has for the workers. As having intermediate importance the following was mentioned: importance of the program for the organization; value given to the program by workers; interest of workers in the program; priority assigned to the program by the organization; workers' satisfaction with the program and legitimization of the program by the workers. A low level of importance was given to the recognition of workers' participation in the program; to workers' initiative; to workers' knowledge and to workers' participation. The relationship between the importance of the program for workers and for the organization was very similar.

The low importance given to the recognition of workers' participation; to workers' initiative; to workers' knowledge and to workers' participation can be explained by the non-existence, in most hospitals, of a MQLW policy, of QLW programs and of specific management for QLW. Isolated actions were developed in these hospitals, the result of organizational initiatives, but without the involvement of the customers, i.e., the workers, in these actions.

Regarding the MQLW approach preferred by the workers in these hospitals, 37% did not choose any approach; 15% chose the transformation approach; 12% chose the legal approach; 12% chose the environmental approach; 9% chose the performance approach; 6% the citizenship approach and 9% others. The predominant choice for no approach can also be explained by the non-existence of a MQLW and of a QLW policy in most hospitals.

Generally speaking, it was difficult to see the difference between the priority levels assigned to the different objectives of the QLW actions and programs in these hospitals. The only exception was the identification of a greater importance given to productivity than to the company image. Productivity and happiness were the only objectives that showed a perceptible level of priority.

The "reciprocity" relationship that permeates the philosophy behind the investment in QLW could be seen due to the fact that productivity, in its qualitative and quantitative dimensions, as well as happiness, were given the same importance as the objectives of QLW actions and programs.

Generally speaking, it was difficult to find a difference between the levels of the different types of impact these QLW actions and programs had on these hospitals.

The only statistically significant exception was the identification of a greater impact on motivation than on the connection with the organization. The Wilcoxon Matched Pairs test showed that the impact on motivation tended to be greater than on productivity and on the meaning of life.

A QLW program has at its theoretical center the needs of its users. Promoting harmony between what the organization offers and the expectations linked to the needs is one of the objectives of the QLW programs related to motivation assumptions. Motivation results from reasons or needs that generate willingness and action and this can explain the result.

It was difficult to establish a difference between the levels of recognition given to workers' needs. The only exception was the identification of a greater importance given to workers' health than to their training and education. Health was the only need that presented a visible priority level.

In sum, the main focus of hospitals' mission was "health", and the priority of these organizations, as well as of people management, was the improvement of healthcare services and the development of skills. This can explain the recognition of the workers' health needs by the QLW actions and programs in the Hospitals. Another explanation is the legal requirement, which ultimately influences the nature of actions and programs implemented by hospitals.

Internal customer satisfaction and quality/productivity were the only indicators that presented a level of recognition, without any statistically significant difference between them. Internal customer satisfaction presented a marginally significant difference vis-à-vis the importance given to citizenship. Internal customer satisfaction and quality/productivity presented a recognition level clearly above that given to the environment. Citizenship presented a level of recognition above that given to the environment. Responsibility and meaning of life were the only concepts that presented a clearly superior level of priority. Responsibility presented a marginally significant difference vis-à-vis the meaning of life and a statistically significant difference vis-à-vis risks/iatrogenic effects and reciprocity.

Autonomy presented a statistical difference vis-à-vis the priorities given to the concepts meaning of life, risks/iatrogenic effects and reciprocity, but not in relation to the concept subjectivity. The concept subjectivity was the only one to present a clearly low level of priority.

Results show coherence regarding the profile and characteristics of the respondents and of the organizations. Therefore, the MQLW policy, even if incipient, or still characterized by focal and contingency actions, considered the dimensions of responsibility and meaning of life, which in itself has an important potential of alignment with the other initiatives and steps to be taken by these organizations for the consolidation and formalization of a MQLW based on values pertaining to modern and future organizations.

Around 24% of hospitals did not measure the results achieved with QLW actions and programs. Among them were those that did not develop any actions or programs. Among those that did have actions and programs, 53% said they used a single indicator to measure their results and 24% mentioned the use of two or more indicators. Only 18% of the organizations used specific QLW indicators to measure their results. 32% of the hospitals used observation and "feeling" to assess results and 41% of them used general organizational indicators. 9% mentioned indicators other than the general organizational indicators, specific QLW indicators, observation and "feeling".

Generally speaking, all elements of the QLW programs implemented had an impact, with relatively little difference among the different types of impact they had. Clearly, QLW initiatives were considered as highly successful, with the positive impact being more often the rule than the exception.

When analyzing the key success factors for the QLW initiatives in these hospitals and their impact on motivation, productivity, the meaning given by workers to their own life and to their work and the workers' connection with the organization, some associations can be established. There was no statistically significant difference between public and non-public organizations regarding the success of the initiatives through QLW actions and programs and their impact on motivation, productivity, the meaning given by workers to their own life and to their work and the workers' connection with the organization. The time the hospital has been in operation, its constructed area, the number of active beds did not have any impact on the success of QLW actions and programs regarding motivation, productivity, the meaning given by workers to their own life and to their work and the workers' connection with the organization.

The workforce composition did not show any relationship with any of the indicators measuring the impact of the success of QLW actions and programs in hospitals. Women presented a marginally greater tendency than men to be involved in QLW programs with great impact in terms of meaning given by workers to their own life and to their work, to the their connection with the organization and to the overall indicator of program success. Age and educational level of the respondents did not show any relevant correlation with any of the impact indicators analyzed.

The comparison between organizations that, in people management, prioritized workers and those that prioritized the organization showed that the former group had more positive impacts resulting from their QLW programs than the latter in all indicators considered.

The most significant results showed that the focus of the mission of the surveyed hospitals was "health", still directed towards external customers, i.e., the users of the healthcare services. The organizational priority was the "the improvement of healthcare services" and the organizational priority for people management was the "development of skills". Hospitals have not yet placed QLW and its management as a priority through a formal and institutionalized policy followed by programs. Most hospitals mentioned isolated actions as being MQLW initiatives.

No difference was found among organizations with and without a formal MQLW policy regarding the success of their programs. This result shows that even those respondents who said that the hospital had a formal policy and formal programs in fact referred to both planned and implemented isolated intentions and proposals, and not to a set of guidelines resulting from the mission that had an impact on the organizations priorities related to QLW and MQLW.

This information is in agreement with that related to the focus of the mission and organizational and people management priorities. However, organizations with a specific QLW management had programs with greater impact on productivity than those organizations that did not have a specific management, with no difference between them regarding the other impact indicators.

Regarding the other organizations, those whose isolated QLW actions were directed to the operational workforce showed a marginally significant trend regarding more positive impacts on productive and the meaning given by workers to own life and to their work, with no difference regarding the other indicators.

The recognition of workers' participation and workers' satisfaction showed a statistically significant correlation with all success indicators considered. This result can be understood as related to the theoretical concepts and the assumptions behind MQLW. A policy that guides a QLW program and QLW actions should start from the needs of the users of this policy and program. Therefore, stressing workers' participation and satisfaction is an important requirement that impacts the quality of the process and the success of the institutionalized proposal.

The legitimization by workers and workers' knowledge did not show any relevant correlation with any of the success indicators considered. Even in those hospitals where such initiatives existed, the latter were actually isolated actions generated by managers who had the workers as "receiving users" of their actions. The comparison between organizations that showed a preference for a certain approach in their QLW programs and those that did not have any preference showed that the former group has more positive impacts resulting from their QLW programs than the latter group in all indicators considered. It should be underlined that 37% of respondents informed that there was no preference regarding MQLW approaches in their hospital.

The emphasis on objectives related to workers' productivity and happiness showed a positive and statistically significant correlation with all impact indicators considered. The emphasis on the organizational image was positively and significantly correlated with all impact indicators, except for the workers' connection with the organization, which showed a marginally significant difference. The emphasis on the well-being at work was positively and significantly correlated with all impact indicators, except for the workers' connection with the organization, which did not show any correlation. The emphasis on complying with the legal requirements was significantly correlated only with motivation and did not relate to any of the other indicators. Attention given to every need assessed showed a positive and statistically significant correlation with all impact indicators. The only exception was the relationship between the concern with the internal customers and the impact in terms of meaning given by workers to their own life and to their work where, in spite of that, a marginally significant correlation was found. The emphasis on concepts related to responsibility—commitment, reciprocity and risks-iatrogenic effects showed a positive and statistically significant correlation with all impact indicators.

Greater effort placed on the concepts of respect to workers and decision-making autonomy showed a positive and statistically significant correlation with all impact indicators, except for the meaning given by workers to their own life and to their work, where the correlation was only marginally significant. The importance given to the concept of subjectivity-concessions did not show any correlation with any of the impact indicators, except for a marginally significant correlation with motivation. These are concepts that support the theory on MQLW and that, as principles, add the notion of value to the organizational policy.

The comparison between organizations that measure the results of their QLW programs and those that do not showed that the former presented more positive impacts with their QLW programs than the latter in all indicators considered. The assessment of the success of QLW actions requires the establishment, improvement and application of specific indicators that analyze the impact on the various factors and areas involved. Availability of resources, the importance of the policy, availability of people with a focus on and competence in QLW, a target related to the development of the QLW program, organizational mission, interest and will by top management, workers' participation and interest, assessment of processes and results, projected organizational image and autonomy of managers were factors associated with the success of QLW actions and programs in place in these hospitals.

ORGANIZATIONAL AND PERSONAL CONCEPTS AND VALUES THAT GUIDE MANAGERS IN THE MANAGEMENT OF QUALITY OF LIFE AT WORK IN HOSPITALS IN SÃO PAULO

Everything that is precious, true and beautiful is inside the natural being
—TULKU, 2007, p. 89.

The key words most frequently used by responding managers to mean QLW in the present survey were professional satisfaction, followed by well-being, co-responsibility, health, recognition, respect, involvement, leadership, motivation and productivity. Managers defined QLW as the process and the result arising from conditions that favor choices related to well-being, satisfaction, happiness, respect, positive affective links, trust, credibility, recognition, benefits, cooperation, reciprocity, infrastructure, compensation, autonomy, achievement, good mood, creativity and innovation, perspectives for the future, participation in the fate of the organization, meeting targets, making the mission come true, relating to one's job and the meaning of work, transparency and communication, legitimacy by users, fulfillment, passion for one's work, healthcare and promotion.

From the analysis of the answers given by the respondents, QLW was understood as the balance between workers' expectations and needs and the opportunities to fully or partially meet them by providing the satisfaction factors during the work process and through the established relationships. A connection can be made between the fact that most respondents have a background in humanities and their perception that QLW is related to opportunities of experiences that would meet workers' needs.

The QLW concepts highlighted by respondents as present in their organizations were associated with QLW actions performed in their organizations designed to promote health, well-being, integration, togetherness, training, commitment, humanization of the work environment, ethical relationships and organization of an environment that is adequate to work.

QLW was associated with a pleasant ethical-legal environment of opportunities, integration, individual and organizational responsibility, productivity, satisfaction, self-achievement, respect, recognition, humanization, ability to choose, physical and mental health, development, leisure, motivation, commitment, infrastructure, trust, solidarity, reciprocity, alignment of individual and organizational objectives, expectations and success.

The QLW concept represented by respondents as a whole associated the diagnosis of needs with interventions that would enable the achievement of the factors leading to satisfaction and well-being. However, organizational practices do not yet take into account these proposals made by respondents, they rather focus on the operational workers without, however, involving them in the decision-making process. Therefore, the dimensions of individuality, subjectivity, needs, meaning of one's own life and of life at work and motivation were not underlined as relevant elements in the actions currently being taken by the organizations. Concepts such as reciprocity, resilience, commitment and legitimacy would still be under construction in a process that should generate a level of awareness that could turn ideas into a management strategy.

SUMMARY

MQLW had not yet been consolidated in the surveyed organizations. The time it would take each hospital to formalize a MQLW policy would depend on the attitude of managers at different levels of the organization and on workers.

The survey showed that QLW was not part of the management strategies; QLW was not a priority for hospitals so far; the relationship of reciprocity and commitment could be better worked on and explored; MQLW was not yet associated with a competence for people management to be able to generate well-being at work, thus impacting productivity and the meaning of work; QLW was not the focus of the mission at these hospitals; and that people managers could include values that guided MQLW strategies and programs.

Organizational learning could help formalize a MQLW policy if assumptions and values supported the changes, aligning them with the respective organizational missions. Corporate education could also be used to change reality.

Dejours (2003, p. 22–4) discusses some important aspects for the construction of the collective process "The banalization of what is bad goes through several intermediate phases, all of them depending on a human construction. In other words, this is not an irrepressible logic, but rather a process that implies responsibilities."

According to Tulku (1994, p. 101), the relationship between objectives, success and responsibility exists when objectives at work are expanded, challenges are increased, responsibility is deepened and either success or failure is the result of this synchrony. "Assuming responsibilities naturally increases our level of understanding and care, our degree of participation and our commitment to protect the results of our efforts and of other people's efforts".

The first limitation and the greatest challenge in this study was to capture the experienced by not informed reality. Fischer (2001, p.16) discussed this issue by saying that:

> We should take into account, therefore, that surveys capture more the formal than the real model and is based on different opinions about the formal model. Making a survey of the real model would require a methodological effort that would hardly be accessible to experts and to which organizations seldom open themselves.

Respondents that are assessed by the effectiveness of their actions usually restrict themselves to analyzing them for the purpose of the scientific study, also aiming at disseminating them, even if this is not stated explicitly. Organizations try to understand the QLW concept and its complexity requires them to review their policies, programs and practices, including people management. This can be an interesting contribution given by this study: providing information that can be used to revise policies, programs and actions linked to people management and MQLW at these hospitals. The diagnosis that has been made could also eliminate the risk of this study being considered the result of a passing management fad because it has the potential to provide the input for a reflection on the strategies to formalize a policy that also includes QLW and that leads to the construction of specific indicators for the assessment of the process and the results.

Although there is no consensus about the QLW concept, what is known is that it goes beyond just meeting legal requirements that protect workers including, above all, meeting workers' needs and aspirations, the humanization of work and the corporate social responsibility (Walton, 1973).

The change process to be experienced by organizations should include the incorporation of a humanist philosophy based on values that guide new management practices that have QLW as a priority. Garcia and Dolan (1997), when discussing "management by values", consider it an indispensable tool for strategic leadership. Quality of life and QLW are politically, socially and economically determined and this fact emerges as the single greatest challenge for organizations to manage. Including QLW in missions, policies and programs can seem a simple alignment process, but when we consider that QLW involves individual, subjective and time-related concepts, the limits start to be outlined. The challenge embedded in this reality would be to identify effective and efficient management strategies for the implementation and maintenance of practices that included the emphasis on QLW in actions and decisions at the organizational level. This challenge is clear in the words of Spink (1997, p. 313):

> Principles are being negotiated at the intersection between the system and the world lived, in a procedural movement that advances from alliances and conflicts, but with the implicit recognition of the possibility of communicative action.

"When we consider freedom as something intrinsic to our being, we realize that life is what we make out of it. All options are open, our choices are unlimited. When we have knowledge, time presents us with infinite possibilities of change" (Maitland, 2003, p.145).

NOTE

1. Research presented as a partial requirement for the completion of the Post-Doc Program at the Administration Department of the School of Administration, Economy and Accounting at São Paulo University, Brazil.

REFERENCES

Agudelo, S.F. (1997). Violência, cidadania e saúde pública. In: Barata, R.B.; Barreto, M.L.; Almeida Filho, N.; Veras, R.P. (org.). *Eqüidade e saúde: contribuições da epidemiologia.* Rio de Janeiro: Fiocruz/Abrasco, p. 39–62.

Agudelo, S.F. (1989). *Violencia e salud: elementos preliminares para pensarlas e actuar.* Washington DC: PAHO/OMS. [mimeo].

Albuquerque, L.G. de & Limongi-França, A.C. (1998). Estratégias de recursos humanos e gestão da qualidade de vida no trabalho: o stress e a expansão do conceito de qualidade total. *Revista de Administração.* São Paulo. v. 33(2), p. 40–51, abril/junho.

Albuquerque, L.G. de. (2002). A gestão estratégica de pessoas. In: Fleury, M.T.L. (coord.). *As pessoas na organização.* São Paulo: Gente, Parte 1, p. 35–50.

Anabuck, M.H. (2001). *Situações geradoras de estresse: a percepção das enfermeiras de um hospital de ensino.* Dissertação. Escola de Enfermagem, Universidade de São Paulo. São Paulo.

Araujo, T.M. et al. (2003). Aspectos psicossociais do trabalho e distúrbios psíquicos entre trabalhadores de enfermagem. Rev. *Saúde Pública*, São Paulo, v. 37(4), p. 424–33, agosto.

Bachion, M.M. et al. (1998). Estresse, ansiedade e coping: uma revisão de conceitos, medidas e estratégias de intervenção voltadas para a prática de enfermagem. *Rev Min Enf.* Belo Horizonte, v. 2(1), p. 33–9.

Barros, A.L.B.L. et al. (2003). Situações geradoras de ansiedade e estratégias para seu controle entre enfermeiras: estudo preliminar. *Rev Latinoam Enfermagem*, Ribeirão Preto, v. 11(5), p. 585–92.

Beckhard, R. (1997). Perfil da organização saudável. In: Hesselbein, F. *A organização do futuro.* 5.ed. São Paulo: Futura, p. 349–52.

Bianchi, E.R.F. (1990). *Estresse em enfermagem: análise da atuação do enfermeiro de centro cirúrgico.* Tese. Escola de Enfermagem, Universidade de São Paulo, São Paulo.

Bianchi, E.R.F. (1999). *Stress entre enfermeiros hospitalares.* Tese (Livre Docência). Escola de Enfermagem, Universidade de São Paulo, São Paulo.

Bianchi, E.R.F. (2000) Enfermeiro hospitalar e o stress. *Rev Esc Enf USP*, São Paulo, v. 34(4), p. 390–4.

Borges, L.O. et al. (2002). A síndrome de *burnout* e os valores organizacionais: um estudo comparativo em hospitais universitários. *Psicologia: Reflexão e Crítica*, Natal, v. 15(1), p. 189 –200.

Brasil. Ministério da Saúde. (2007). Secretaria de Gestão do Trabalho e da Educação na Saúde. Departamento de Gestão e da Regulação do Trabalho em Saúde. *Indicadores de gestão do trabalho em saúde: material de apoio para o Programa de Qualificação e Estruturação da Gestão do Trabalho e da Educação no SUS–ProgeSUS/ Ministério da Saúde, Secretaria de Gestão do Trabalho e da Educação na Saúde, Departamento de Gestão e da Regulação do Trabalho em Saúde.* Brasília: Ed. Ministério da Saúde, p. 290.

Chanlat, J.F. (coord.). (1996). *O indivíduo na organização: dimensões esquecidas.* São Paulo: Atlas, v. 2 e 3.

Chizzotti, A. (1991). *Pesquisa em ciências humanas e sociais.* São Paulo: Cortez.

Cordeiro et al. (2006). Impacto do múltiplo vínculo empregatício do enfermeiro. Paper apresentado como Trabalho de Conclusão de Curso de Especialização em Gerenciamento de Unidades e Serviços de Enfermagem, Faculdade Santa Marcelina. *CD Anais Semana Científica*–Faculdade Santa Marcelina.

Costa, J.R.A., Almeida, P.C. & Lima, J. (2003). Stress no trabalho do enfermeiro. *Rev. Esc. Enferm USP*, São Paulo, v. 37(3), p. 63–71.

Cunha, K. de C. (2003). The perception of stress associated with the work environment of nursing related employees. *Anais.* 27th International Congress on Occupational Health–ICOH. Foz do Iguaçu.

Cunha, K. de C. & Limongi-França, A.C. (2003). Perceptions of bullying from students employed in the nursing workplace. *Anais.* 27th International Congress on Occupational Health–ICOH. Foz do Iguaçu.

Cunha, K. de C. & Souza, L.A de. (2004). Impacto da violência urbana no processo e nas relações de trabalho em unidades básicas de saúde da cidade de São Paulo. *Anais.* 4º Congresso de Stress da ISMA-BR e 6º Fórum Internacional de Qualidade de Vida no Trabalho. Porto Alegre.

Cunha, K. de C. (2004). *Gestão da qualidade de vida no trabalho em hospitais da cidade de São Paulo.* 2004. 247f. Relatório de Pesquisa. Programa de Pós-Doutoramento do Departamento de Administração, FEA, Universidade de São Paulo, São Paulo.

Cunha, K.de C. et al. (2007) Qualidade de vida no trabalho: percepções dos enfermeiros. *Anais do VII Congresso de Stress da ISMA-BR*, Porto Alegre.

Cunha, K. de C. et al. (2007ª). Policronia no processo de trabalho da enfermagem. *Anais do I Congresso Científico da* Faculdade Santa Marcelina.

Cyrulnik, B. (2001). Resiliência: essa inaudita capacidade de construção humana. Lisboa: Horizontes Pedagógicos.

Dahlberg, A.W. et al. (1997). Construindo uma empresa saudável. In: Hesselbein, F. et al. *A organização do futuro.* 5ª.ed. São Paulo: Futura, p. 383–91.

Dejours, C. (1992). *A loucura do trabalho: estudo de psicopatologia do trabalho.* 5ª ed. São Paulo: Cortez/Oboré.

Dejours, C. (2003). *A banalização da injustiça social.* 5ª.ed. Rio de Janeiro: Ed. FGV.

Di Martino, V. (2002).Workplace violence in the health sector—country case studies (Brazil, Bulgaria, Lebanon, Portugal, South Africa, Thailand, and an additional Australian study): Synthesis Report. Ginebra (SWZ): *OMS/OIT/CIE/ISP.*

Dolan, S.L. (2006). *Estresse, auto-estima, saúde e trabalho.* Rio de Janeiro: Qualitymark.

Drucker, P.F. (2000). A nova sociedade das organizações. In: Howard R. et al. *Aprendizado organizacional: gestão de pessoas para a inovação contínua.* Rio de Janeiro: Campus, p. 3–17.

Dutra, J.S. (1997). Autonomia para o desenvolvimento profissional: utopia ou realidade no contexto brasileiro. In: Motta, F.C.P.; Caldas, M.P. (org.). *Cultura organizacional e cultura brasileira.* São Paulo: Atlas.

Eboli, M. (coord.). (2001). *Educação para as empresas do século XXI: desenvolvimento e alinhamento de talentos humanos às estratégias empresariais.* USP/FEA/PROGEP/FIA. São Paulo: Schumuckler.

Faria, A.C. de, Barboza, D.B., & Domingos, N.A.M. (2005). Absenteísmo por transtornos mentais na enfermagem no período de 1995 a 2004. *Arq Cienc Saúde,* Umuarama, v.12(1), p. 14–20, jan./março.

Fernandes, E.C. & Gutierrez, L.H. (1988). Qualidade de vida no trabalho (QVT): uma experiência brasileira. *Rev.Adm.* São Paulo, v. 23(4), p. 29–38, out/dezembro.

Fischer, A.L. (2001). O conceito de modelo de gestão de pessoas—modismo e realidade em gestão de recursos humanos nas empresas brasileiras. In: Dutra, J, S. (org.) *Gestão por competências.* 3ª ed. São Paulo: Gente.

Fischer, A.L. (2002). Um resgate conceitual e histórico dos modelos de gestão de pessoas. In: Fleury, M.T. L. (coord.). *As pessoas na organização.* São Paulo: Editora Gente.

Fleury, M.T.L. (2001). Aprendizagem e gestão do conhecimento. In: Dutra, J.S. (org.). *Gestão por competências.* 3ª ed. São Paulo: Gente.

França, A.C.L. (2007). *Práticas de recursos humanos: conceitos, ferramentas e procedimentos.* São Paulo: Atlas.

Freire, P. (1983). *Educação e mudança.* 12ª. ed. Rio de Janeiro: Paz e Terra.

Freitas, M.E. (1997). Cultura organizacional: o doce controle no clube dos raros. In: Motta, F.C. P. & Caldas, M.P. (org.). *Cultura organizacional e cultura brasileira.* São Paulo: Atlas.

Garcia, S. & Dolan, S. (1997). *La dirección por valores: el cambio más allá de la dirección por objetivos.* Madrid: McGraw-Hill.

Gaspar, P.J.S. (1997). Enfermagem profissão de desgaste: perspectivas do enfermeiro do serviço de urgência. *Nursing.* Edição Portuguesa. v. 10(119), p. 23–4.

Gatti, M.F.Z. (2005). A música como intervenção redutora da ansiedade do profissional de serviço de emergência: utopia ou realidade? *Dissertação.* Escola de Enfermagem, Universidade de São Paulo, São Paulo.

Gil, A.C. (1995). *Métodos e técnicas de pesquisa social.* 4. ed. São Paulo: Atlas.

Hoga, L.A.K. (2002). Causas de estresse e mecanismos de promoção do bem-estar dos profissionais de enfermagem de unidade neonatal. *Acta Paul Enferm,* São Paulo, v. 15(2), p.18–25.

Kanter, R.M. (1997). Recolocando as pessoas no cerne da organização do futuro. In: Hesselbein, F. et al. *A organização do futuro.* 5ª. ed. São Paulo: Futura, p. 155–67.

Lemos, J.C., Cruz, R.M. & Botomé, S.P. (2002). Sofrimento psíquico e trabalho dos profissionais de enfermagem. *Estud Psicol,* Natal, v. 7(2), p. 407–9, jul./dezembro.

Lima Jr., J. H.V. & Ésther, A.B. (2001) Transições, prazer e dor na trabalho de enfermagem. *Rev Adm Emp,* São Paulo, v. 41(3), s.p., jul./setembro.

Limongi-França, A.C. (1996). Indicadores empresariais de qualidade de vida no trabalho: esforço empresarial e satisfação dos empregados no ambiente de manufatura com certificação ISO 9000. 1996. *Tese-Faculdade de Economia, Administração e Contabilidade,* Universidade de São Paulo, São Paulo.

Limongi-França, A.C. (1997). Qualidade de vida no trabalho: conceitos, abordagens, inovações e desafios nas empresas brasileiras. *Rev.Bras.Med.Psicossomática,* Rio de Janeiro, v.1(2), abr/mai/junho.

Limongi-França, A.C. (2001). Interfaces da qualidade de vida no trabalho na administração de empresas: fatores críticos da gestão empresarial para uma nova competência. 2001. 246f. *Tese de Livre-docência–Faculdade de Economia, Administração e Contabilidade, Universidade de São Paulo,* São Paulo.

Limongi-França, A.C. (2003). *Qualidade de vida no trabalho-QVT: conceitos e práticas nas empresas da sociedade pós-industrial.* São Paulo: Atlas.

Loomis, D.P. (1998). Epidemiologia da violência em locais de trabalho nos EUA. In: Barreto, M.L., Almeida Filho, N., Veras, R.P. & Barata, R.B. (org.). *Epidemiologia, serviços e tecnologias em saúde.* Rio de Janeiro: Fiocruz/Abrasco, p. 153–66.

Lüdke, M. & André, M.E.D. (1986). A. *Pesquisa: abordagens qualitativas.* São Paulo: EPU.

Maitland, A. (2003). *O trabalho como mestre: sabedoria do budismo tibetano para o sucesso empresarial.* São Paulo: Dharma.

Marconi, M. de A. & Lakatos, E.M. (1996). *Técnicas de pesquisa.* São Paulo, Atlas.

Martins, L.M.M. et al. (2000). Agentes estressores no trabalho e sugestões para amenizá-los: opiniões de enfermeiros de pós-graduação. *Rev Esc Enfermagem USP,* São Paulo, v. 34(1), p. 52–8.

Martins, L.A.N. (2003). Saúde mental dos profissionais de saúde. *Rev Bras Med Trab,* Belo Horizonte, v. 1(1), p. 59–71.

Marziale, M.H.P. (2004). A violência no setor saúde. *Rev Latino-am Enfermagem,* Ribeirão Preto, v.12, n.2, p. 147–8, mar/abr, Editorial.

Maslach, C. & Leiter, M.P. (1999). *Trabalho: fonte de prazer ou desgaste?* Campinas: Papirus.

Maslach, C. (2005). Conseqüências do stress ocupacional no trabalho e na saúde. In: Rossi, A.M., Perrewé, P.L. & Sauter, S.L. (org.). *Stress e qualidade de vida no trabalho: perspectivas atuais da saúde ocupacional.* São Paulo: Atlas, p. 41–55.

Mauro, M.Y.C. (1996). Saúde mental do trabalhador e o enfermeiro. *Rev. Enfermagem UERJ,* Rio de Janeiro, Extra, p. 81–8, outubro.

Mendes, R. (1995). *Patologia do trabalho.* Rio de Janeiro: Atheneu.

Menzani, G. (2006). Stress entre enfermeiros brasileiros que atuam em pronto socorro. *Dissertação. Escola de Enfermagem da Universidade de São Paulo.* São Paulo.

Minayo, M.C.S & Souza, E.R. (1993).Violência para todos. *Cadernos de Saúde Pública,* v. 9(1), p. 65–78.

Minayo, M.C.S. (1994). A violência social sob a perspectiva da saúde pública. *Cadernos de Saúde Pública,* v. 10(19), supl. 1, p. 7–18.

Minayo, M.C.S. & Souza, E.R. (1999). É possível prevenir a violência? reflexões a partir do campo da saúde pública. *Revista Ciência & Saúde Coletiva,* v. 4(1), p. 7–23.

Minayo, M.C.S. (1992). Violência e saúde. In: Spínola, A.W.P., Sá, E.N.C., Westphal, M.F., Adorno, R.C.F. & Zioni, F. (coord.). *Pesquisa social em saúde.* São Paulo: Cortez, p. 257–67.

Morgan, G. (1996). *Imagens da organização.* São Paulo: Atlas.

Motta, P.R. (2001). *Desempenho em equipes de saúde.* Rio de Janeiro: OMS/OPS/FGV.

Murofuse, N.T., Abranches, S.S., Napoleão, A.A. (2005). Reflexões sobre estresse e *burnout* e a relação com a enfermagem. *Rev Latino-am Enfermagem,* Ribeirão Preto, v. 2(13), p. 255–261, mar./abril.

NIOSH. CDC (2002). Workplaces safety and health violence: occupational hazards in hospitals. Department of Health an Human Services. Center for Disease Control and Prevention. *National Institute for Occupational Safety and Health.*

Nonaka, I. (2000). A empresa criadora de conhecimento. In: Howard, R. et al. *Aprendizado organizacional: gestão de pessoas para a inovação contínua.* Rio de Janeiro: Campus, p. 43–58.

OIT. (2002). Un informe de la OIT estudia la salud mental en el trabajo en Alemania, Estados Unidos, finlandia, Polonia e Reino Unido: aumentan los coston del estrés en el trabajo y la incidencia de la depresión es cada vez mayor. *Comunicación. OIT/ 00/37.* file://A:\OITassediomoraltrabalho.htm.

OIE/OMS/ISP   . Directrices marco para afrontar la violencia laboral en el sector de la salud. Ginebra (SWZ): *OIT/CIE/OMS/ISP,* 2002.

Peniche, A.C.G. & Nunes, L.M. (2001). Estresse-ansiedade do enfermeiro em sala de recuperação anéstica. *Rev SOBECC,* São Paulo, v. 6(3), p.19–23.

Platt, L.E. (1997). O equilíbrio entre a vida profissional e pessoal do funcionário. In: Hesselbein, F. et al. *A organização do futuro.* 5ª ed. São Paulo: Futura, p. 339–348.

Quick, J.C. et al. (2003). *O executivo em harmonia.* São Paulo: Publifolha.

Robayo-Tamayo, M. (1997). Relação entre síndrome de *burnout* e os valores organizacionais no pessoal de enfermagem de dois hospitais públicos. *Dissertação.* Universidade de Brasília–UNB, Distrito Federal.

Rossi, A.M. (2005). Estressores ocupacionais e diferenças de gênero. In: Rossi, A.M., Perrewé, P.L. & Sauter, S.L. *Stress e qualidade de vida no trabalho: perspectivas atuais da saúde ocupacional.* São Paulo: Atlas, p. 9–17.

Ruas, R. & Antunes, E. (1997). Estruturação, programas da qualidade e práticas de benefícios e incentivos: a questão do comprometimento. In: Carleia L, L. & Valle, R. (org.). *Reestruturação produtiva e mercado de trabalho no Brasil.* São Paulo: Hucitec.

Santos, K.J. & Soler, Z.A.S.G. (2003). Absenteísmo na enfermagem: enfoque nas causas de ordem psicológicas. *Enfermagem Brasil,* v. 2(6), p. 336–43.

Santos, M.S. & Trevizan, M.A. (2002). Sofrimento psíquico no trabalho do enfermeiro. Nursing, São Paulo, v. 5(52), p. 23–28, setembro.

SES. Secretaria de Estado da Saúde. São Paulo. *Programa de melhoria da qualidade de vida e ambiente profissional. Implantação das COMSATs.* Disponível em: <http://www.recursoshumanos.sp.gov.br/qualidadevida/secretarias/saude>. Acessed January 2008.

Sethi, D. (1997). Os sete rs da auto-estima. In: Hesselbein, F. et al. *A organização do futuro.* 5ª. ed. São Paulo: Futura, p. 195–206.

Silva, V.E.F. da. (1996). O desgaste do trabalhador de enfermagem: relação trabalho de enfermagem e saúde do trabalhador. 289 f. *Tese–Escola de Enfermagem, Universidade de São Paulo,* São Paulo.

Souza, E.R. & Minayo, M.C.S. (1995). O impacto da violência social na saúde pública do Brasil: década de 80. In: Minayo, M. C. S. *Os muitos brasis: saúde e população na década de 80.* 2ª ed. São Paulo/Rio de Janeiro: Hucitec/Abrasco, p. 87–116.

Spink, P.K. (1997). Discurso e ideologia gerencial: reflexões a partir da experiência brasileira. In: Motta, F.C.P.& Caldas, M.P. (org.). *Cultura organizacional e cultura brasileira.* São Paulo: Atlas.

Stacciarini, J.M.R. & Tróccoli, B.T. (2001). O estresse na atividade ocupacional do enfermeiro. *Rev. Latino-am Enfermagem,* Ribeirão Preto, v. 9(2), p. 17–25, março.

Stalk Jr., G. et al. (2000). Competindo em capacidades: as novas regras da estratégia empresarial. In: Howard, R. et al. *Aprendizado organizacional: gestão de pessoas para a inovação contínua.* Rio de Janeiro: Campus, p. 19–113.

Triviños, A.N.S. (1995). *Introdução à pesquisa em ciências sociais.* São Paulo: Atlas.

Tulku, T. (1994). *A excelência da realização no trabalho: o caminho da habilidade.* São Paulo: Dharma Publisching.

Tulku, T. (2007). *A liberdade oculta da mente.* Rio de Janeiro: Dharma Publishing.

Walton, R.E. (1973). Quality of working life: what is it? *Sloan Management Review,* Cambridge. v. 15(1).

Welch, J. (2005). *Paixão por vencer: a bíblia do sucesso.* 5ª ed. Rio de Janeiro: Elsevier.

WHO (2006). Working together for health. The world health report. Geneva: *WHO Press,* hhttp://www.who.int/topics/health_workforce/en/. Acessed February 7, 2008.

CHAPTER 12

HEALTH PROMOTION AND QUALITY OF WORK LIFE

The Challenge of Integrated Management

Ana Cristina Limongi-França

Wealth means education (...) competence (...) technology.
Wealth is knowledge. Yes, we have money.
But we are not rich. We are like the son who
inherited money from his father, whom he never met.
He was not raised and prepared to spend it.
He has it in his hands, but does not know how to use it.
If you do not know how to spend the money,
then you are not rich.
We are not rich.

—Report by a banker from the Persian Gulf
in *The Wealth and Poverty of Nations*, Landes, 1998

In this chapter we present concepts that have contributed to the construction of policies and practices, especially regarding the integration of health promotion with quality of work life. We hope to contribute to the effective trend of the last ten years, which have been fertile in the discussion of this

Stress and Quality of Working Life, pages 235–256
Copyright © 2009 by Information Age Publishing
All rights of reproduction in any form reserved.

subject. There is a new horizon, with values and concepts in the scope of management, regarding health promotion; fairness, social inclusion and diversity; psychosocial care and resilience, specialties aimed at the occupational well-being.

Integrating Health Promotion and Quality of Work Life–QWL represents political and organizational challenges, even today. It is a political challenge due to the absence of values, strategy, goals and an agenda. This absence paralyzes the sectors of occupational safety and health of a major portion of companies, both national and internationalized. On its turn, the organizational challenge refers to the lean staff, overloaded with reports, records and suppliers, which almost never have priority placed on the educational aspects that the health promotion integrated with quality of work life requires. Hence, it has not been common to conciliate the new knowledge on health and well-being, the professional qualification, and the technological pressure with new life and work styles. The challenge for integration is essentially systemic.

The debate in the sphere of health and well-being has generated organizational changes. Changes that have made a more attentive and responsible organizational management viable, which reveal an effective evolution of management. There is often an integration of traditional procedures and tools, such as: sensitization, diagnoses, definition of procedures, programs, implementation and assessment of the results. There will be a great advantage in the results if the criteria for processing change incorporate the certifications and the tools that are already a part of the corporate obligations.

What is observed, still today, in most of the public and private organizations are actions that are soothing, random or reactive to the requirements of civil and criminal responsibility. However, specifically within the sphere of people management, there are programs and studies regarding the reduction of physical and mental fatigue, a traditional subject of ergonomics. Regarding the attention to the worker, there are managerial efforts in terms of understanding the morale of the work group, the reasons for demotivation and, more recently, the programs on the balance between personal and professional life.

Among the studies on this subject, the construct Quality of Life has been abstracted from a group of specialists of different cultures: subjectivity; multidimensionality; presence of positive (mobility, for example) and negative (pain, for example) dimensions. The development of these elements has led to the definition of Quality of Life in the WHOQOL Group (in: site: www.hcpa.ufrgs.br, 1998), as "the perception of the individual on his position in life, within the context of culture and the system of values in which he or she lives and in relation to his or her goals, expectations, standards and concerns".

The recognition of the multidimensionality of the construct has reflected on the structure of the instrument, based on six domains: physical, psychological, level of independence, social relationships, environment, and spirituality/religion/personal beliefs–psychosomatic medicine, with that of the vision of the biopsychosocial person, where psychosocial factors are fundamental to explain the health and illness of modern society. It is located in the same conceptual proposal of the holistic vision of man, including by the most critical sociologists, such as *Giddens* (2000), who states:

> Living in a global era means to face a diversity of risk situations. Very often we may have to be daring, and not cautious, and support scientific innovation and other forms of change. (Giddens, p. 45)

The corporate social responsibility and the aging of the population strengthen the vision of sustainable development. New paradigms for the QWL issues unveil at the beginning of the millennium.

The convergence of these challenges is in the biopsychosocial vision of the person. This approach originates in the Psychosomatic Medicine, which proposes an integrated vision of the human being that acts under the principle that every person is a socio-psychosomatic complex, i.e., has biological, psychological and social potentialities that respond *simultaneously* to the conditions of life. The specific domains we have specified here should be worked upon from this vision. Normally, we have adopted the term layer, criteria or indicator. However, in order to align this debate with the discussions regarding the sphere of qualify of life, we started addressing these competencies as domains (Limongi-França, 2004), which are defined below:

The *biological* domain refers to the physical characteristics inherited or acquired at birth and during the whole course of life. It includes metabolism, resistances and vulnerabilities of the organs or systems.

The *psychological* domain refers to the affective, emotional processes and to those of reasoning, either conscious or unconscious, that shape the personality of every person and their mode of perceiving and positioning themselves before people and circumstances they perceive.

The *social* domain incorporates the values, the beliefs, and the role of the family at work and in all the groups and communities to which each person belongs and in which they participate. The environment and the geographical location also set up the social dimension.

While aiming at integrating the concept with elements of work in organizations, we developed the organizational domain. The *organizational* domain refers to the organizational culture, the size of the company, the economical segment in which the company acts and the standards of competitiveness.

The Set of these domains constitutes the vision of the person at work: BPSO, in continuous interaction, interdependence, but with their own intrinsic and extrinsic processes, as per the figure: The vision of the BPSO person:

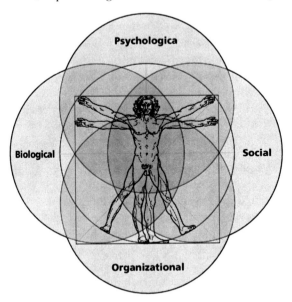

The approach of the integral BPSO vision is associated with ethics and the promotion of the human condition. This integrated attitude meets demands related to:

First: identification, elimination, neutralization and control of occupational risks that can be observed in the physical environment,

Second: definition of standards for work relationships,

Third: knowledge and assessment of the physical and mental load required for each activity,

Fourth: explanation and guidance on the political and ideological implications,

Fifth: qualification of the corporate leadership dynamics and of the informal and formal power,

Sixth: awareness of the meaning of work in s,

Seventh: importance of the relationship and satisfaction of persons in their everyday life.

The administrative awareness on the needs of people and new challenges at work have stimulated the arrangement of the activities of quality of life in the companies, and characterized a new competency, a new managerial specialization, the Management of Quality of Work, which we have defined as:

The capacity to manage the set of actions, including diagnosis, implementation of improvements and managerial, technological and managerial innovations in the work environment, aligned and constructed within the organizational culture, with an absolute priority to the well-being of the people in the organization.

A FEW HISTORICAL ROOTS OF QUALITY OF LIFE

Quality of Life is the *perception of well-being, from the personal needs, the social and economical environment and life expectations, while considering the individual forum.* The relationships between Work and Quality of Life represent, nowadays, a growing need of appreciation of the working conditions. This demand attracts the discussion on: procedures of the task itself, care for the physical environment, attention to interpersonal relationship, meaning of work and problems of adapting to the positions and life conditions inherent to it.

The subject Quality of Work Life has been treated in a broad range. QWL is defined from medical care established by legislation on health and security up to voluntary activities of employees and employers. The majority of these paths lead us to the discussion of the conditions of life and well-being of people, groups, communities and even of the planet, as a whole, and of its insertion in the universe. In reality, we believe that the basis of the discussion of the concepts of quality of life encompasses choices on well-being and the perception of what can be done to meet the expectations, both of managers and users of the QWL action within the companies.

Nowadays, maybe the most revealing contribution in the field of social-political organization of nations is the one called "third path". Giddens (2000), its main idealizer, situates the dilemmas of society in the last 15 years: globalization, individualism and the left and right political positions that appear no longer to make sense.

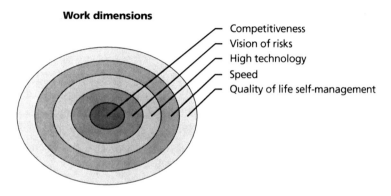

Work dimensions

- Competitiveness
- Vision of risks
- High technology
- Speed
- Quality of life self-management

The awareness on sustainable growth and the future of the new generations is growing, which endangers the process of globalization. For the author, the general goal of the third path policy should be to help citizens to open their path through the most important revolutions of our time: globalization, transformation in personal life and relationship with nature. The values propagated by the "third path" are fundamentally based on the principle of social equality, the protection of the vulnerable, the freedom with autonomy, the rights with responsibility, the authority with democracy, the cosmopolitan pluralism, among others. These principles affront neoliberal conservatism, which is the ideological source behind globalization. In a schematic manner, Giddens (2000) lists the basic principles of this new political current:

- development of citizenship;
- social responsibility and projects;
- equality with freedom;
- conservation of the environment;
- sustainable development.

"Of course, the dilemmas are not separate, but we need to tie the threads", asserts Giddens (2000). "Tying the threads", when talking about Quality of Work Life, starts with the analysis of the work relationships in this era of globalization and their paradoxes. Globalization has impelled new work relationships, which bring along trends that are certainly reflecting on security, on health and on expectations of the worker. Technology, increasingly advanced, provides safer protection equipment and preventive medicine, on its turn, can rely on studies and more solutions. At the same time, new challenges emerge from the revolution in the relationships of production and occupational forms, such as, for example, remote work. Demands to reduce working hours take place in many countries and, when met, this free time, available for the worker to rest or perform other activities, is directed toward tourism and consumption. Simultaneously, the inclusion of new technologies may result in the exclusion of people from the productive sphere.

These paradoxes of modern age indicate the constitution of a new paradigm in social sciences. National society is being overlaid, assimilated or submitted by the global society, a reality that has not yet been sufficiently encoded. Global society presents empirical and methodological, or historical and theoretical challenges that demand new concepts, other categories, and different interpretations. The conceptual references change quickly. According to political scientist Octávio Ianni (1994:147):

There has always been an enormous debate on how society and the state relate to each other, who should submit the other and who should embody the highest moral values. Thus, we became accustomed to thinking that the boundaries of society and the State are the same, or if they aren't, they could (and should) be the same. (...) We live in States. There is a society under every State. States have a history, and therefore, traditions. (...) The only problem was that, as time went by, more and more anomalies revealed unexplained in this reference scheme; and more and more gaps (of unresearched human activity zones) seemed to emerge.

In the field that we investigate here, Quality of Work Life, regardless of the analytical layer, either biological, psychological or organizational, new references or new paradigms are emerging. Here is what happens in the area of health, following the positions of Santos & Westphal (1999:75):

The new public health emerges from the recognition that everything that exists is a product of human action, except what could be called untouched nature, in opposition to the hegemony of therapeutics, as a solution to all evil that can reach the human body. The health of an individual, of a group of individuals or of a community also depends on things that man has created and does, on interactions of social groups, of policies adopted by the government. The very mechanisms of attention to illness, of teaching medicine, of teaching nursing, of education, of interventions on the environment.

With these studies, we can verify the awareness of the need of social construction of public health, by several social players that become an integral part of the process of health and illness of people, in the view of Berger & Luckmann.

The denomination Quality of Work Life has been used in administration since the 1970s, especially in the United States, in organizational activities related to healthy service to the employee. The term and the practice are also present in Public and Social Policies in Canada. France has one of the most critical cultures dedicated to the study on the conditions of life at work, which gained higher expression after the 1980's. The French specialists propagated concepts on psychopathology at work, disaggregating suffering, and creative suffering at work, questions on power, myths, and envy within organizations. They also introduced methods of improvement of working conditions through research-action, participatory research and discussion practices, such as the "collective space", for awareness-raising and organizational change through decisions made by the workers and the company on ergonomic conditions and occupational diseases. Dejours (1994), one of the most important experts and leaders of these thoughts, defines working conditions as "*the physical, mechanical, chemical and biological pressures of the working position*". *The working pressures aim mainly at the body of workers, where they can cause burnout, aging and somatic* diseases (Dejours, Abdoucheli, Jayet, 1994:125).

Besides, among the Europeans, the works performed at Volvo–the Swedish automobile industry, stand out, with the social-technical model, with participatory practices in the design of the plant and the positions. Alvesson (1987) highlights paradigms for the modern working life: self-determination *versus* control, monotony *versus* variability and qualified demand *versus* generalist view. Another stream of actions regarding Quality of Work Life on the human condition at work has turned toward the question of the morale in the group, from de demonstration that a factory is a social institution (Mayo, 1945 in Tratemberg, 1985:88), for the needs and its various hierarchies and classes, such as basic needs of security, association, prestige and self-achievement, and motivation with incentives. Maintenance with benefits that generate stability of interest and a behavior of continuity (Herzberg, 1966). Styles of leadership and results between the leader, the subordinates and the targets to be achieved, maturity and decision-making processes. The authors are: McGregor, 1944, Cris Argyris, 1953, according to Hersey and Blanchard, in the classical publication Psychology for Managers, with its first Brazilian publication in 1977.

In the 1990s, along with the actions related to process and product quality management and the evolution of social awareness and of the right to health–reinforced by the need of life style renovation, actions, studies, practices and managerial efforts toward personal quality multiply. New designs of Management of Quality of Work are constructed in this scenario. This scenario has the systemic approaches, the participatory management, the diagnostics of the organizational climate, nutritional education, health promotion, the consolidation of preventive proposals, ergonomic actions and mental health care at work, as well as the importance of leisure, sports and cultural activities. More recently, the questions on citizenship and social responsibility have been proposed in the quality of life programs within the companies.

Among the studies on quality of work life QWL, the Walton model (1975) stands out, which defines Quality of Work Life as *"environmental and human values, neglected by the industrial societies in favor of the technological advancement, as well as the advancement of productivity and economic growth"*. On his turn, Roberto Crema (1992), a Brazilian expert in the subject, provides evidence to the existential aspects and indicates toward the moment of challenges, of change and of the need of *entirety* of the human being, linked to the *interconnected dimension of knowledge and love,* so as not to fragment before the "traumatisms of all times". During the same period, the psychoanalyst C. Dejours, refers specifically to Quality of Work Life as *social and psychological conditions* of work, specifically regarding creative suffering and pathogenic suffering.

There are studies that confirm the importance of the *participation* factor. In the published works of Werther and Davis (1983:70–87), the authors state that the QWL is one of the great challenges of management and personnel development. The authors describe factors that affect QWL: *"supervision, working conditions, pay, benefits and position design... a good working life means an interesting, challenging and rewarding position"* that lead to commitment and productivity.

Eda Conte Fernandes (1992), the most important pioneer of the quality of work life movement, says that the expression *Quality of Work Life* is associated with improvement in the physical conditions, leisure programs, life style, facilities, meeting workers' demand, and extension do package of benefits. The author says: *"QWL is intimately linked to industrial democracy and humanization of work, and its strongest stream is the French stream, which uses the systematic testimony of the employees on their activities as a scientific methodology"*.

THE CONTRIBUTION OF THE SCIENCES

Post-Industrial Society, Competing for the Future, The Banker of the Poor, Networks of Connections, Sustainable Growth, The Individual in the Organizations–forgotten dimensions, Beyond Virtual Organizations, among other titles, demonstrate that society as a whole is experiencing new paradigms on the ways of life in and out of the work place, and is building a culture related to the demands of Quality of Work Life. We highlight a few subjects of the sciences that have influenced and contributed toward the construction of the concept of Quality of Work Life, as follows:

QWL: Contribution of Sciences

Health: In, 1986, the World Health Organization—WHO (Dejours, 1994) defined health as the conservation of physical, mental and social integrity—a complete biopsychosocial well-being—and not only the absence of illness, with a longer life expectation and biomedical advances.

Ecology: where man is an integral part and is responsible for the conservation of the ecosystem of the living beings and the provisions from nature.

Engineering: through *ergonomics:* with a higher capacity to build objects and environments—extension of human needs—in an increasingly more comfortable, effective and harmonious manner, in the people–work interface.

Psychology: along with philosophy, by demonstrating the influence of the internal attitudes and the perspective of life in the analysis and insertion of each person in their work and the importance of the intrinsic meaning of individual needs and to the psychological working contract.

Sociology: by rescuing the symbolic dimension of what is socially shared and constructed, by demonstrating the implications of who influences and who is influenced in the several cultural and social contexts.

Economics: by emphasizing the social awareness that all goods are finite and that the distribution of goods, resources and services must involve social responsibility and globalization.

Law: concerning the right of the personality, the right to life, to health and legal contracts, as well as civil institutional figures.

Administration: with the increase in the capacity of mobilizing resources, increasingly sophisticated and impacting in technological terms, before more specific, quick and changing goals.

LEVELS OF ACTIVITY OF HEALTH PROMOTION INTEGRATED WITH MQWL

Considering the multiple possibilities of approach in the Management of Quality of Work Life (M-QWL), we can define the following levels:

- *Strategic Management of QWL* (SM-QWL) when it is declared in the mission and policy of the company, along with the corporate image.
- *Administrative Management of QWL* (AM-QWL) when it appears as a responsibility and an attribution of the leaders and heads of specific areas and departments in the second or third hierarchical level, with emphasis on goals, objectives and the organizational productivity.
- *Operational Management of QWL:* when there are specific actions—random, reactive or planned—aiming at the well-being and the awareness-raising of new life style practices for the people at the company, but not in line with the purposes of competitiveness or optimization of management, productivity and performance for work.

Hierarchic Decision Levels

These managerial demands have anchors in specific sectors, such as, for example: Benefits, Health, Hygiene and Safety, Quality, Human Resources, Internal Communication, among others, which characterize focuses of actuation. It may also be organized on specific demands originating from the organizational culture, on facts occurred, or on legal demands. These are, for example: drug-usage prevention programs, AIDS, cancer, labor-related accidents, employee image, citizenship, etc. We must note that there are QWL actions that emerge on specific occasions, in function of choices of their executives, of the culture of the company, on the product that is on the market and of the behavior of competitors.

The analysis of specific phenomena of work, such as health, safety, motivation, adaptation of expectations to general determining factors, among countless others, limits the understanding of the investigation. In strict terms, Quality of Work Life involves a specific dimension of the location where the production relationships take place. It is a matter of recognizing that a major part of work relationships, of their practices and values comes from experiences on the **shop floor**, from **production control** processes, from **times and movements,** and evolves to **total quality** and **criteria of excellence**. Although influenced by the general conditions of the social and economical organization, it is on this dimension that we can call **organizational** that many researchers supported their reflection.

Maybe the paradoxical reference of this school is Taylor, with his studies on the best ways to rationalize mass production, a typical phenomenon of the 20th Century. Taylor's reason for knowing was of a technological nature, by means of the use of better techniques and methods by the employees, the employees considered as one of the parts of the complex productive gear work. After this fragmented standpoint, a movement emerges that emphasizes human relations, which later on gave way to the questions related to the physical and mental, or psychological health of the worker.

This movement was started by Elton Mayo and his collaborators, in Hawtorne. The real centers of leadership would be supported on the interpersonal relationships of the work unit. The administration theory models X and Y of McGregor were to follow, as well as the conceptions of maturity-immaturity of Chrys Argyris. These studies had a new landmark with Maslow, with the development of the concept of **hierarchy of needs**. Next, Hersberg introduced the **hygiene and satisfaction** needs as focal points of the work process (in: Hersey & Blanchard, 1986). After the 1970's the quality gurus, and among them Juran and Deming, are the pioneers of the discussion of the questions regarding **personal quality** as part of the organizational quality processes. In the 1990's, the North American works of Schein, Handy, Mintzberg and Ulrich approached new concepts on the **human condition** at work, in an extensive set of contributions under the organizational perspective, regarding competence, strategy, culture and talent.

Tools and Focuses of QWL Integrated with the Health Promotion

The management tools of health promotion integrated with quality of work life, fit into the competencies and deliveries of the specialists and managers of the personnel management departments and its functional derivations related to the alignment of the performance of people with the conditions offered by the organization. The following are the most frequently used diagnostic tool, as from the 1990s:

- Diagnosis of the organizational climate;
- Topical teams for improvement;
- Self-management of health;
- Quality of life commissions;
- Medical reports;
- Absenteeism index;
- Mapping of socio-family profile;
- Compensations and benefits group;
- Opinion survey upon the community;
- Enforcement of legal requirements;
- Assessment of satisfaction and performance of internal and external clients, on a specific quality of life product or service;
- Educational campaigns;
- Incentive programs.

All managerial tools mentioned above translate into efforts of managerial activity and, in general terms, are associated with: *quality systems, human potential and work safety and health.*

The managerial effort on *quality systems* involves the Total Quality and ISO 9000 Certification policies and programs, as well as many other managerial methods and practices centered on customer satisfaction.

The managerial effort on *human potential* refers to qualification, motivation and professional development of the work force, education for social coexistence, for the use of potentialities and for organizational learning—this is where the actions and policies fit in.

The managerial effort on *occupational safety and health* refers to conservation, prevention, correction or repair of human and environmental aspects that neutralize risks in the working conditions.

The BPSO-96 indices for the health promotion with emphasis on QWL

Indices are planning and decision-making tools that allow clarity in the criteria, assessment objectiveness, easy collection of information, visibility of data and effects of certain actions.

The idea is to—via indices—make a higher strategic, managerial and operational capacity viable for questions related to quality of work life. The consolidation of quality of work life management indices may lead the personnel management area to a conceptual and methodological maturing with the same importance of the other areas in the organization, by locating and describing aspects that allow to make records, comparisons and evaluations in the construction of a method of analysis based on indices.

The economy in the digital era, the new paradigms of organizational management and the difficult union between quality of life and economical stability impel complex actions. These complex actions take place in situations that are typical of the third millennium, and among them are the following:

- instant circulation of information, with the intensive use of virtual systems,
- pursuit of new values to overcome the Freudian classic: *civilization discomfort*,
- stimulation of innovation and competitiveness in individual and collective activities.

Communities and work organizations—both public and private—do already recognize a great variety of actions, practices and policies related, either directly or indirectly, to quality of work life. In spite of the recognition of the need to act effectively on all aspect of personal and collective well-being, there are concerns regarding pressures, conciliation of expectations between work, family and consumption, differences between the types of stress: eustress—healthy adaptation and distress—unhealthy adaptation, eating habits and physical care, life styles, and technological impacts. There are many stimuli and few values for the awareness of well-being as part of life—in and out of the work place.

The quality of life actions are not random. As a principle, they should generate sustainability. The QWL actions presume needs to be met, in the sense of personal preservation and the survival of the species. It was only in the last decade that the idea of quality of life concept expanded. In some countries, the QWL demands are called working conditions (for example, in France). The question is: was QWL an ignored phenomenon or did it simply not exist at the companies? The most probable attitude is to believe that QWL was an action that was not recognized as a responsibility of the internal environment of the organization, both by employers and by employees. It is worth mentioning a few initiators of quality of work life that are typical in our post-industrial society, as follows:

- personal life structure: family, leisure and sports activities, living habits, life expectation, health care, nourishment, fight against sedentary life, affinity and support groups;
- social-economical factors: globalization, technology, information, unemployment, government policies, class organizations, privatization of public services, expansion of the health insurance market, more sophisticated consumption standards;
- corporate goals: competitiveness, product quality, speed, costs, corporate image;
- organizational pressures: new power structures, information, agility, co-responsibility, variable remuneration, transitoriness at the job, investment in social projects.

By using the biopsychosocial view (Limongi-França, 2004) we prepared Table 12.1, based on criteria and focuses that can be operationalized for the construction of M-QWL indices.

TABLE 12.1 Corporate Indices of M-QWL

Criteria	Focus
Organizational	Image, Training & Development, Processes and Technology, Decision-Making Committees, Absence of Bureaucracy Personnel Routines
Biological	Internal Accident-Prevention Week, Ergonomic Risk control – PPRA, Medical First Aid Post, Corporate Wellness Meals (cafeteria), Health – PCSMO, Commission–CIPA
Psychological	Recruitment and Selection, Performance Evaluation Companionship–Organizational Climate, Career, Salary, Personal Life
Social	Commercial Agreements, Free Time – Leisure, Children, Basic Needs Private Pension Plan, Financing of Courses

EXTENSION OF HEALTH PROMOTION AND QWL INDEXES

The Human Development Report of Brazil (1996:4) emphasizes three basic options of human development:

- enjoy a long and healthy life,
- acquire knowledge, and
- have access to the necessary resources for a decent standard of living.

These options are incorporated to the index through variables that measure longevity, educational level and income.

The Social Development Index–IDS is made up of:

- Indices of: life expectancy,
- Degree of literacy,
- Income distribution.

On its turn, the Human Development Index–HDI is made up of:

- Food,
- Health,
- Life insurance,
- Knowledge,
- Working conditions,
- Safety against crime,
- Leisure,
- Economical participation,
- Cultural and political participation.

The studies on the Human Development Index (HDI), the Social Development Index (SDI) and the Living Conditions Index (LCI) and, more recently, risk, ergonomics in the questions of work health and safety, mental load, repetitive efforts, occupational risks and technological communication and the psychology of work: in the studies on psychopathology, meaning of work, behavioral processes, such as psychological work contract, motivation, and expectations. The activities refer to Primary health care, Promotion of health, Eating habits, ergonomic improvements, occupational safety and risks, Psychopathology of work and psychic load. From here, the QWL Concept is structured, with a focus on the person. Below we summarize this panorama of the main pressures on the management and sustainability of well-being in organizations.

**Pressures on the Management
of Quality of Work Life**

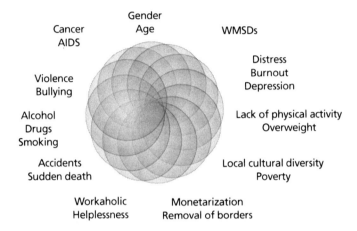

Gender
Age

Cancer
AIDS

WMSDs

Violence
Bullying

Distress
Burnout
Depression

Alcohol
Drugs
Smoking

Lack of physical activity
Overweight

Accidents
Sudden death

Local cultural diversity
Poverty

Workaholic
Helplessness

Monetarization
Removal of borders

Some authors have presented a study with new criteria of indices. In Brazil, Fernandes, E.C. (1992:7) points to the following focuses of Quality of Work Life–QWL programs:

- Rearrangement of working positions,
- Improvement in organizational culture,
- Creation of autonomous or self-managed groups.

One of the mostly used criteria models of quality of work life in Brazil is the one proposed by Walton (1975), which should and may be operationalized according to the QWL program proposal of each company. These criteria are as follows:

1. Fair and adequate compensation
2. Working conditions
3. Social integration within the organization
4. Opportunity for growth and safety
5. Use and development of personal skills
6. Citizenship
7. Work and total living space
8. Social relevance of work

Levering (1995:18) mentions the studies by Arthur D. Little, originally published in 1993, on companies with a good working environment which tend to have a better financial performance related to the types of relationship at work based on these motivators: employees have more confidence in the board of the company, employees that are proud of their work and the companionship climate.

The Regulatory Standards of Health and Safety Legislation were consolidated in 1978. They are indices of quality of life, since they determine programs of elimination, control and conservation of health and, consequently, of well-being at the working environment. Among the standards, some programs are stated as mandatory, such as: Internal Commission on Accident Prevention (CIPA), Internal Week on Accident Prevention (SIPAT), Program on the Prevention of Environmental Risks (PPRA), Medical and Occupational Health Control (PCSMO).

The new trends of the concept of compensation and benefits have *impellers* regarding external and internal pressures. Wood Jr. (in Coopers & Lybrand, 1996:31) considers as *external pressure* the competition, industrial policy, import and export, consumer demands, community demands, expectations of the shareholders and *internal pressures* the power conflicts, the demand for more autonomy at work, the demand for more creative and motivating activities, information technology, improvement in the general education of employees. These trends signal the construction of new indices.

Career is a powerful index of perception of quality of work life: Dutra (1996:16–19) defined career as occupational mobility or profession: *"A path structured and organized in time and space, a result of the established relationship between the person and the company, comprising the perspectives of both"*.

Other aspects of human resources management are the Corporate Indices of Quality of Life:

- *Culture:* leisure and art activities and cultural information that companies develop and that interfere positively on the organizational climate and on the motivation of employees.
- *Courtesy:* courtesy at work translates into an act of recognition and appreciation of our fellow men and *Humor* are indices of the culture and of the level of integration between the people of a group.
- *Ecologically correct products:* consumers are more and more concerned with the environment. In the future, we will not be able to have products that are aggressive to the environment. Therefore, some arrangements are necessary:
  - use packaging made of recycled material,
  - implement a system for collection of rain water,
  - reduce energy consumption,
  - use mass transportation, instead of private cars,
  - not use chlorine to whiten paper, separate garbage (glass, paper, plastic) for recycling,
  - restrict products with high lead content.

We still face many challenges to the integration of health promotion and quality of work life management, and we highlight those that reflect reports and studies carried out by companies and experienced professionals that work in this area. The following are the challenges:

- People management practices little consolidated in most companies.
- Emphasis on the market environment, with demands more associated with product quality requirements and processes, to the detriment of the personal-professional quality.
- Fear of employees to express their real opinion and becoming unemployed.
- Lack of habits of survey upon employees, with great impacts on latent expectations.
- Belief that qualified and healthy *performance* must be achieved naturally and on their own.
- Quality of work life considered simply as philanthropy.
- Actions toward quality of work life are ignored within the companies.
- The meaning of work as a source of enrichment and existential accomplishment, but not as a practice in people management.

Faced with these challenges, endless alternatives for the expansion of health promotion integrated with quality of work life have been constructed. When these alternatives are achieved in an administrative environment, such as visible and legitimized architecture, there will be greater chances of perceiving results. Therefore, there is a growing need to build a model and a procedure that consider the expansion of the concept of health, including Health Promotion, along with the mandatory care of illness. The figure below highlights a few points that can make up a model of integrated management of health promotion with quality of work life:

Element for the Healthy Working Environment

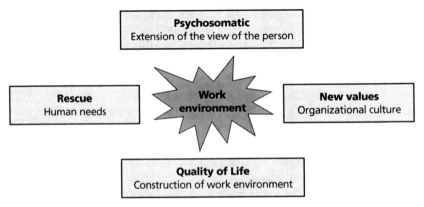

The understanding of the human being, in which the individual is his or her body, reveals conditions of life and marks of endured and desired experiences. It is situated in the same holistic and integral vision of the person. The biopsychosocial school integrates the concepts of Philosophy, Psychology, Physiology, Biology, Sociology, and knowledge concerning human life. The concept that we propose for Quality of Work Life—QWL is set up by three aspects, which are the following that are vital:

- Self esteem,
- Perception of balance
- Well-being and healthy habits.

DEFINITION OF QWL

In our point of view, Quality of Work Life is: the set of choices of single and individualized well-being that provides positive self esteem, perception of balance, healthy habits and readiness for the healthy performance at work.

Quality of work life, as an element of organizational management and of performance at work provides consistency for healthy work, with the elements of psychosocial integration, social and community credibility, mapping of expectations through the psychological contract, qualifies and achieves. It generates economic and financial conditions for our own survival, as well as the survival of our family and of the community. This is the virtuous circle of sustainable work.

Perception of a good organizational climate, personal feeling of well-being and happiness, harmonious integration of people and their teams, among other signals of individual and collective behavior signal the profile of a modern company; the modern company that is integrated with the view of social, economical and sustainable evolution, besides the highly positive impact on its image. Widening the view and the practices of health promotion integrated with quality of life is part of the great contemporary movement of humanization of the quality of work life.

REFERENCES

Albuquerque, L.G. (1996). Administração participativa: modismo ou componente de um novo paradigma de gestão e relações de trabalho. *Revista da ESPM*, São Paulo, v. 3(1), maio.

Alvesson, M. (1987). *Organization theory and technocratic consciousness*. Berlin/New York: Walter de Gruyter.

Arendt, M. (1983). *A condição humana*. Trad. Celso Lafer. Rio de Janeiro : Forense.

Berger, L. P, & Luchmann, T.A. (1987). A construcao Social da realidade. Trad. Floriano de S.Fernades. Petrópolis: Vozes (Colecao Antropologia, v. 5), 7 Ed.

Bolles, R.N. (1981). *The three boxes of life*. Berkeley : Richard Nelson Bolles.

Chanlat, J.F. (Coord.). (1996). *O indivíduo na organização*: dimensões esquecidas. Trad. Sette, O. (organização e revisão).São Paulo: Editora Atlas, (três volumes).

Coda, R. (1992). *Pesquisa de clima organizacional: uma contribuição metodológica*. Trabalho apresentado no Concurso para Professor Titular, São Paulo.

De Cicco, F.A. (1994). ISO 9000 e outras exigências da maior potência do mundo. *Revista de Administração de Empresas da FGV*, São Paulo, v. 34(2), mar./abril.

Dejours, C., Dessors, D. & Desriaux, F. (1993). Por um trabalho, fator de equilíbrio. Maria Irene S. Betiol. (trad.). *Revista de Administração de Empresas da FGV*, São Paulo mai./junho.

Dejours, C., Dessors, D. & Desriaux, F. (1994). *Psicodinâmica do trabalho*. São Paulo: Atlas.

Dejours, C., Dessors, D. & Desriaux, F. (2000). Novas formas de organização do trabalho e lesões por esforços repetitivos (LER): abordagem através da psicodinâmica do trabalho. In Sznelwar, L.I. & Zidan, L.N. (orgs.). *O trabalho humano com sistemas informatizados no setor de serviços*. Departamento de Engenharia de Produção da Escola Politécnica da USP. São Paulo: Plêiade.

Dutra, J.S. (1996ª). *Administração de carreiras*: uma proposta para repensar a gestão de pessoas. São Paulo : Atlas.

Fernandes, E.C. & Rendón, J.V. (1992).Sondagens de opinião interna como instrumento de informação. *Revista de Administração da USP*, São Paulo, v. 27(1), jan./março.

Fleury, M.T.L. (1987). Estórias, mitos, heróis: cultura organizacional e relações de trabalho. *Revista de Administração de Empresas da FGV*. Rio de Janeiro, v. 27(4).

França, A.C.L. (1996). *Indicadores Empresariais de Qualidade de Vida no Trabalho: esforço empresarial e satisfação dos empregados no ambiente de manufaturas com certificação ISO9000*. Tese de Doutorado. FEA/USP.

Frosini, L.H. & Carvalho, A.B.M. (1995). Segurança e saúde na qualidade e no meio ambiente. *Revista Proteção*. São Paulo, nº. 38, julho.

Giddens, A. (2000). *A terceira via : reflexões sobre o impasse político atual e o futuro da social-democracia*. Tradução Maria Luiza X.de A Borges. Rio de Janeiro: Record, 3ª ed.

Hersey, R. & Blanchard, T. (1986). *Psicologia para Administradores*. Tradução e revisão técnica: equipa CPB – Edwino A. Roger. São Paulo, EPU.

Ianni, O. (1994). *Globalização: novo paradigma das ciências sociais*. Estudos Avançados *21*, São Paulo: USP.

Kehl, S. (1995). *Metaqualidade: um novo conceito de qualidade global*. São Paulo: Fundação Carlos Alberto Vanzolini, julho. Rede Vanzolini de educação continuada à distância. Manual do Participante.

Kochan, T.A. et al. (1995). Total quality management and human resource systems: an international comparison. *The International Journal of Human Resource Management*, 6:2, May.

Landes, D.S. (1998). *Riqueza e a pobreza das nações*. Tradução Álvaro Cabral. Rio de Janeiro: Campus.

Levering, R.A. (1995). Definição de um excelente lugar para se trabalhar. *Revista de Administração de Empresas da FGV*. São Paulo, v. 2(4).

Limongi-França, A.C. & Rodrigues, A.L. (2004). *Stress & Trabalho – uma abordagem psicossomática*. São Paulo: Editora Atlas, 4ª. ed.

Limongi-França, A.C. (2004). *Qualidade de Vida no Trabalho – práticas e conceitos na sociedade pós-industrial. São Paulo*. São Paulo: Editora Atlas, 2ª. ed..

Lipowski, Z.J. (1986). Psychosomatic medicine: past and present. *Can. J. Psychiatry*, v. 1.

Marx, R. (1992). Processo de trabalho e grupos semi-autônomos: a evolução da experiência sueca de Kalmar aos anos 90. *Revista de Administração de Empresas da FGV*, São Paulo, abr./junho.

McGlothlin, J. (1998). Niosh research priorities in ergonomics and the present and future impact on the quality of worklife in the united states. *Anais do 1º Encontro Internacional de Gestão de Competências em Qualidade de Vida no Trabalho*. São Paulo: Progep–FEA-USP.

McGlothlin, J. (1999). *Gestão ergonômica*: espectro internacional gestão ergonômica: espectro internacional. 2º Encontro Internacional de Gestão de Competências em Qualidade de Vida no Trabalho. 2. QVT. São Paulo: FEA/USP.

Mello filho, J. et al. (1992). *Psicossomática hoje*. Porto Alegre: Artes Médicas.

Mendes, R. (1996). A promoção da saúde nas empresas: o futuro da medicina do trabalho, já existente. *Revista Práticas Bem-Sucedidas*. São Paulo: Centro Brasileiro de Segurança e Saúde Industrial, v. 1(1), jul./agosto.

Net. http://newciv.org/worldtrans/BOV/BOV/BV-364.html. Best ways of measuring quality of life.

PNUD, IPEA, IBGE, FJP. (1998). *Desenvolvimento Humano e Condições de Vida: Indicadores Brasileiros*. Coleção Desenvolvimento Humano. Brasília, setembro.

Rodrigues, M.C.P. (1993). O índice do desenvolvimento humano–IDH da ONU. *Revista Conjuntura Econômica*, Rio de Janeiro, julho.

Rodrigues, M.V.C. & Amorim, T.A.A. (1994). *Qualidade de vida no trabalho*. Petrópolis: Vozes.

Roitman, A. (1996). A Ética da Globalização. *Revista Trevisan*, Nº 101, ano 9, julho.

Santos, J.L.F. & Westphal, M.F. (1999). Dossiê saúde pública. *Estudos Avançados*, v.13(35), jan./abril.

Schein, E.H. (1984). Coming to a new awareness of organization culture. *Sloan Management Review*, Massachusetts Institute of Technology.

Spink, P. (1975). Some comments on the quality of working life. *J. occup. Psychol*, 48.

Tratemberg, M. (1985). *Burocracia e ideologia*. São Paulo: Ática.

Walton, R. (1975). Criteria for quality life. In: Davis, L.E., Cherns, A.B. *The quality of working life. problems, prospects and state of the art*. New York : The Free Press, v. 1.

Werther Jr., William B. & Davis, K. (1983). *Administração de Pessoal e Recursos Humanos*. A. B. Simões (trad.). São Paulo: McGraw Hill do Brasil.

Wood, J.RT. (1995). *Mudança organizacional*. São Paulo: Atlas/Coopers & Lybrand.

WHOQOL Group. (1998). Site: www.hcpa.ufrgs.br.

ABOUT THE CONTRIBUTORS

Burnout and Workplace Injuries: A Longitudinal Analysis

Michael P. Leiter (BA Duke; PhD Oregon) is Professor of Psychology at Acadia University in Canada and Director of the Center for Organizational Research & Development that applies high quality research methods to human resource issues confronting organizations. He holds the Canada Research Chair in Occupational Health and Wellbeing at Acadia University. He is a registered psychologist in Nova Scotia, Canada

Christina Maslach (A.B. Harvard-Radcliffe, Ph.D. Stanford) is Vice Provost for Undergraduate Education and Professor of Psychology at the University of California at Berkeley. She is best known as one of the pioneering researchers on job burnout, and the author of the Maslach Burnout Inventory (MBI), the most widely used research measure in the burnout field. In addition to numerous articles, she has written several books on this topic.

The Impact of International Business Trips on the Travelers and Their Spouses

Mina Westman is an Associate Professor, at the Faculty of Management, Tel Aviv University. Her primary research interests include job stress, work-family interchange, crossover in the family and the workplace, the effects of vacation on stress and strain, and the impact of short business trips and expatriation on the individual, the family and the organization.

Stress and Quality of Working Life, pages 257–263
Copyright © 2009 by Information Age Publishing
All rights of reproduction in any form reserved.

Dalia Etzion, Ph.D. in Psychology, has been with the Faculty of Management, Tel Aviv University since its establishment and is one of the founders of the OB Program; she headed the program during 1979-81 and 1988-92. Etzion is a certified psychologist and authorized trainer in the areas of social, industrial and organizational psychology. Her current research focuses on respite from work and well being; gender and the work/life interface; and the crossover of job stress and burnout between spouses.

Shoshi Chen received her Ph.D. in Organizational Behavior at the Faculty of Management, Tel Aviv. Her current research interests are: work and stress, the effects of vacation on stress and strain, preventive stress management, and IT implementation.

Occupational Stress and Workplace Sleepiness

Sarah DeArmond is an assistant professor of Human Resource Management at the University of Wisconsin Oshkosh. She obtained her Ph.D. with a specialization in Occupational Health Psychology from the Industrial/Organizational Psychology program at Colorado State University. Her research interests include occupational stress, workplace sleepiness, job performance, and training.

Professor **Peter Chen** heads the Occupational Health Psychology (OHP) training in Mountain and Plains Education and Research Center. He is the past President of Society for OHP and the Associate Editor of Journal of OHP. His primary research programs are safety training, program evaluation, and safety and health behaviors.

The Experiences of Work-Related Stress across Occupations

Sheena Johnson is a Chartered Psychologist and lecturer in Organisational Psychology at Manchester Business School, UK. She holds a Masters in Occupational Psychology from UMIST and a PhD from the University of Liverpool, in which she investigated the risk culture of financial organisations and its subsequent impact on financial loss events. She is a member of the British Psychological Society, European Association of Work and Organizational Psychology, British Academy of Management, and is an International Affiliate of the American Psychological Association. She is a reviewer for journals such as *Journal of Management Studies* and the *International Journal of Stress Management*.

Cary Cooper (same as above)

Susan Cartwright is Professor of Organizational Psychology and Head of Department at Manchester Business School, UK. She is a Fellow of the British Psychological Society and a Fellow of the British Academy of Management. Susan is currently President of the British Academy of Management, past Editor of the *Leadership and Organization Development Journal* and a former Associate Editor of the *British Journal of Management*. Susan has been researching and consulting in the area of stress, health and wellbeing for over twenty years and has been an expert advisor to the Health and Safety Executive and the UK Government's Foresight Programme on Mental Health

Professor Ian Donald holds a chair of Organizational Psychology and is Head of the School of Psychology, University of Liverpool. Ian has carried out research around the world, examining such factors as risk and risk management, organizational climate, culture and change, and stress. He has advised many major public and private sector organizations and government on industrial and social issues. He has been awarded and managed research grants and contracts worth over £3million. Ian was recently invited keynote speaker to the Graduate University of Chinese Academy of Science, Beijing, also giving an invited lecture on his work at Peeking University. During 2007 Ian was Visiting Scholar at the Centre for Asian Pacific Studies, Lingnan University, Hong Kong. He has published on research methods, social, forensic, environmental, occupational and occupational health psychology.

Paul Taylor is now a Senior Lecturer in Psychology at Lancaster University, UK, where he directs the Department's MSc in Investigative Expertise. His research examines communication and sensemaking in high-stress environments, particularly in relation to negotiation, where his research has earned the Earl Scheafer best paper award and the 2007 and 2008 IACM best applied paper awards. Paul works on these issues with academics and professionals from Europe, the Middle East, and North America, and he is an honorary research associate of the Police Research Laboratory at Carleton University and the Laboratory for Bounded Rationality and Law at Memorial University. More details are at: http://www.lancs.ac.uk/staff/taylorpj/.

Clare Millet Cook is a Chartered Psychologist and consultant at The Occupational Psychology Group. She holds a Masters in Occupational Psychology and is a member of the British Psychological Society. Clare undertakes research and consultancy in the areas of stress management, resilience, personality profiling, team dynamics and individual development.

Work-Related Mental Disorders: A Perspective of the Brazilian Occupational Medicine and Psychiatry

Duílio Antero de Camargo—occupational physician, psychiatrist at the Psychiatry Institute, *Clínicas* Hospital of the São Paulo University School of Medicine and chairman of the Technical Committee on Mental Health and Work of the National Association of Occupational Medicine (ANAMT). He is a founding member of the Mental Health Laboratory at UNICAMP.

Leadership from a Positive Health Perspective: A Qualitative Study

Marilyn Macik-Frey is an Assistant Professor of Management at Nicholls State University in Thibodaux, Louisiana. She was previously the Elvira Fuller Faust/Goolsby Doctoral Fellow in Leadership and Communication, Goolsby Leadership Academy, University of Texas at Arlington. She has published in the *Journal of Management, Journal of Management Studies, Consulting Psychology Journal, Journal of Organizational Behavior,* and *Journal of Business and Leadership.*

James Campbell Quick is John and Judy Goolsby Distinguished Professor, The University of Texas at Arlington and Visiting Professor, Lancaster University Management School. His current research is on executive health and the career transitions of retired U.S. Navy admirals. He was awarded The Legion of Merit by the United States Air Force.

Phillip Shinoda is Associate Director of the Memnosyne Foundation. He was the Director of Corporate and Community Relations at the University of Texas at Arlington, and taught at Wake Forest University and Oregon State University. He received his BA from the University of California, Santa Barbara and MBA and PhD from the University of California, Berkeley.

Dr. **David A. Mack** is Assistant Dean for Program Development and the Director of the Goolsby Leadership Academy at The University of Texas at Arlington's College of Business. He received his Ph.D. from UT Arlington in May 2000. He previously earned an MBA in Entrepreneurship from DePaul University in 1993.

David A. Gray, Ph.D. is Associate Dean of the College of Business and Professor of Management. His teaching and research interests are in the areas of human resource management and labor relations. Results of his research efforts have been published in the Academy of Management Review, Academy of Management Executive, California Management Review, OMEGA: The International Journal of Management Science, and national proceedings of the Academy of Management and Industrial Relations Research Association.

Nathan Keller, Major, U.S. Army is Chief of Mental Health for the 1st Cavalry Division, United States Army. He earned his Ph.D. in social work at The University of Texas at Arlington where he was a Goolsby Doctoral Fellow, Goolsby Leadership Academy. His research interests include leadership and combat stress.

Cary L. Cooper is Distinguished Professor of Organizational Psychology and Health and Pro-Vice Chancellor (External Relations) at Lancaster University. Author of over 100 books and over 400 scholarly articles for academic journals. He is Editor-in-Chief, The Blackwell Encyclopedia of Management and editor, Who's Who in the Management Sciences. Professor Cooper was awarded a CBE for his contribution to organizational health.

The Role of Political Skill in Neutralizing the Dysfunctional Impact of Negative Affectivity on Psychological and Physiological Strains

Kelly Zellars, Ph.D., is an Associate Professor of Management in the Belk College of Business at the University of North Carolina–Charlotte. Dr. Zellars has focused her research on job stress, coping, personality, and organizational justice.

Pamela L. Perrewé (Ph.D.) is the Distinguished Research Professor and Jim Moran Professor of Management in the College of Business at Florida State University. Dr. Perrewé has focused her research in the areas of job stress, coping, organizational politics, emotion and personality.

Ana Maria Rossi, Ph.D., president of the International Stress Management Association in Brazil (ISMA-BR) and a Brazilian representative for the Occupational Health Section of the World Psychiatric Association (WPA). She is the director of the Clínica de Stress and Biofeedback, in Porto Alegre, and the pioneer of self-control and biofeedback techniques in Brazil.

Charles (Chuck) Kacmar is an Associate Professor in the Information Systems, Statistics, and Management Science Department at the University of Alabama. His Ph.D. is in computer science from Texas A&M University. His research interests include perceptions of trust in the use of information systems, individual affectivity, and tele-mentoring.

Wayne Hochwarter, Ph.D. is currently the Jim Moran Professor of Management at Florida State University. His research, which has examined stress processes in organizations, can be found in the *Journal of Applied Psychology*, *Organizational Behavior and Human Decision Processes*, the *Journal of Management*, and *Administrative Sciences Quarterly*.

Gerald R. Ferris is the Francis Eppes Professor of Management and Professor of Psychology at Florida State University. He received a Ph.D. in Business Administration from the University of Illinois at Urbana-Champaign. Ferris has research interests in the areas of social influence processes in organizations, and the role of reputation in the organizational sciences.

Meditation in Health: Definition, Operationalization, and Technique

Roberto Cardoso, Ph.D. candidate, a physician specialized in Gynecology and Obstetrics. He was a collaborating professor at the module "Techniques for Altered Consciousness Status" of the Graduate Program in Behavioral Medicine at the Department of Psychobiology of UNIFESP, with the subject "Meditation". He is author of medical articles in the behavioral field and of the book *Medicina e Meditação* (Medicine and Meditation).

Eduardo de Souza, Ph.D., associate professor at the Department of Obstetrics of the Federal University of São Paulo–São Paulo School of Medicine and scientific coordinator of Gynecology and Obstetrics of the São Luiz Hospital and Maternity.

Luiz Camano, Ph.D., professor at the Department of Obstetrics of the Federal University of São Paulo–São Paulo School of Medicine and Obstetrics professor. He has published over 300 scientific papers.

Biobehavioral Mediators of Stress and Quality of Life in Occupational Settings

Robert J. Gatchel has a Ph.D. in Clinical Psychology and is a Diplomate of the American Board of Professional Psychology (ABPP). Dr. Gatchel is Chair, Department of Psychology, The University of Texas at Arlington and Director of Clinical Research, The Eugene McDermott Center for Pain Management, The University of Texas Southwestern Medical Center at Dallas.

Andrew Baum is the Jenkins Garrett Professor of Psychology at the University of Texas at Arlington, Director of the Center for the Study of Chronic Illness, and Director of the health psychology graduate concentration. He has more than 350 scientific articles, books, and chapters and is a Fellow of the American Psychological Association.

Qualitative and Quantitative Methods in Occupational-Stress Research

Irvin Sam Schonfeld is a professor of psychology at the City College of New York. He has published in the *Journal of Occupational Health Psychology*, *Genetic*, *Social*, *and General Psychology Monographs*, the *Archives of General Psychiatry*, *Developmental Psychology*, and *Organizational Research Methods*. His research interests include occupational stress in teachers, youth psychopathology, the psychology of teaching evolution, and bullying.

Edwin Farrell received his Ed.D. from Harvard University. His books, *Hanging in and dropping out* and *Self and school success*, offer a qualitative researcher's analysis of the lives and stresses of urban adolescents. Adel Assal and Farrell's ethnography, "Attempts to Make Meaning of Terror" (*Anthropology and Education Quarterly*) was based on data collected during the Lebanese civil war. Farrell is professor *emeritus* at the City University of New York.

Management of Quality of Life at Work in Healthcare Organizations

Káthia de Carvalho Cunha, Ph.D. (FEA/USP, Department of Administration), holds a Nursing Degree, with specialization in Occupational Nursing and Hospital Administration. Her doctoral and Post-Doc work focus on People Management.

Health Promotion and Quality of Work Life: The Challenge of Integrated Management

Ana Cristina Limongi-França, Ph.D., is a senior associate professor at the Universidade de São Paulo (USP) at the Department of Administration of the Faculty of Economics, Administration and Accounting (FEA). She directs the Nucleus for Studies and Research in Management of Quality of Work Life (NEP-MQWL), and is the coordinator of the Administration Institute Foundation (FIA).

Lightning Source UK Ltd.
Milton Keynes UK
20 January 2011

166060UK00001B/23/P

9 781607 520580